HOW TO DIVORCE

A NARCISSIST

AND SUCCEED IN THE FAMILY COURT

DIANA JORDAN LLB

Book design by: Nicola Humphreys
www.nicolahumphreys.co.uk/

Printed in the United Kingdom
First Printing, 2021

ISBN: 978-1-7398159-0-5 (Paperback)
ISBN: 978-1-7398159-1-2 (eBook)

Diana Jordan
www.dealingwithdivorce.co.uk

Disclaimer:

This book is intended as general information and guidance only. Readers should not place any personal reliance on the material or views expressed; no two cases are ever the same, and the law in this complex area changes frequently. For specific advice, you should consult a solicitor or financial advisor, who can advise you based on your own individual circumstances.

WHO THIS BOOK IS FOR

This book is for women and men, married or unmarried, who are:

- Wondering if their partner or ex is a narcissist
- Leaving, or thinking of leaving, a narcissist
- Facing children proceedings in the family court
- Being alienated from their child by a narcissist
- Trying to co-parent with a narcissist
- In divorce and/or financial proceedings with a narcissist
- Litigants in person
- Represented by a solicitor and/or barrister

CONTENTS

INTRODUCTION

When you're dealing with a narcissist, you're never going to have a 'normal' divorce. Nor will you ever have a 'normal' co-parenting relationship. Those are the first things to accept when you leave a narcissist.

The second thing to accept is this: knowledge is power. The very fact that you know (or suspect) your ex is a narcissist is of enormous help to you because you'll be able to plan your separation, divorce proceedings, financial proceedings, and children proceedings accordingly. And you'll be able to parent your children in the best way possible, without being continually caught off guard by the narcissist's tactics. This book is designed to help you do all that and more – to navigate the legal side of things effectively, deal with the narcissist's behaviour, support your children, and maintain your sanity.

What to expect from this book

I wrote this book with the litigant in person – someone who doesn't have a lawyer (solicitor or barrister) representing them and therefore self-represents – very much in mind. Most of my clients don't have solicitors so I'm aware of their struggles and frustrations when divorcing a narcissist. That said, if you have a solicitor, you will still benefit from understanding the processes involved and tactics to use when going through court with a narcissist, and will be able to educate your lawyers accordingly – which should, in turn, help to save time and money. In addition, anyone who is supporting a loved one through the painful process of divorcing a narcissist will also get plenty from this book. If that's you, this book will help you provide both the practical and emotional support your loved one needs.

I want you to treat this book as a workbook, not a coffee table book you need to keep in pristine condition. So get your pens, highlighters and Post-it notes out. Scribble in the margins. Highlight what's most relevant to you. That way, you can easily find the information that's most important to you when you need it in future. You'll also find plenty more helpful information via the Resources section at the end of the book.

In addition to this book and the recommended resources, Google is your friend. You can find a wealth of information online – including the necessary court forms mentioned in this book and how to submit them – but do keep in mind that, depending on the source, not everything you read online is correct.

I recommend combining any internet research with the trusted resources mentioned in this book.

You'll notice that I've included lots of quotes in italics throughout the book. These quotes are from my clients and others who have lived this experience of divorcing a narcissist. Where possible, I have asked permission from my clients and others to use their words, but I've been collecting quotes for several years and apologise to those whose words I've used without asking. Rest assured that all the quotes used are anonymous and any names have been changed. If you think you recognise your words, they may indeed be yours – but as I hear the same experiences over and over again, they could have been said by many people.

I should also clarify that this book talks about the legal system in England and Wales. If you're in Scotland or elsewhere, you will still find lots of useful strategies, but you'll obviously need to follow the appropriate legal steps for your jurisdiction.

Is there a gender bias in the family court (and in this book)?

Women get drunk and abused and it's their fault.
Men get drunk and abuse and it's the alcohol's fault.

Both fathers' and mothers' groups complain about the dreadfully wrong decisions made about children in the family courts. And both the women and the men are right, because the awful truth is that the abusive parent is the one most likely to win in court proceedings. And of course the real losers are always the children.

For the most part (although not exclusively), I've written this book using 'he' and 'him' for the narcissistic perpetrator and 'she' and 'her' for the victim. I had to make a choice in order to preserve the conversational style and flow of the book (and for it to not be too full of 'thems' and 'theirs'). I make no apology for writing it this way; there is most certainly a gender bias towards the patriarchy in the legal system, as well as society as a whole, and this is my attempt to restore the balance just a little. This will no doubt enrage the fathers' rights groups, but this book isn't written for those men (who, unfortunately, often make things harder for the decent fathers trying to protect their children from narcissistic mothers).

That's not to say this book isn't useful for men who are divorcing a narcissist. It absolutely is. About a third of my clients are men so I'm well aware of the abuse they suffer too. Men can be as badly controlled and emotionally abused by women as women are by men, and this book is very much for them too. (The stories of Mrs Gibbs and Mrs S in Chapter 9 prove all too well the damage women can do.) I also recognise that people in same-sex partnerships and marriages can and do experience abuse.

Bottom line, although I often (not always) use gendered pronouns in this book, it is written for anyone who is going through the process of separating from a narcissist.

I also recognise that many people don't like to be referred to as a 'victim' and prefer to be called a 'survivor'. I've used both words in this book. I tend to refer to someone having been a victim during the relationship, but once they make the decision to escape and disengage they become a survivor.

Carol's story

My previous life as a solicitor came back to haunt me recently. I acted for Carol almost 30 years ago and Sarah, her daughter (now 38), tracked me down via LinkedIn. She wanted help to piece together what happened when she was a child as she still feels confused and conflicted by it, and she wasn't able to talk to her mother about it before she died. She told me it's 'tough, because I'm choosing to relive my traumas' and 'as hard as this has been, I'm glad I kept digging as the smoking gun that I suspected was there all along'.

I'm sorry to say that although I remember their names, I don't remember this lady, although I do remember most of my clients. I can only think that this case was so awful, or that I felt I'd totally failed to help Carol or her children, that I erased it from my memory. Sarah sent me some of the court papers and letters I wrote to her mother, and this very sad story has made painful reading. Although I knew Jay, her partner, was violent to her, it's now so clear to me that Carol was also suffering narcissistic abuse and coercive control. But I didn't have a clue about narcissists at the time (most lawyers still don't) and coercive control was unheard of. I can only hope that I was kind to her, as I know I wouldn't have been happy about her failure to protect her children, and I wouldn't have begun to understand why she couldn't fight for them the way most mothers would.

These are the signs I can see now that I would have missed then:

The debts
So far as I can see, Carol only came to me because Jay owed a lot of money and one of his creditors had a charge on the house and was applying to the court for it to be sold. They weren't married, which made it all more complicated.

Many narcissists have lots of debts and there were lots of charges on this property in addition to the mortgage.

The lies
It seems from the correspondence that Carol was obsessed by Jay's lies, and that the only thing she was interested in was proving that he had lied. She even brought me tapes she had recorded of him. The problem was that the lies just weren't relevant to the issues we had to resolve, but she seemed unable to focus on anything else. And I doubt that I had any understanding of why the lies were worse than all the other dreadful things Jay did to her, including 'dragging her around by her hair, hitting her over the head with squash shoes, having his hands around her throat, and smashing glass doors in anger'. Not to mention turning her children against her and encouraging them to abuse her just as he did.

The gaslighting
I realise many of the lies are part of the gaslighting and no wonder lots of victims say they feel they're going crazy. An example of Jay's gaslighting is where he says Carol accused him of stealing her purse and the children later found it in her room. Where he had no doubt put it, and then sent the children to look for it. It's hard to imagine two children both coming upon one purse in a room they presumably wouldn't normally be in, but I doubt I spotted that at the time.

Refusing to take any responsibility
Narcissists are perfect and never do anything wrong! Which means they never take responsibility. Jay blamed his son for letting one of their dogs out during a visit by Carol's friend, who had brought along her daughter who was afraid of dogs. Jay said he was well aware of this and ensured that the dogs were kept shut in a room, but unfortunately his son accidently let them out. 'I have been blamed for the incident ever since although no fault can be attributed to me,' Jay insisted. And this despite saying elsewhere that 'I am left with no alternative but to take a very active role in the children's upbringing as Carol has all but washed her hands of looking after them'.

Involvement of police and other agencies
Carol had called the police several times and social services had some previous involvement with the family. This is a tell-tale sign of a desperate parent trying to get help for themselves and their children, usually without success as the narcissist always talks a better story and is able to manipulate professionals as well as their family.

Sometimes it is the narcissist who engages agencies, because they like nothing better than a drama. So involving the police or other agencies isn't necessarily indicative of which of the two is the abusive partner.

Isolating her from her friends

When Carol tried to negotiate with Jay to have friends come to the house, Jay refused to agree to give her privacy, stating that he must stay in the room the entire time. Carol lost all her friends as a result of his behaviour and threats towards them, and her family did not know what was going on.

Jay changed his car from an automatic to a manual, which Carol no longer had the ability to drive, and took her off the insurance, which was another tactic to isolate her.

Loss of her own identity

Carol said she didn't call the police before because it was not the Indian way – but as Jay was quick to point out, she was not Indian, he was. It's not unusual for a woman to be completely taken over by a man like this, who never stops telling her what she is and isn't, until she has completely lost herself in the relationship.

Sarah, Carol's daughter, says: 'She didn't have a business career like Dad. She didn't know how to form legal arguments. She was just a mum losing her health, whose partner ran her into the ground and convinced everyone in her life she was the enemy until she had no one she could lean on. She had started taping him but was trying to find a legal forum to share them with us because she didn't want to share without approval and that never happened.'

I say: Mother knows best (even when Father tells her she doesn't). If you feel something is right, go ahead and do it. Don't wait for approval. However, in this case, I'm not sure that making the children aware of their father's lies would have helped; they were clearly frightened of him and controlled by him, and it's unlikely they would have done much differently as a result, although maybe they would have felt less confused.

Financial control

When he went away to India, Jay gave money to his 11-year-old son instead of Carol. It seems all she had for herself was the child benefit, which she did well to hang on to as I'm sure Jay would have tried to talk her into handing it over to him. In response to her allegation that he refused to provide them with sufficient bedding, Jay states that Carol and the children were never cold. This is typical of a narcissist to know how someone else feels better than the person knows themselves ... although by the time he's finished they often really don't know how they feel.

The failure to give instructions

I wrote several letters asking Carol how I should reply to things and how she wanted to proceed, but didn't receive a response. However, when I asked her to attend a conference with counsel in London, she was able to get herself there without a problem.

I now understand that people who have been traumatised by abuse are not able to make decisions or have clarity about what to do next. However, if you give them simple instructions – such as to be somewhere at a specific time – they are able to respond to that. It would be a little easier now that we all have mobile phones, but Jay refused to allow Carol to use the home phone to call me when she asked, so she had to make calls from a pay phone or the neighbour's house. His solicitors then accused her of seeking to delay matters.

The failure to follow legal advice
Poor Carol just couldn't do what both her barrister and I were telling her she needed to do to protect her children and herself. And I could not understand why she wouldn't; I'd never heard of trauma bonding or Stockholm syndrome. Now I realise she had him in one ear and me in the other – and he was shouting louder and longer and she'd long been brainwashed and totally controlled by him.

So even if I had been more aware of what was really happening, would it have changed anything? I doubt it, because I think it would have been impossible for Carol to leave – even if Jay wasn't threatening her that she would lose custody of the children. There simply wasn't the awareness of abuse and coercive control that there is now, nor the help for it.

The narcissist always wins
I wish I could report something more positive from this whole sorry tale but, as is most often the case, Jay managed to manipulate everything to go his way. Much of the legal case I dealt with was about who owned how much of the house and it's unclear from the papers remaining whether this was ever resolved. What is clear, however, is that they both continued to live in the house, and when Carol's mental health was failing, Jay took her to his own solicitor (rather than back to me) to make her will. This left everything to him, rather than to her children as she wanted. Jay continues to live in the house to this day.

You can read Sarah's story and how she experienced all this as a child in Chapter 6. But for now, let's explore the narcissist's modus operandi in more detail.

CHAPTER 1:
RECOGNISING THE NARCISSIST'S ABUSE

It can be very hard indeed to recognise and then admit, even to yourself, that you're in a relationship with a narcissist. Accepting and admitting that you're being abused may be even harder as that sort of thing doesn't happen to people like you, and the shame you feel can be overwhelming.

The different types of abuse

Abuse is almost always done to control you and this can be achieved in one or more of the ways described in this chapter.

No matter what they may tell you, the abuser rarely loses control of themselves when they do any of these things. On the contrary, they control:

- Who they abuse, i.e. probably only you.
- When they abuse you, i.e. when no one else is around to see or hear it.
- Where they hit you, i.e. where the cuts or bruises won't show.
- Whose possessions they damage, i.e. yours, not their own.

Physical abuse

Pushing and shoving is physical abuse and may escalate to more serious assault or even strangulation. Backing you into a corner whilst shouting in your face is also physical abuse, even if they don't touch you. Harming pets or damaging your possessions are also aspects of physical abuse.

Emotional abuse

Some people consider emotional abuse to be less serious than physical, but those who have suffered both almost always say the emotional abuse is worse. Emotional abuse includes blaming and shaming you, intimidating you, isolating you, controlling you, shouting at you, calling you names and belittling and humiliating you.

Sexual abuse

Forcing you to have sex, even if you do so willingly at other times, is rape. Sexual abuse is any situation where you are forced or coerced to participate in unwanted, unsafe or degrading sexual activity.

Financial or economic abuse

Economic abuse includes not letting you have access to money or credit cards (whether yours or his), restricting you to a certain amount of money, and making you account for everything you spend. You may be prevented from working, or told when and where you can work. He may jeopardise your job by making you late for work or calling you all the time while you're there. He may even steal your money or possessions or force you to transfer your assets into his name. Or stop you having access to basic essentials, such as food, medicine or clothing. You may earn the money yourself, but still not be free to spend it how you wish or on yourself.

When we first met I had a successful music career, had toured the world and released many records, earned enough from my music to pay off my mortgage, employed managers, agents, accountants, publicists, musicians, engineers and so forth, and was totally financially self-sufficient. My husband is a lawyer and seemed so trustworthy and good at accounts and business that it wasn't difficult for him to convince me that it was easier if he took on the responsibility of handling all our money, and as we were married I felt this was safe. I trusted him completely.

He gradually took control over my bank accounts, credit cards, savings, phone contract, all household business, in fact anything concerning money/ bills/expenses, etc. When my mother died, he took complete control of her estate and my inheritance. I have been left with no legal or financial records from this time, including my bank statements, her will – nothing. Nor copies of any documents I may have signed. Nor where my Premium Bonds went as I have no paperwork to trace these. He has continued to control all matters regarding my finances since.

My husband could, on occasions, make grandiose gestures of generosity (especially in front of other people in bars, restaurants, parties, etc.) and sometimes a gift for me (my computer and iPhone) but these would be balanced out by months of extreme penny pinching, vigilance and nagging me over absolutely everything I needed to buy. He always treated himself very generously though.

When he left, he took all our savings and pension, and almost every document concerning our personal and home finances went with him.

I knew I needed to regain control of my own money/housing/accounts, etc. but as I had almost no paperwork to reference, it has been a nightmare making sense of it all and very frightening and stressful. I was advised by the police and my IDVA [independent domestic violence advisor] to contact my bank and credit card providers in order to stop my husband continuing to have access to my accounts. When I did I was horrified to discover that I had been left with only £28.75 in my accounts and large credit card debts with absolutely no savings, no family to help me, no rich friends and nothing personal of any value to sell to raise funds. That was the night I reached rock bottom and I seriously considered suicide. I called the Samaritans which I think saved me. The next day I told my IDVA and she very kindly arranged for me to use a food bank. Kind friends and neighbours also dropped off small food parcels from time to time to help out.

Narcissistic supply (or what fuels the narcissist)

The narcissist is a damaged individual who feels empty inside; with no sense of internal value he has to derive his worth from outside of himself. His emotional life is different from most people's and he's unable to empathise with others. He feeds off other people's emotions, but you can never give him enough admiration, attention, affection or validation; he's like an addict, always looking for his next fix and sucking the life out of everyone around him.

Narcissistic 'supply' is anything that feeds a narcissist's ego. It's his life blood, his fuel. Your fear is a good source of supply for the narcissist, as are any of the following:

- Keeping the focus of attention on himself
- Compliments, praise, adulation
- Status and reputation
- Winning, or achieving something
- Feeling powerful (having power over you)
- Feeling in control (being able to control you and his world)
- Conflict
- An addictive substance or activity
- Sex
- Emotional energy (which can be positive or negative)
- Money and financial resources
- A family structure
- Messing people around

- Withholding information
- Using the court system and his children as weapons of destruction

Narcissists obtain this supply from their victims by seduction, manipulation, anger and bullying behaviour. They use the conflict they create in different ways: sometimes so they can play the victim, sometimes to gain control, sometimes to upset or intimidate you, sometimes to get people scrambling to do what they want and sometimes so they can be the hero and save the day.

> *This is classic George the narcissist: mess everything up, step in as the rescuer and blame the original mess on someone else. I had to stop myself from thanking him for sorting it out!*

The entire purpose of your relationship and the one goal of everyone involved (including your children) is to feed the narcissist. This form of psychological manipulation works because when the narcissist is 'fed' and calmed, everyone involved is lulled into a false sense of security.

Every time you are fearful or angry you stimulate and entertain him, which makes him feel powerful and in control. And he won't hesitate to use his own children to make you react. Don't feed the monster!

How the abuser operates (watch and learn!)

Let's delve into more detail and explore the typical ways in which a narcissist behaves.

Relationships in general

> *You are incompatible from the start*
> *because you want a partner who makes you feel good.*
> *They want one who makes them look good.*

The narcissist isn't good at relationships – his personality is disordered so he doesn't relate to other people the way most of us do. But he's a good actor so he can fool you into thinking he does for quite a long time. Sooner or later, though, his relationships – work, family, friends, as well as intimate – will break down, which is why a disproportionate number of narcissists end up in divorce proceedings.

The narcissist is very needy. But like a bottomless pit, you can never fill that black hole. He will see you as having failed him and may soon move on to the next person. And the next .... he's a predator.

The narcissist defines the terms of his relationships so it will never be mutual or co-operative and you will not have been listened to. He lives by a set of double standards and he won't resolve conflicts. Like a toddler, he has great difficulty in managing his emotions when he's upset or frustrated, but unlike the toddler, he won't grow out of it. He's stuck in this stage of emotional development. In other words, you're not in an adult relationship.

Although demonstrations of physical affection and amazing sex may have been part of the 'love bombing' phase (more on this coming up), many narcissists are disinterested, often cruelly so, in this side of their relationships. They don't make love, they take it.

> *The lack of physical warmth and connection in my marriage was always the worst thing to cope with. There was no nurturing physical connection of any kind. He just wasn't interested. If I asked for a hug this would be done in a distracted, irritated fashion, which was worse to bear than no hug at all so I stopped asking. If penetrative sex wasn't the end result of touching there was no touching.*
>
> *The last time I tried to initiate sex he froze and looked really disgusted so I stopped and hurriedly left the room. Afterwards and over the subsequent years he has referred to this incident as sexual assault and attempted rape. The hurt and utter injustice I feel about this is so enormous I can hardly bring myself to face it even after so very long. As in all other matters, my husband was in control. If it wasn't totally his way it didn't happen at all.*

Love bombing, devalue, discard

Did you have a whirlwind romance with a person you thought was your soulmate as he smothered you with praise and attention, intense sex, exotic holidays, and promised you the moon for your future life together? Did the narcissist charm you into moving in together, or even marrying or having a child very quickly? This is the love bombing phase, characterised by overwhelming displays of attention, affection and grand romantic gestures. His aim here is to get you locked in as soon as he can so he doesn't have to keep up the pretence for too long.

The relationship begins to change soon afterwards. He starts to neglect you, withhold affection, take you for granted and make you feel devalued or unimportant. The only feelings he cares about are his own.

Narcissists are skilled at reading people and know how to love bomb, manipulate and devalue others, but they don't see the hurt they cause; they think they can sweep it under the carpet and that you'll forget. They deny and deflect. Or, when they do admit something happened, they dismiss it as of no importance and persuade you that you should just move forward.

The narcissist doesn't want your love. (He doesn't know what love is.) He wants your admiration and your obedience as a player in his make-believe world.

Narcissists are black and white thinkers; you are either with him (friend) or against him (foe). If you're an enemy, he's not happy unless he destroys you, and what better way to destroy someone than with a courtroom full of witnesses and drama. He thrives on drama.

Within the relationship, this drama may include dramatic exits, or sometimes just disappearances as he discards you, followed by his reappearance as if nothing had happened. Then the cycle begins again.

One of his first comments to me was, 'When I saw you at Michael's party I thought she looks hard work I'm steering clear of that one!' Followed by a constant drip feed of, 'You're no walk in the park', 'You're too high maintenance', 'You're no picnic', 'You're weird', 'You're selfish', 'You're too sensitive', 'You don't care about other people', 'You can't be left to travel alone as it's too dangerous', 'You don't know how to behave appropriately' and 'I'm the only person who really loves you', etc. The years and years of this constant verbal poison are devastating and I ended up believing all the negative things he kept drilling into me. I felt utterly alone, unloved and unlovable and really felt grateful to have him as no one else could possibly tolerate me.

The outside charm vs the inside horror (Jekyll and Hyde)

The abuse is hidden in plain sight.

No one else will see it, except maybe your children, so you end up questioning your own reality and sanity.

The narcissist charms anybody and everybody – including your friends and family if he can, and, of course, all the professionals involved in your court proceedings. But his charm and confidence is a mask that hides his insecurities and, behind closed doors, he turns into someone none of these other people would recognise.

You called the police after he hit you. They arrested him but he was so calm and polite and full of 'yes sirs' and 'no sirs' that they decided he couldn't possibly be abusive. They believed him when he said it was actually you who had lashed out at him. He hates the police and says they're all stupid (and worse) but is able to flip a switch and turn on the charm when he needs to. Remember, he loves drama, and he's a brilliant actor.

Not only charming, the narcissist is often highly intelligent and successful in the world; a high-profile job with a salary to match is just what he needs for his entitlement to admiration. No one wants to believe what a respected doctor, lawyer, teacher, police officer or MP is actually like behind closed doors. And he'll be telling you repeatedly that no one will believe you.

Some narcissists are 'do-gooders' who boost their self-esteem by doing wonderful things to help other people; Jimmy Savile springs to mind. Others are 100% anti-social and boost their self-esteem by putting others down in a destructive and hurtful way.

To the outside world he seems the perfect upstanding and morally blemish-free husband. He always did just enough to keep up appearances, particularly if he felt he might be observed or judged by outsiders, particularly anyone he considered powerful or upper class. I know he is writing his communications to me via texts and emails to be read by a third party and is consequently continuing the 'honest citizen' charade, which at first seems polite, reasonable and conscientious but which I know from bitter experience cannot be trusted in any way.

Isolation

An isolated partner is easier to victimise and control so it's common for narcissists to remove their victims from their support system.

A narcissist may isolate you by:

- Persuading you to move a long way away from your home town
- Persuading you not to see your friends as he can't cope without you
- Denigrating your family and friends to set you against them
- Stopping you from working
- Stopping you from driving
- Conducting smear campaigns that make you embarrassed to see people

Sometimes the need to isolate their partner stems from the insane jealousy the narcissist feels, for no reason that any 'normal' person could fathom; he may not even be able to tolerate you being alone with your own brother.

My husband worked very long hours, often including weekends, and usually socialised with work colleagues/clients/friends in the evenings on several nights a week, and sometimes weekends too. I was rarely invited to these events with the excuse 'Wives aren't invited', 'You wouldn't like it' or 'It's inappropriate'. My husband was usually unavailable in the evenings so I eventually stopped socialising as I was afraid to travel alone on public transport at night due to PTSD from a brutal attack I had experienced in the early 80s, which my husband knew about.

Over the years, through exhaustion and a complete lack of self-worth, I have become more and more isolated from my friends and other musicians and artists. Before we moved I had a large social circle and a lot of fun, surrounded by open, usually creative people who were on the same wavelength as me. There were good bars, clubs, music venues, etc. and I felt connected, supported and energised. It was a shock when we moved to an area he considered worthy of him and his status and that would impress his work colleagues and clients, and I realised it was a social desert for someone like me. It was lonely, I missed my old neighbourhood and I felt alienated, and some of my other friends drifted away as a result of my reclusiveness and his behaviour towards them.

People occasionally came to stay but my husband wasn't always as welcoming as he could be and he would often choose these rare occasions to be particularly vile to me just prior to their arrival. I would be upset, stressed and exhausted from trying to play happy families and present a front to the world. It was a nightmare trying to second guess whether or not he would be pleasant to people, boorish and provocative or simply refuse to join in at all. He could go upstairs in a huff and ignore them or behave sulkily, for example, sitting at the dinner table reading the paper and totally ignoring everyone else or being patronising if he thought someone wasn't clever enough or from the right sort of class background.

He only invited work friends back to our house once during the last 16 years. I had enjoyed meeting them and they seemed to enjoy the evening very much too. It was so lovely to get a brief glimpse into his 'other world' and share it for a while and I had hoped this would happen more often. When I asked him why he didn't invite more people over he replied that he was too ashamed of our house (with six bedrooms in a fashionable part of London) and that I wouldn't be able to get on with them anyway. I could regularly go for five or six days a week without seeing another living person and would pathetically anticipate the window cleaner or gardeners coming as I would have some company for a while.

Communication – welcome to the world of 'narc speak'

*I feel his aim is for me to have him
in the forefront of my mind at all times.*

The narcissist dominates the conversation and, if someone else does manage to get a word in, they will soon interrupt or make it clear they are not interested by looking away, fidgeting, or tapping their fingers. If you do manage to get your point across, they will simply ignore it if it doesn't suit them. They will turn the conversation back to themselves and what they want, whilst making negative remarks about you or those close to you.

Obfuscation or making things unclear is a hallmark of the narcissist and best ignored if you can. Simple conversations become crazy-making marathons. Where most of us speak logically, the narcissist uses word salad, or 'narc speak' (i.e. gobbledygook), which is intended to make him sound knowledgeable. And when you don't understand it – which of course you're not supposed to – it's your fault, not his, because you're not as intelligent as he is, which is why the poor man has to keep repeating himself. If you try to challenge him about anything, he throws all sorts of words and phrases together, some of which contradict each other, as he takes you round and round in circles. His aim is to frustrate you so that you give up and do things his way, and don't bother trying to hold him to account for anything he does in the future.

'I'm sorry' aren't words you'll hear the narcissist say very often. If he does, he's likely to say 'I'm sorry you feel that way' rather than actually take responsibility for his actions. Or the unspoken words after 'I'm sorry' might be 'that I got caught out'.

Your narcissist may promise you the world, and then fail to deliver. That's when you realise you've been manipulated into doing something you didn't want to, or punished for not doing something he wanted you to do. Either way, if you complain about what he's failed to do, he'll either lie and tell you he never promised he would, or turn it back on you saying your expectations are unreasonable and so it's all your fault.

A narcissist only ever talks about himself. He doesn't have any other topic of conversation. So whatever he's accusing you of, you can be pretty sure he's doing it himself. And if he says he's not doing something, be very suspicious that he is. One of my clients received an email from her ex saying 'I have paid your credit card bill and will continue to do so until we make some other arrangement. I have no wish to punish you or make you destitute.' That told me very clearly that he did wish to punish her and/or make her destitute. Any 'normal' person would have ended the message after the word 'arrangement'.

It's worth making a careful study of the words the narcissist uses as they can give you valuable clues as to his actions and intentions. Just be sure not to react to them. Play the sleuth. Look for a pattern in his emails. Maybe he first compliments you, then puts you down, before ending with a victim statement. Once you see the pattern, it's easier to ask yourself what his point is. Usually it's just to get a reaction from you, in which case, you can see that no reply is necessary (or advisable). There's more on communicating with a narcissist in Chapter 5.

The lies

The lies trip off the tongue, like butter off a hot knife.

Of all the dreadful things narcissists do, their lies seem to distress their victims and cause them more pain than anything else. And they lie a lot! A person with borderline personality disorder (BPD) or narcissistic personality disorder (NPD) – see Chapter 3 for the different types of narcissist – may lie to distort reality into something that fits with the emotions they are feeling, or with their version of the facts. A sociopath often lies for their own personal gain, or just for pleasure.

Perhaps the lies, even more than their other behaviours, highlight the huge divide between the narcissist and their victim because it's in such stark contrast to the latter's own honesty.

I feel I have to prove I'm telling the truth.

And although the victim is well aware that her partner frequently bends the truth, even when not telling outright lies, she still seems to be outraged, if not poleaxed, by his lies, especially when they're about her. Her biggest fear may be that everyone will believe his lies.

How does the narcissist convince everyone else that what he says is true, even though you know he's lying through his teeth? He's clever. He's worked it all out and he mixes his lies with a few grains of truth, possibly facts that can be checked and therefore lend credence to the rest. And he's probably rehearsed it so many times that he's come to believe his lies himself and therefore sounds all the more credible.

I get sucked in by a grain of truth.

Although you will see how well the lies work for him, and the truth doesn't work for you, don't be tempted to sink to his level. At least, never say anything that he could possibly know or find out is not true or he will dismantle your story before not only your eyes, but the judge's too.

If you're able to change your mindset a little, it can really help; for example, start looking for the truthful statements rather than the lies. Expect the lies, they're who he is; you wouldn't waste your time and energy trying to get a leopard to change his spots, so use the same acceptance with the narcissist. Nothing you say will change him. You can only change how you react. So deciding not to let it stress you, and focusing on you, rather than him, will make your life happier. The lies are used to distract from the real issues so try not to get side-tracked.

You feel and know that for the narcissist that is their absolute truth.
That they wholeheartedly believe their lies as fact. There would be no
defending of yourself. It would be a battle you could never win. And you
know that their personality is so all-consuming, that anyone listening would
believe them without question. And so you have someone that speaks
untruth. An injustice on everything you are. Everything that makes you
you. And there is nothing you can do about it. Except sit back and let
their words seep out of their mouths like a leaking oil vat.

Gaslighting

'A lie once told remains a lie,
but a lie told a thousand times becomes the truth.'
Joseph Goebbels, Nazi propagandist

Gaslighting is yet more lies, but even worse. It's a pattern of manipulation used by narcissists, dictators and cult leaders to gain control of people. It's a common tactic in coercive control and makes the victim question their own reality; you start to think you're going mad and then they can get you to believe absolute absurdity. He humiliates you but you blame yourself and defend him when anyone else challenges you. You end up not knowing where you are and having to depend on him.

The term 'gaslighting' comes from the 1944 film *Gaslight*, where the husband kept turning down the gas supply so the lights dimmed, and insisting that his wife was imagining it.

Gaslighting is not a one-off event. It's a series or pattern of behaviour and it's unlikely to happen every day, or even every week – narcissists play the long game. They use this form of psychological abuse to cause confusion, disorientation and anxiety, to the point where their victims don't trust their own memory or judgement and have to depend on the perpetrator, who can then take control of their life.

They do it to keep you off-balance, and sometimes just to amuse themselves. They try to convince you that you're wrong about something, even when they know, and you know, that you're not. They tell blatant lies, denying that something just happened: 'I didn't hit you, you're making it up, it was you who hit me.' They manipulate everything. They eat your sandwich while your back is turned and then convince you that you ate it yourself. The more you lose confidence in yourself, and start to question your own reality, the less likely you are to challenge your partner and the more he will be in control of you.

Donald Trump, the narcissist we all know, used classic gaslighting behaviour when he told us that what we were seeing and what we were hearing was not what we were seeing and hearing. How many times did he repeat that the 2020 presidential election was 'stolen' or 'fraudulent', despite the evidence to the contrary (i.e. that Joe Biden won with 7 million more votes)? And when his lawyers were asked for proof of any alleged fraud they produced none; there was nothing to produce, but that doesn't deter a narcissist.

Gaslighting is often done by perpetrators who are not violent, but instead use gaslighting as well as other forms of controlling behaviour, such as surveillance or isolating their victim, in order to gain control over them. It's done over a long period of time, and it can be subtle and hard for you or others to spot. It's also hard for you to be believed by others; who would trust your version if you said your husband kept dimming the lights – why would anyone do that? In the end you come to believe his lies, fairy tales and re-writing of history.

Perhaps you agreed to go shopping with your partner on Saturday, but when you ask what time they want to go they tell you they said Sunday not Saturday. You think you heard or remembered it wrongly and it's no big deal.

You prepare a special meal for them: prawns, their favourite. They tell you they hate shellfish and boil themselves an egg instead. Did you mishear or misremember what they told you about prawns a few weeks ago?

You left your keys on the table by the front door when you came in yesterday. Now you're late for work and they're not there. You empty your handbag and rush round the house searching everywhere, until he tells you they're on the table where you left them. Did you imagine they weren't there before?

You've got friends coming to dinner and, as you're working from home with a deadline to meet, he said he'd pick up the lamb chops on his way home from work. He arrives late, and without the meat. He denies ever saying he'd get it; he told you he'd be late and clearly remembers you saying you'd go to the shop. You get upset and angry, and he tells you you're always overreacting. But he says he'll go and get the chops now, even though he's supposed to be sending an urgent email for work. When your guests arrive he apologises for the meal not being ready and explains that you've been on a spa day with a friend and had completely forgotten to buy the food and how he'd had to make a heroic dash to get it before the shop closed.

Gaslighting allows the narcissist to remain blameless, and to look like either a hero or a victim, depending on which fits the bill in the particular circumstances.

And then he starts to gaslight your friends and family by telling them you're struggling with your mental health.

If the narcissist is also gaslighting your children, it's important to help them as much as you can to know what is normal and right, and to be able to trust themselves. The narcissistic parent may tell them that what they are feeling is not how they feel, or make fun of them if they're upset or angry. Your ex will convince the children that they're always wrong and he is right, and will blame the children for anything that goes wrong, even when they know it's not their fault. And if it really is their fault, their 'offence' will be blown out of all proportion. They may be told:

- You're making a big deal out of nothing.
- Don't be so dramatic.
- You're being too emotional.
- You're just tired, go to sleep.
- You're so sensitive.
- You should have known …
- I'm only punishing you because I love you.
- You're not upset about your friend hitting you, you're just bad tempered.

Read more about the narcissist's effects on your children (and what to do about it) in Chapter 6.

If you manage to escape this dreadful relationship and find yourself before the family court, you could be subjected to more gaslighting there. Your accounts of the abuse are disbelieved or minimised, and you're effectively told that it is more harmful to a child not to see their abusive parent than it is to be further abused by them. In other words, despite his dreadful abuse of his children's mother, he is still a 'good father'.

You will be told that your case is 'high conflict', meaning the court and/or Cafcass (Children and Family Court Advisory and Support Service) believe you are as responsible as your ex for the angry exchanges and damage to your children, whilst refusing to recognise the abuse you have suffered. You'll be told you have to co-parent with your ex, which of course isn't possible (see parallel parenting, Chapter 6, instead). You may be told you have to stop breastfeeding because it's more beneficial for your baby to spend extensive time with her father than to be breastfed. If your children complain of abuse, you may be told that you are encouraging the children to lie.

If you think you may be a victim of gaslighting, it might help to keep a journal and write everything down so you can check back as to what's been said before – though it won't help to argue with the narcissist or point out their gaslighting as they will just tie you in even more knots. A trusted friend may be able to help you sort out reality from the narcissist's fantasy, but otherwise professional help is invaluable to help you recover from this insidious form of abuse.

He was fond of 'gaslighting' or saying I am mad or imagining things, hiding silly things like backdoor keys or household items and pretending not to. Telling me that I need help, that I am mentally unstable, am just too much to bear and that is why I never see him. Maybe if I was different he might still care. Saying again and again that I drink too much or am drunk which is totally untrue and makes me feel angry and bitter as, ironically, he is the one with an alcohol problem and could hardly get through dry January and drinks spirits and beer every day when he is in his room upstairs. It's almost as if he is using my imaginary 'drinking' as a reason to justify his callous disregard for my needs and concerns; using this fake excuse to pass them off as the unreasonable rantings of a drunken woman. Like blaming a girl's choice of skimpy clothing as an excuse for raping her.

I may be protesting too much but this new game has been particularly hurtful as my father was an alcoholic and it killed him. I was his primary carer towards the end and the wounds from that experience are still very raw.

Each time he uses this tactic to discredit me it is deeply cruel of him and very, very painful. Because of my father's drink problem, I have always been hyper-vigilant regarding alcohol and any possible inherited addiction issues but I am lucky not to have this illness. For almost three years I didn't touch any alcohol at all as I was on a Weight Watchers' diet and didn't need the calories. During this period I didn't crave a drink or even think about alcohol. My husband continually tried to sabotage my efforts by leaving tempting foods and drink in obvious view even after my repeated requests for him to take them away so I wouldn't be tempted. I succeeded in spite of his efforts to sabotage me. I used to joke about it at the WW meetings.

Hoovering

Just as you hoover the carpet, he hoovers (sucks) you back in if you try to leave. He will start to behave as he did when you fell for him at the beginning of your relationship, telling you how wonderful you are and all the things he loves about you. And he insists he's going to change and things will be different this time. They will be different, but unfortunately worse different not better different as you go through the cycle of love bombing/devalue/discard once again.

Police involvement

Even in cases where there's no physical violence, the police will often be involved. The narcissist loves a drama and to have the blues and twos screech up to his door gives him a hefty dose of narcissistic supply. If he threatened or hit you, he'll swiftly claim that you did just that to him, and call the police. He's a brilliant actor and he'll be totally cool, calm and collected when the police arrive, whilst you're more likely a gibbering wreck so he can say that you're crazy or violent. He'll have you arrested, and sent to prison if he can.

He'll then use all that against you in children proceedings, saying that you're a danger to your children as well as to him. You then spend all your time trying to defend yourself, and his abuse gets lost in the chaos.

We had an argument and I snapped and tore up a small photograph on display in the house. I destroyed it because it had his father in it and his father had sexually molested me as often as he could during the first five or six years of our marriage. Out of kindness and to stop him feeling conflicted about his father, I didn't tell my husband about the abuse until both his parents had died but by the time of our fight he was well aware of what had happened. I couldn't stand to see the photograph each time I went into the room as it caused flashbacks of the abuse. I didn't understand why he couldn't display it in his own bedroom or in a drawer or album where I wouldn't have to keep seeing it on a daily basis.

After I had torn up the photo, he grabbed my arms very tightly and wouldn't let go. He caused my arms to bleed and was really hurting me and pushing me towards the corner of the room. Eventually I scratched his face with my arthritic hands and very short 'gardener's nails' and he let go. I ran downstairs and locked myself in the living room then hid in the pantry. I was terrified and in shock. He called the police who smashed through the sitting room door and had me arrested for criminal damage to the photo and ABH. I was handcuffed and marched along the street in the middle of the day in front of all the neighbours and put into the back of a police van.

The police were so, so kind to me even though I freely admitted that I had done something wrong and accepted that I would be punished for it. I sensed that they could tell that there was more to the situation than a few scratches on his face especially when they photographed my arm marks. I asked the man at the desk if I was going to prison and he looked at me so kindly but with such pity that I just couldn't stop crying. I was so traumatised that large sections of that day are still a blank.

I spent about 12 hours locked in a cell and when the lady in charge arrived for the night session she opened the hatch in the door and talked to me for ages. Her kindness tore me apart. I'm sure she and everyone else knew what may really have occurred. She said that some things happen in life which are signposts and we can take notice of them or not as we choose, but that this experience may well be a sign for me. She also mentioned her own marriage breakdowns and told me that I needed to look after myself and stop worrying about other people. I experienced more kindness and understanding from the police that day than I had at home for so many years that I told the officer that I felt safer and more at peace in that cell than I have ever felt in our home and at that point I almost wanted to go to prison just to escape my husband and the torture of my marriage.

Eventually I gave my statement to a detective who said she suspected that what had happened prior to my arrest was simply my acting in self-defence and that, if I wanted, the police could press charges against my husband for me. I said no as I was too afraid to provoke him. He dropped the charges against me as I guess he thought I had been taught enough of a lesson for that day. The detective called me a number of times at home to check I was okay and kindly put Women's Aid in touch with me for continued counselling and support. As it wasn't safe at home, I had my first support/counselling session sitting on the floor of my next door neighbour's communal hallway.

When the person from Women's Aid told me that my husband's behaviour was domestic violence and coercive control, I didn't believe her and still vacillated, even though four professionals had by now said the same thing. I loved my husband and was still resistant to the idea of him as an abuser and was almost ready to stay in the marriage, get some therapy and forgive him.

However this changed when he went back to the police a second time the following week. I have subsequently learned a lot and that using the police for harassment is a common tactic used by abusers.

Debts

They just spend, spend, spend ....
and leave everyone else to pick up the pieces!

Narcissists often have huge debts, because they're worth it. And because they can talk people into lending them money. Most of us wouldn't be able to sleep at night owing that much money, but the narcissist doesn't bat an eyelid and will borrow still more to cover his legal fees.

How they get away with not repaying debts is still a mystery to me, but they do! If you're going through financial proceedings in court (Chapter 12), analyse his debts carefully so they're not put on to you as 'matrimonial debts'.

I don't look at bank statements because I'm afraid to look.

If the debt is in his name only then you're not liable to his creditors. They will only go after him. But if he can persuade the family court his debts were accrued for the benefit of his family, they will be taken off before the capital is divided and you'll lose out.

Keith did get a better job after taking a degree course,
but he does not have a student loan. It's what he and his
solicitor are calling his credit card debt!

And if he hasn't issued financial proceedings when it would have been the logical thing to do, or if he's threatened it several times but never gone through with it, consider whether he doesn't want to have to disclose all his debts. Some narcissists hide assets, others hide debts.

You too may have debts. You may well have been persuaded to lend or give him money, or to sign a loan agreement. Or you may find you've 'signed' for things you had no idea about. Or he may not have allowed you to work but kept you so short of money you had to take out debts to survive. He'll do all he can to make sure you can't afford legal representation.

Blaming, shaming and narcissistic rage

Hell hath no fury like a narcissist scorned.

Nothing is ever the narcissist's fault; he's perfect and therefore can't ever be wrong. Even when faced with incontrovertible evidence to the contrary, a narcissist won't accept responsibility. Somehow he will turn it around and make it your fault, or say you made him do it. If you blame a narcissist, they rage, often behaving like a toddler throwing his toys out of the pram. His black and white thinking extends to himself; he's either all good, or all bad, unlike most of us who understand that we all have good and bad traits. Being in the wrong means to him that he's worthless. He can't stand that so he has to make you wrong instead.

Usually he'll throw you under the bus to save himself but occasionally he'll admit to what he's done – if it suits him and he can use it to his advantage. Survivors are often desperate for this validation and can be devastated to find that an admission lasts only minutes or days before being turned on its head. He didn't stab you at all, it was you who was violent to him and he shows everyone the scar to prove it. And only you know he's had that scar since he fell off his bike aged 15.

The narcissist loves to humiliate other people. It's another way he can feel he's won and he loves to inflict on others the pain he is desperate to avoid himself: his own humiliation. He believes he's perfect and better than everyone else and he needs to cling tightly to this delusion as his larger-than-life persona is all he has; it's his cover for his empty inner core which is devoid of meaningful values and attachments.

It's a survival mentality, essentially. Narcissists have a fragile sense of self and they really can't take responsibility for anything that could make them look bad in any way, which is why they never apologise. They would feel exposed and could shatter. They came to the conclusion as a child that the world is not a safe place and that it's a 'me or you' world. And if it's got to be one of us it's got to be me, so I'm not going to give you anything.

When he calls you fat or ugly, he does it to save his own fragile ego. He has no intuition or inner sense of what's wrong but he doesn't want to look stupid in front of you. So instead he just puts all the blame for the failing sex life onto you.

He may believe that he's unfairly maligned by other people, which can make him play the victim and seethe with resentment. He can't stand any blow to his ego or status and his reactions to shame tend to be grossly disproportionate to the 'offence' he feels has been committed against him; he may hold a grudge or continue to punish the 'offender' for years to come.

Sometimes a mere prick of shame could literally burst his bubble and threaten to destroy him, whilst the 'offender' (i.e. you) has little idea of why their innocent comment or request to please pick up his dirty socks has provoked such a violent reaction. His rage serves to deflect attention from his inner emptiness, which needs to be constantly filled with admiration and ministrations.

Narcissistic rage is not a pretty sight and you'll want to close your ears to the insults hurled at you. But try to note them objectively because in his rage the narcissist will let slip some useful clues about himself. (He always talks about himself, even when he's pointing at you.) Sometimes the rage can take the form of physical violence in the narcissist's attempt to make you pay; others will take you to court instead.

A narcissist's rage can also be brought on by the weakness of others, which the narcissist finds contemptible and worthy of punishment in his bid for superiority. Again, this can be his attempt to hide (especially from himself) an aspect of himself, in this case perhaps his traumatic childhood. If you can listen objectively and keep in mind that it's not really about you at all, there may be clues in the words he uses.

Failing to follow his 'rules' or 'behave' as he dictates may remind him of his loss of control over you and make him lash out. Leaving a narcissist causes them a big narcissistic injury, and you will be punished accordingly. If they 'had' to leave you because of your 'behaviour' (i.e. because you weren't, or didn't do, all they wanted during the relationship), you will also have to pay for this.

Smear campaigns and revenge porn

Smear campaigns are common at the end of a relationship with a narcissist; they can be his tactic to take you down before you can do the same to him, or part of his ambition to destroy you. And of course it's a great source of narcissistic supply for him. He still wants to control you and your life, and the stronger you get and the less you engage in his nonsense, the more he finds other ways to hurt you.

If you have a history of mental health problems, he'll use them against you, even if they were caused by his abuse. If you don't, he'll make them up if he wants to prove you're an 'unfit mother'. If it's not your mental health, he'll tell people you're drinking to excess, taking drugs or sleeping with a different man each night. Either way, he may well say you're not fit to be a mother to his children and they should therefore live with him. He seems not to remember that you cared for them for years, almost single-handedly, before you separated – with none of these complaints.

Smear campaigns can go on for years because they don't want to see you happy or doing well as that would indicate that he had been the problem in the relationship, not you as he insists. He won't move on after the divorce as normal people do, he'll continue to make problems in any way he still can to keep you feeling vulnerable and scared.

Unfortunately, you have to accept that there's little you can do; you can't stop him telling anyone what he wants to tell them. He's an awful person and you can't control what he says, only how you respond. And the answer is don't respond, and don't dwell on what he's doing or he's still at the forefront of your mind (which is, after all, what he wants). Don't give him your thoughts or energy. Don't feed the monster, in other words; focus on your new life instead.

Of course you'll be worried about the damage to your reputation, but don't be tempted to engage or fight back. That's just what he wants you to do and it will only fuel the fire. The harsh reality is that yours is not a normal divorce and there's likely to be a lot of collateral damage. You may lose friends, a job, or even family in your bid for freedom and a new life. The smear campaign may be another smoke screen behind which he's doing all sorts of other things, so don't get distracted by trying to clear your name. Don't take your eye off the ball. Hold on to your truth and let everyone else work it out for themselves in their own good time.

It's more common than you might imagine (just google 'revenge porn') for abusers to threaten to share intimate images with a victim's family or friends or on social media as a way of controlling and frightening them.

If you're not aware that he has any images, and he's just told you he's secretly recorded you having sex, do ask him to show you what he has before you panic. If he refuses, you can be pretty sure he has nothing.

Whether you were recorded in secret or not, it's a criminal offence (punishable with up to two years in prison) to show a private sexual photograph or film of you to another person, or to share it via social media, without your consent and with the intention of causing you distress. Threats to share intimate or sexual images are also now a crime under the Domestic Abuse Act 2021 (see Chapter 16) so don't hesitate to report his threats or actual disclosures to the police.

Threatening suicide, guns

Threatening suicide is another form of narcissistic manipulation. Please don't fall for it. As with everything else, you should just ignore it. Sometimes it's part of the daily drama to get narcissistic supply, sometimes it's part of the 'poor me' victim playing.

Very, very occasionally, they mean it and do kill themselves. But a death is very rare indeed compared with the number of threats that are made. Of course, if it does happen, it's usually awful for everyone involved but that may depend on how dreadful the abuser was. If you've read Rachel Williams's *The Devil at Home,* or have heard of her #dontlookback hashtag or SUTDA (Stand up to Domestic Abuse) organisation, you'll know that she was shot and beaten by her ex, and you won't imagine that she felt anything but relief at his death. Either way, if it should happen to you it's not your fault. Or even your responsibility; their disordered personality was not down to you, but was probably a result of their upbringing (or possibly their genes). If you have a child old enough to understand what's happened then some therapy will be essential to ensure they are not feeling any guilt, which children commonly do for far less than a death.

Guns are a common possession of narcissists. But like actual suicides, it's very rare that they're used. You just have to have seen it and know it's there for him to establish his control over you. It's enough for you to fear what might happen if you were to step out of (his) line.

The silent treatment/stonewalling/ghosting

This is a particularly cruel form of passive-aggressive emotional abuse used to punish and control a partner whilst giving the message of how insignificant and unworthy of any attention they are. Your increasingly frantic efforts to communicate are just the reaction he wants: a wonderful source of narcissistic supply together with a feeling of domination and control over you.

Recognise it for the immature manipulation it is from a person unable to communicate in the normal way. It can be a form of gaslighting if he suddenly starts talking to you again while acting as if nothing happened.

Projection

He projected so much on to me I felt like a cinema screen.

Projection is when you split off a part of you that's too painful or shameful for you to own and project it on to someone else, believing your stuff is their stuff. This is another way of not taking responsibility and shifting the blame on to someone else. It's a survival mechanism for someone with a fragile sense of self. So when a narcissist is accused of something, they have to push it away and push it onto you to deflect it away from themselves.

Your first inclination is to fight back, to defend yourself and point out that he's accusing you of exactly what he's doing. But your anger and outrage is feeding the monster with narcissistic supply, which is just what he wants. So stop, breathe and think before you react. Ask yourself if he's projecting his stuff on to you. If so, don't take the bait, just say calmly and without emotion 'I hear what you're saying' or 'I understand your position'. After all, there's absolutely nothing you can say that'll convince him he's wrong, so walk away.

Although you mustn't react to the names the narcissist calls you, it's good to take note of them because they're usually talking about themselves (their favourite subject, which they rarely depart from). You can learn a lot from their accusations; for example, if he's accusing you of having an affair, it probably means he's having or has had one (and often more than one).

Remember it's not about you; he's confessing to something he's done and projecting it on to you, so be grateful for the information and work out how best to use it in the future.

Flying monkeys

Flying monkeys are people recruited by the narcissist to do his dirty work, usually to abuse a victim on his behalf but sometimes to persuade her to do something he wants, such as go back to him.

The term comes from *The Wizard of Oz*, where the Wicked Witch dispatched monkeys to fly and get Dorothy and her dog. The monkeys obeyed her command, doing her dirty work for her, taunting and terrorizing Dorothy as she tried in vain to get back home. Flying monkeys may be his friends, family members, or even his own children. They may be minor narcissists themselves, but often they are just charmed and misled by the narcissist. Or maybe they're frightened into doing his bidding.

The narcissist's new partner may unwittingly be a flying monkey. He can play the long game with his great acting skills so that she remains convinced that he's a great dad, desperately missing his children who are being unjustly kept from him by you. In court proceedings, her narrative may be extremely valuable to him, to show he's not a risk and has a stable home for the children.

Understand who and what your ex's flying monkeys are, develop a tough skin, anticipate them, and do all you can not to respond emotionally.

Triangulation

This is another narcissistic manipulation tactic. It's used to divide and conquer two people and pit them against each other, and your ex may do this with you and his new partner (for example, by telling the children his new partner is a better parent than you). It doesn't work to argue with your children when they come home and tell you this; you'll want to rise above it and not join in with the narcissist's games. You can tell the children that it hurts you that they feel the new person is better, and remind them that you're their mother and are always there for them. And you can demonstrate that by making sure your home is always calm and welcoming and that you still love and accept them no matter how hurtful they are at times.

Sometimes the narcissist will triangulate his own children by playing one off against the other, where one is the golden child and the other the scapegoat (see Chapter 6).

Affairs

It's very common for narcissists to have affairs, often more than one as they have no boundaries. Their sense of entitlement justifies their departure from the social norm, and their lack of empathy means they don't know or care how hurt you might be.

If you confront him, he's likely to deny it and turn it back on to you – you've been acting suspiciously and he suspects you're seeing someone else, or you have trust issues due to your poor relationship with your father, or even how could you blame him for an affair seeing how fat and ugly you are?

Not all narcissists cheat, but for those who don't it's because they're not very sexual or they didn't want to risk damaging their public reputation, not because they value their partner. Some are sex addicts, while others are addicted to shopping, gambling, etc.

Narcissists have double standards; they demand your loyalty and monogamy – you can't even say hello to another man without them being insanely jealous – but it doesn't apply to them and they don't understand why you'd be upset by their affairs.

It's much less common for the partner of a narcissist to have an affair. But it certainly does happen as they can become desperate for the real love, attention and intimacy that they are never going to get from the narcissist.

Harassment, stalking and recording

*I started to detach from him in a way that I have
never done before.*

*He started to be even more controlling,
stalking me and following me.*

*I found him behind my back on more than one occasion
while returning home from work, even if on the phone
he'd said he'd be somewhere else.*

Stalking is any persistent (as in, it happens at least two or three times) and unwanted attention that makes you feel pestered, harassed, alarmed or distressed. It includes cyber-stalking or online threats.

It's a criminal offence so don't hesitate to report it to the police. You can also get help from the National Stalking Helpline.

As well as sending you incessant texts and emails, the narcissist will use all sorts of authorities to harass you. He'll report you to social services (probably more than once) for abusing or neglecting the children – or for something much more trivial, but they'll still have to investigate. He'll ring the police with some story about how worried he is about his children so they have to come round and do a welfare check, frightening both you and the children. He'll report you to your boss, and if you're a professional, to your professional body. He may report you to HMRC. If you're not a British national, he'll report you to the Home Office.

And much of the time, the abuser doesn't actually report you at all, but continues to blackmail and control you with his threats to do so. Some of them won't stop at you; they'll threaten to report your family to the authorities, or they'll report your solicitor to the Solicitors Regulation Authority (SRA). It's one of his best control tactics to ensure you comply with his demands.

Court proceedings

Our adversarial legal system allows the narcissist to take you back to court for another fight every time he gets bored, or feels he's losing control over you. He'll start with getting an order for contact with the children, but soon be back applying for more. You'll just catch your breath and he'll make another application, asking for shared care (50/50 custody) this time.

The court enables the narcissist to continue his abuse of you and the children. This is horrific, but it's a fact. It's a little-known fact, because family court proceedings are held in secret, but the truth is beginning to come out now thanks to the Harm Report. Read more about the family court system in Chapter 9 and the Harm Report in Chapter 16.

CHAPTER 2:
CONTROLLING RELATIONSHIPS AND COERCIVE CONTROL: HOW DOMESTIC ABUSE ISN'T ALWAYS PHYSICAL

I was not even able to go to the shop to buy bread without him getting super anxious and questioning me:
Where did you go? What did you buy? Where is the bread you bought? How much did you pay for it? Where's the receipt?

Bullying, cruelty and all varieties of abuse can be going on behind the most ordinary facades. They want you unstable so they can control you better. The US writer Evan Stark first coined the phrase 'coercive control' to help explain that domestic abuse is not just about physical abuse.

Coercive control (the formal name for what's more usually referred to as a 'controlling relationship') has been a criminal offence since 2015, although unfortunately there have not been a great number of prosecutions yet. That's in the criminal courts. The family court is even slower to catch up.

Recognising controlling and coercive behaviour

If you feel controlled, frightened, isolated or dependent because of the way your partner behaves towards you, this may amount to coercive control.

In 2019, Sally Challen's successful appeal against her conviction for murdering her controlling husband brought coercive control into public awareness. So much so that it's now recognised as a common feature in many abusive relationships.

According to the law:

- **Controlling behaviour** is an act or pattern of acts designed to make a person subordinate and/or dependent by isolating them from sources of support, exploiting their resources and capacities for personal gain, depriving them of the means needed for independence, resistance and escape and regulating their everyday behaviour.

- **Coercive behaviour** is an act or a pattern of acts of assault, threats, humiliation and intimidation or other abuse that is used to harm, punish, or frighten the victim.

That's what the law says, but what does it mean in everyday life? Firstly, as it's usually a pattern of behaviour rather than actions, it's much more subtle than, say, punching someone, leaving blood and bruises visible to all. Physical abuse can happen alongside coercive control, but controlling abusers are often too clever to leave any evidence. Which is why I believe rape is a more common form of physical abuse in these cases – the ultimate act of control and coercion, but very hard for a woman to prove.

Although more women than men are said to be victims of coercive control, women can be equally controlling, even if not so physically intimidating; they may, for instance, threaten their partner with never seeing their children again. Regardless of the perpetrator's gender, their aim is to take away their partner's freedom, and to strip away their sense of self.

Other forms of control and coercion include:

- Isolating you from your friends and family, for example, by not speaking to you for a week if you go to see them, or limiting the time you're allowed to spend with them, so it becomes easier not to go and you eventually become dependent on your partner.
- Depriving you of your basic needs – not just food and shelter, etc. I've even heard of someone not being allowed to use the toilet.
- Constantly checking up on you, monitoring you with online communication tools or hiding a camera in the house, tracking your movements on an iPhone, or stalking you.
- Surveillance can continue even when your partner is not present, either by constant phone calls or texts, using the children to report back, or having brainwashed you to continue behaving in the way they want.
- Controlling how much money you have and how you spend it.
- Micro-managing your everyday life, such as where you can go, who you can see or speak to, what you can wear, what you can eat, etc.
- Questioning your behaviour.
- Putting you down in public.
- Repeatedly telling you you're worthless, stupid and unattractive. Or that you do everything wrong or badly and would be nothing without him, as no one else would love you.

- Changing how they are towards you, i.e. nice one minute and nasty the next, so you don't know where you are with them.
- Constantly monitoring and criticising you, with every move being checked against an unpredictable, ever-changing, 'rule-book', such as rules about how you cook, housekeep, parent, perform sexually and socialise.
- Financial control, such as allowing you little or no money, or demanding that you explain all your expenditure.
- Threats to hurt or kill you, your child or pets.
- Threats to reveal or publish your private information.
- Threats to report you to the police or other authorities.
- Threats to take you (back) to court.
- Damaging your belongings, or house/contents.
- Preventing you from having access to transport or from working in certain places.
- Keeping you (and the children) waiting by arriving late.
- Mind games and gaslighting.
- Not discussing your needs (because they are not important).

The effects on victims

You can see how the forms of coercion and control track so closely to narcissistic behaviour. But what does it feel like to be in a controlling or coercive relationship?

- Walking on eggshells. You have to say or do things in a particular way or your partner will get angry.
- Living in a world of shifting sand or moving goalposts.
- Being taken hostage – a captive in an unreal world created by your partner.
- Trapped in a world of confusion, contradiction and fear.
- Adapting your normal behaviour in order to survive.
- Loss of self-confidence and constantly doubting and questioning yourself.

When children are involved, perpetrators often continue to control their former partners even after the relationship has ended. I hear stories of cameras being hidden in children's bags or teddies to monitor what's going on at home when the children are too young to be used as spies.

Evan Stark described controlling behaviour as 'akin to terrorism and hostage taking'. But his research has shown how hard it can be to recognise, as it's often the man controlling his female partner by micro-regulating some of the daily activities commonly undertaken by women in their traditional roles as homemakers, mothers and sexual partners. And it can be easy to confuse control with romantic love, especially when he tells her that his jealous behaviour, along with telling her what to wear, is because he loves her so much.

Coercive control doesn't leave bruises or broken bones, which are the traditional signs of domestic abuse. And once the abuser has gained control of his partner, he often needs to use no more than a look, movement or phrase that will be totally innocuous to an outsider but enough for his victim to know that she's about to break one of his (frequently changing and often unspoken) rules. The power and dynamics in a relationship are hard for others to analyse, which is why there have been so few prosecutions, and why the family courts get it so wrong.

The key takeaway here is that, if your ex was or is using controlling or coercive behaviour, that is domestic abuse. Whether he was physically violent or not. And whilst you may struggle to get others to recognise the abuse, recognising yourself that you have been a victim of abuse is a key step on the road to recovery.

CHAPTER 3:
THE DIFFERENT TYPES OF NARCISSIST

We can all be narcissistic and some narcissism is healthy. Whether or not it is healthy can be gauged by a person's capacity for empathy. Empathy is something most of us have naturally but narcissists are tuned out of caring. Although they may intellectually understand someone is hurt or upset and react accordingly, they cannot feel it themself or put themself in someone else's shoes.

There are people who are just plain selfish, but who are not narcissistic. Both can be hurtful or damaging to the person on the receiving end of their behaviour. So how can you tell the difference? A narcissist causes conscious damage – they know exactly what they're doing because they're doing it deliberately. A selfish, self-centred person causes unconscious damage – they didn't mean or want to hurt you, they just didn't think about the consequences of their actions.

Narcissism and other personality disorders

There are various different personality disorders. Those described in this chapter are Cluster B personality disorders and, although they are different disorders, they all involve some degree of unhealthy narcissism. This means many of the symptoms overlap.

Note that a personality disorder is different from other mental illnesses, such as depression or schizophrenia – these impair the life of the sufferer, who usually wants to get better. In contrast, someone with a personality disorder damages the lives of those around them but, because their behaviour works well for them, they have no wish to change or get treatment. Although the narcissist knows what they're doing, most of them don't realise that they have a problem, let alone a personality disorder; they simply don't have the sort of introspection that someone who has bipolar disorder, for instance, would have.

The childhood wounds which have caused the changes in his brain, thereby resulting in the narcissism, are no excuse for him not taking responsibility for his behaviour now. But hurt people will hurt people. Not all narcissists were abused in childhood, though. Some were over-indulged.

Personality disorders are on a broad spectrum of severity from high- to low-functioning. At the less severe end, people have just traits of narcissistic personality disorder (NPD) or borderline personality disorder (BPD) and actually function pretty well in the world. Many are extremely intelligent, hold down high-powered jobs and do a lot of good in the world (whilst causing mayhem at home). At the other end of the spectrum are low-functioning people living in crisis, estranged from their families, perhaps with addiction problems, perhaps suicidal, and unable to hold down a job. No matter where the narcissist sits on the spectrum, they can be hurtful and destructive in their relationships.

When it comes to separation and divorce, most people are distressed by such a huge life event and may act totally out of character for a while. That doesn't make them a narcissist overnight; a personality disorder is typically caused by the person's upbringing and there will have been signs of it since their teenage years. As they've lived with it for so long, they may have learned to adapt or control much of their behaviour and it may have been hidden from you for extended periods of time. However, the stress of a divorce is likely to tip them over the edge of what they can control so you will be on the receiving end of more extreme behaviour than usual.

Identifying your narcissist – privately (don't publicise it)

In this chapter, I'll set out some brief descriptions of the different types of relevant personality disorders. Understanding what you've been through and what you're dealing with is key to being able to heal and move on with your life. You may not be able to make an accurate 'diagnosis' of your ex because some of the traits are common to more than one personality disorder, especially borderline personality disorder and covert narcissism. That doesn't matter; all you need to know is that he's a narcissist, he operates in a certain way because of that, and you can, in fact, learn to navigate the chaos he causes.

As I said at the start of this book, knowledge is power. The fact that you know your ex is a narcissist is of enormous help to you, but don't make the mistake of thinking it will be helpful to anyone else. It won't be, and it will damage your case if you mention it to the court. Whilst it's important for you, and your healing, to know what you're dealing with and to act accordingly, judges don't understand narcissists or their abuse. Therefore, it's not helpful to use the word narcissist in court, however desperate you are to expose your ex for what he is.

If you try to label your ex as a narcissist, the court will say you're not a psychiatrist so you can't diagnose anyone, and they won't take kindly to you appearing to do so. If your ex does have a professional diagnosis of a personality disorder then absolutely do go ahead and use it, but such a diagnosis is sadly very rare. I've had a couple of cases where a borderline personality disorder has been diagnosed but I've not seen a narcissistic personality disorder, sociopath or psychopath diagnosis – although I live in hope.

It's fine to tell your therapist or your own lawyers in private that you believe your ex is a narcissist – indeed, it will help you to gauge whether they have any understanding of the issue, and how helpful they're likely to be to you. It might even encourage them to do a little research on the subject. But don't mention the word to your ex's lawyers, Cafcass or other professionals involved in your case. They're likely to view you as vindictive and out to cause trouble, and they'll be against you from the outset. And you can be sure your ex or his lawyers will use your 'diagnosis' against you further down the line.

Your ex may well have labelled you with all sorts of 'diagnoses' but please take the high road and don't try telling him he's a narcissist. Instead of labelling him, give the court descriptions of his patterns of behaviour and its effect on the children and you, and how each of you react as a result. A narcissist can't change his behaviour so you have to decide what you're going to do about it, and treat him very differently to a 'normal' person.

Before we get into the relevant personality disorders, let me stress that I'm not a psychiatrist or psychologist. The signs of personality disorder I describe are based on my own research and experience of working with clients, but are not intended to form the basis of a 'home diagnosis'. I include these descriptions purely to help you recognise what you may or may not be dealing with – for your own clarity and healing. Just as with the term 'narcissist', unless there is a formal clinical diagnosis in place, it will probably harm your case to bandy these personality disorders around in court, so resist the temptation.

Narcissistic personality disorder (NPD)

The word comes from Narcissus, a mythical Greek character who fell in love with his own reflection. He stared at it until he died and a narcissus flowered in his place.

I've already described at length how the narcissist behaves in a relationship, but let's briefly explore their personality traits.

The narcissist can be charming, flattering, charismatic and alluring. He has delusions of grandeur and a big sense of entitlement, which means he believes he deserves to be treated differently to other people. But underneath his confident surface may lurk a secret excess of worry and anxiety. He is obsessed with himself and his fantasy world, and has no empathy for anyone else, even his own children. You may try telling him how his behaviour affects you or the children but he won't really get it, and he won't change if what he does is working for him. He'll preach at you, but won't listen to a word you say.

Narcissists are driven by 'dreams of glory'. They are bored by routine and, in the absence of a difficult challenge they can rise to, they'll create drama and chaos. They're ambitious and competitive and drawn to high-profile jobs with executive pay and glamour where they can use their talents to much acclaim. They are less risk-averse than many of us and can perform well under stress, whether in the boardroom or the courtroom. They don't mind who they exploit or trample over to get to the top because they want to be admired rather than liked or loved – though they still think of themselves as likeable.

The narcissist takes the credit for successes – yours as well as his – but never the blame for his failures. His lack of empathy means he's oblivious to the self-centred abrasiveness that others see in him so clearly. Despite his confident outer self, he lacks self-worth and has an 'inner shakiness', which means he can't afford to listen to criticism. He'll even see constructive feedback as an attack and grasp at evidence that supports his views whilst ignoring facts that refute them.

The narcissist does feel shame, and sometimes even a little guilt. But he feels threatened by shame, or indeed any sort of failure, due to his 'empty shell' – because he has no meaningful values and attachments and nothing of substance within for him to fall back on. Despite this, he sees himself as perfect and has to maintain his grandiose delusion of superiority at all costs (because, ultimately, it's all he has). This is why he'll lash out at anyone who tries to shame him, and the 'punishment' can go on indefinitely.

Narcissism is typically a core wound from early life and he's likely to have had an insecure attachment to his mother in his childhood. Or he may have been unappreciated by his aloof father, who remained unimpressed no matter what his son accomplished. As an adult he craves applause and becomes enraged when he feels under appreciated. Underneath it all, NPD is a disorder of self-esteem.

The victim often has a core wound from childhood too (see the double whammy in Chapter 4) but sometimes they're just a very empathetic person.

Narcissists seek out people who have energy, life and empathy, and then drain them of it as they have none of their own. But it's never enough. They're too empty to fill.

The covert narcissist

This is the hardest personality disorder to spot as the narcissism is covert, i.e. hidden. Covert narcissists differ from the typical grandiose (or overt) narcissist in that they may be more introverted. They will be passive-aggressive rather than outright antagonistic. Unlike the overt narcissist, they're preoccupied by what people think of them; they want people to like and trust them, whereas overts don't care what people think. Because of this desire to be liked and trusted, coverts tend to maintain longer relationships than overt narcissists.

But like overt narcissists, coverts exhibit the same fantasies of self-importance and grandeur. They believe they're special and entitled, but they know it puts people off if they show it, so they try to hide it. They've learned how to act empathetically; they look you in the eye, even though they don't really care. They thrive on the attention of others, and people who think they're special and amazing feed them narcissistic supply. They create drama and thrive on the energy from it.

They won't care for you if you're sick. They won't say it but you can feel their resentment, while giving others the impression that they're taking excellent care of you. The overt narcissist tells you you're ugly, lazy, etc. but the covert won't say it out loud, although you feel they want to, and you know they're thinking it.

He 'forgets' things you ask him to get for you but may give you grandiose presents on your birthdays, though not something you'd want or choose.

Most narcissists will play the victim to manipulate others, often whilst vilifying the real victim. In contrast, the covert narcissist plays the victim to garner sympathy. Whatever's happened to you, they will have suffered something worse and your plight could never be as bad as theirs. Their predicament is what makes them so 'special' in their fantasy mind, rather than the good looks, intelligence, etc. of the overt narcissist.

Coverts can change their behaviour when in public, so they clearly know their behaviour in private is wrong. But they don't want you to know that they know it's wrong, because their image is more important than who they really are. When you know they know, you can stop seeing them as a victim and hoping they'll change. They don't want to change; they enjoy their narcissistic supply.

The covert narcissist often instigates the break up but won't then issue divorce proceedings because of their reputation or how it would look. The survivor has to initiate the divorce as well as everything else: take care of the children, sell the house and furniture, sort out the debts, etc. The covert is gone and unaffected. Meanwhile, you're left to pick up the pieces and make big decisions, at a time when you're an emotional mess.

Things are not as perfect and wonderful as they appear when the covert has moved on with someone else because he's filled with silent rage. His manufactured happiness isn't authentic. It's just a show to rattle you.

Sociopaths and psychopaths

Unlike the overt narcissist with his hot temper, the sociopath is a cold fish and his detachment can be quite chilling. He may have cold, hard and distant staring eyes which can look predatory. He is more likely to use passive-aggressive behaviour than to blow up in a rage, although that doesn't stop him using violence, which he may do in a cold and calculated way. Even if he never gets physical, the threat of harm is somehow hanging in the air.

Nevertheless, the sociopath is usually most charming and can be exciting and seductive, at least in public. This makes them hard to spot. Sociopathy is also known as antisocial personality disorder, meaning these people do not conform to society's normal rules, laws and ways of behaving and treating other people. Their antisocial behaviour may only be unpaid parking tickets and taxes, but will extend to anything else they think they can get away with. If caught out, the sociopath has an endless supply of excuses to draw on as well as his victim mentality and ability to blame you for worse than he's done.

The sociopath views other people, and animals, as objects, so it's easy for him to mistreat and abuse them and he's indifferent to the emotional pain he causes them. He may have been taught by one of his parents to break the rules and, in time, learned to adjust to the behaviour and no longer feel uncomfortable with it.

The aim of the sociopath is to have people fear and obey them. They want power and control over you, not intimacy, which they may avoid once in a long-term relationship. For them, life is a competition to be won at all costs, not a give-and-take exchange for the mutual benefit of people we feel close to. And unlike the narcissist, he doesn't crave admiration and praise.

Psychopaths are similar but can't be diagnosed before adulthood. As children or teenagers, however, they may be cruel to animals, bully and intimidate other children, pick fights, set fires, force sex and commit other crimes against property and people.

> *My brother is a definite casualty of our upbringing. He is three years younger and it always broke my heart that I couldn't help him more but he is a very strange man. He began seeing a therapist at three years old and tried to burn the house down at eight. At one time he asked me, quite honestly, if he should murder our parents for their life insurance!*
>
> *My brother had a total inability to recognise the pain and damage he caused. He also boiled his tropical fish alive when he grew bored with them, left his cats to starve and terrorised his partner, amongst many cruelties. When we were growing up he stole everything of value from the entire family to swap or sell.*
>
> *He is 6ft 6 and terrifying. Totally unpredictable and his addiction to skunk/ cannabis made him much, much worse.*

As adults psychopaths are often involved in criminal activity; they are the serial killers, hired assassins and people who are completely ruthless in business. They also make great salesmen as they can read people well, and then manipulate them. They feel no fear or anxiety, and have no conscience, or internal control system, just a reckless disregard for other people.

Whereas a narcissist may feel shame when they've done something bad, a sociopath or psychopath doesn't care who gets hurt and will feel no remorse. They are virtually oblivious to the threat of punishment, although many will try to stay under the radar. Their worst fear is being controlled or dominated by someone else so prison isn't their favourite place to go.

Unlike the overt narcissist, who you can't fail to spot as he wants to stand out, these people blend in with their glib, shallow charm and hide in plain sight. And like the covert narcissist, they're good at playing the victim. The cause of their emotional deficit is thought to be down to genetics as well as upbringing, whereas narcissists are a product of their environment.

Sociopaths and psychopaths are risk-takers, immune from stress, and remain cool, calm and collected in situations that would make other people panic, including court hearings. It has been shown that while most people's heart rate speeds up in stressful situations, the sociopath's slows down. So you're unlikely to be able to provoke his anger and get him to show himself up like you can with someone with NPD or BPD.

James controlled and goaded me for almost two years. He would say things which he knew would alarm me and cause me to shout and then accuse me of being abusive to him. He told my mother and brother that he had been recording me for two years. I was shocked and frightened by this and I also believe James tried to electrocute me on one occasion and gas me on another.

James bought me a mobile phone with the contract in his name. I later discovered he had set up a Google account on the phone and was following my calls and movements as well as gaining access to all my private passwords. I had no access to the contract and he refused to cancel it. I also discovered he had set up remote access for himself on my mother's laptop, and he set up a false Facebook account under his brother's name and invited me as a friend. We were advised by the police to change email addresses and passwords as well as replace my parents' wi-fi box.

Throughout the latter stage of the marriage I was fearful of James's behaviour and found him to be cold, detached and calculating with his staring eyes. He seemed to take sadistic pleasure in my shock each time a new disaster hit me and it felt like he wanted me to suffer in some way.

James insisted on renovating our home himself but he did not ever finish a job before moving on to the next one and our home became more and more uninhabitable over the years and throughout both my pregnancies and early years with the children. He showed no concern for the stress, difficulties and exhaustion this caused me while trying to bring up a small child and work, including having to do college administration and marking students' work in my car in the winter. My daughter and I were confined to the small back bedroom and she still refers to being 'trapped' there whenever the house is mentioned. James just put his head round the door to say goodnight and slept in the other bedroom. He would rarely spend the night with me or visit whilst I was away.

When I returned after the birth of our second child – the children and I having spent six months with my parents who live on the other side of the country – the house was far worse than when I had left it. James had taken the covers off all the sockets, leaving bare wires in every room, deliberately making it unsafe for a toddler. The outside looked like a building site and every room was covered in rubble and dust. The children and I spent the next six weeks with his mother and then had to move to a caravan with no running water.

On one occasion there were signs of animal neglect and cruelty. Sitting on top of the bed was our cat, looking at the wall. When I went to stroke him I discovered he was covered in some sticky substance making it impossible to wash himself. He looked very sick and depressed. We had brought him back from my parents only three weeks before and he was hardly recognisable. His litter tray reeked of ammonia and had clearly not been emptied since I had left and the dog dirt on the floor indicated that our dog had been left in the house for a long time.

I have not had a key to our house for a long time as I was no longer deemed responsible enough to have a house key. My second car key disappeared and was never found. The key for the allotment disappeared from my car. My paddock field key disappeared from my car and I was no longer able to get the pony out of the field without asking James to open the gate with his key. I was suspected of stealing hospital cutlery and James was 'entrusted' to 'be in charge' of my cutlery for the kitchen staff!

After we separated, James threatened to run up bills for which he said I would be liable and I received letters from the building society month after month warning that the mortgage hadn't been paid on time. I had to pay off a £2,000 overdraft which James had taken out in my name and without my knowledge before I could close our joint account. It was hard to keep track of all the debts he ran up, mostly without my knowledge.

James is still living in the house, and I am still paying the mortgage as he refuses to, while the children and I continue to live with my parents. James has only seen his youngest twice since her birth. When I asked if he wanted to hold her he immediately took out his phone to photograph himself with her, then handed her straight back to me. He rings to speak to the children (but only the landline, I won't give him any more access to a mobile or internet) but pays no maintenance for them. The divorce proceedings have been complicated, not least because of his allegations of abuse against me!

Borderline personality disorder (BPD)

BPD is now also known as emotionally unstable personality disorder (EUPD). If you can't work out whether they love you or hate you, that'll be because they don't know either. It changes from one moment to the next.

Like the narcissist, someone with BPD can be charming and popular, the life and soul of the party.

Those with BPD are very narcissistic but unlike the 'ordinary' narcissist, sociopath and psychopath, they're not in control of their emotions. The others have temper tantrums like a toddler or explode for effect and control, while the borderline rages, screams like a baby, throws things or attacks you because something's triggered them. It's not always easy to tell the difference, but you're more likely to get a heartfelt apology from a borderline than from the other narcissists.

Even more than with the other disorders, you may feel you're walking on eggshells around a borderline because their moods change so quickly that you're never sure who you're going to come home to. One moment they're euphoric, the next they're angry or despondent.

Their mood swings can cause confusion with bipolar disorder, although they tend to change much more quickly. And some borderlines can have bipolar too. BPD can also be confused with PTSD, and some people have both. This is why it's so dangerous to make a 'home diagnosis' as you can get it horribly wrong. Unfortunately, even psychiatrists can misdiagnose both children and adults with bipolar disorder, attention deficit disorder, oppositional defiant disorder or BPD, when in fact they're suffering from complex trauma.

Like bipolars in a manic phase, the borderline may behave in sensational and harmful ways, particularly when they're upset. They may spend money they haven't got, drink or eat to excess, be sexually promiscuous, use drugs, or drive fast and dangerously.

Borderlines are terrified of being abandoned and this can make them needy and cling to you. The narcissist doesn't want to let you go either as he needs your attention and admiration, but he'll keep you there more by manipulation than histrionics and will break up with you first rather than have you make a mortal dent in his ego by leaving him. Whilst the narcissist may threaten suicide to manipulate you, he's unlikely to hurt or kill himself as he thinks too much of himself. Borderlines, however, tend to suffer from depression and anxiety, and may have an eating disorder and/or history of self-harm. So they may mean it when they say they're suicidal. And of course their extreme mood swings, lies and manipulations make people want to abandon them.

The borderline can feel abandoned when you're late for dinner, not just when you're leaving them for good. Even hearing an opinion that they disagree with can feel threatening and trigger feelings of abandonment. When you do leave, they can keep trying for years to get you back, or to get back at you.

When they lose their partner, the borderline may cling to their child and become too enmeshed – a huge burden as the child then feels responsible for their parent. And some children have the misfortune of having one parent with NPD and the other with BPD as they do attract each other.

Unlike the other personality disorders, BPD can be treated if the person really wants to change their behaviour.

The alcoholic

While not a personality disorder, alcoholism is a mental health disorder – and one that often coincides with personality disorders, particularly narcissism.

I think one of the reasons Barry drinks is to deal with the fact that he is often unable to control stuff. His drinking became worse when his dad died – I think some abuse history there was triggered by his early demise. When he is drunk, Barry is less clever with his manipulation and therefore becomes openly aggressive, which is extremely scary and intimidating.

Some people are alcoholics, some people are narcissists, and some people are both. It's not always easy to work out if you're dealing with an alcoholic narcissist, or a narcissistic alcoholic. The alcoholic and the narcissist have a lot in common including:

- Both have distorted views of themselves.
- The lies – the alcoholic denies how much he drinks and lies to cover up his addiction.
- The alcoholic thinks only about his next drink and is as self-absorbed as a narcissist, unable to see or consider the effects of their actions on others.
- An alcoholic is more likely than a narcissist to apologise for their behaviour but both make promises to change, which they never keep.
- Confronting either an alcoholic or a narcissist can result in them attacking you, sulking or stonewalling you.

A narcissist uses drink or drugs to cope with their extreme feelings when they can't solve their problems the way the rest of us do. If your ex is drinking to excess, your concern is going to be protecting your children. But be careful about focusing too much on the alcohol issue as it's no good insisting they get treatment for that if they're still abusive underneath. Alcohol makes them more abusive, but it isn't the root cause.

Playing the victim

One thing that's common among all the disorders and conditions mentioned in this chapter is this: they can all play the victim if things aren't going right for them and they don't see an easier way out.

Some abusers are always the victim, at least in their own minds. In fact, it's another form of gaslighting their real victim. If they're not claiming to be the victim of your abuse, they may claim to be the victim of your false allegations of their abuse.

The narcissist is watching and studying other people's behaviour all the time and is an expert in understanding what makes people tick. He will listen to what real victims say and write, and latch on to every word himself, so don't be surprised to hear him call you a narcissist (see 'projection' in Chapter 1).

He presents himself as a victim to his wider family and manipulates them into acting as his flying monkeys.

It takes years to recover from the abuse, and during that time the survivor is having to deal with the narcissist pretending he is the victim and everyone falling over themselves to protect him.

One of his favourite tricks was an example of extreme passive aggression. He would play what became known as 'The Victim Game'. He behaves particularly badly in some way and I am hurt/frustrated/afraid/crying, etc. and tell him how I feel, being careful not to apportion blame and make things worse. He will respond by adopting his 'cowering, wounded little boy' persona who is being hurt by a shrill, overbearing wife. Thus reneging on taking any responsibility for his actions and the damage they have caused, attempting to distract from the real issues at hand, and punishing me for having the audacity to express my feelings and pain in the first place. The problem will remain unresolved and I will be silenced and disempowered. This will then be followed by days of sulking and geographical absence. I have attempted to honestly and adultly address this ritual with him over many, many years but it seems to be his default setting and it serves a purpose for him in his trying to control me.

CHAPTER 4:
HOW THE NARCISSISTIC ABUSE AFFECTS VICTIMS – AND HOW TO BEGIN THE HEALING PROCESS

The worst thing about it was the growing sense that the more I suffered over the years the more he enjoyed it, and the perversity of being punished for trying to please my husband felt obscene and devastating. He expected me to make the house perfect and to spend thousands of hours online trying to source things for unrealistic prices.

I personally did not have unrealistic expensive tastes as I am pragmatic and not particularly materially acquisitive but my husband had status expectations, which I never really understood but went along with to keep the peace. Invariably he would criticise my choices anyway or capriciously refuse to buy something I may have spent a great deal of time and effort sourcing to please him.

I was constantly on edge, double-checking my decisions, not trusting my judgement, afraid to make a mistake, exhausted, guilty, depressed and ashamed to be such a burden to him.

I had nothing of my own and was constantly told I was lucky to have him supporting me and that no one else would want me anyway as I was too sensitive or difficult.

So far we've talked a lot about the narcissist and what makes them tick. Now let's turn to the victim, and how they are affected by the narcissist's behaviour. Living with narcissistic lies and manipulations makes people feel confused, ashamed and worthless. Trying to explain how you feel about what they do, or don't do, is usually a futile exercise – the narcissist's obfuscation and word salad makes their victims feel angry, whereas the sociopath's extra charm, or extra threats, makes their victims feel anxious.

Who experiences narcissistic abuse?

I've been abused. To type that is the singular most astonishing fact I've come to accept. I finally left after 18 years.

Anyone – both men and women – can be ensnared by the charm of a narcissist. Victims are usually kind people with considerable empathy, often a happy, contented disposition and a certain amount of joie de vivre – all things the narcissist doesn't have himself. Many narcissists play the victim and the kind, empathetic person has trouble saying 'no' when they ask them for help – even when they're in the process of getting divorced.

When there's no physical violence, people can find it hard to recognise that they're in an abusive relationship, particularly when the abuse is quite subtle. And after a few years, the abuse becomes so normal that the victim can think it isn't that bad because they've adapted to it. If you're questioning whether you've read the situation wrongly, do check it out with a domestic abuse professional before you dismiss it.

Surprisingly, many highly intelligent, high-functioning and powerful women can find themselves in an abusive relationship. They may be in a senior position at work, lead a big team of people and be a high earner, while at home they're afraid to put a foot wrong. Rosie Duffield's moving speech in the House of Commons demonstrated this: the stronger the woman, the greater the achievement it is for the narcissist to break her down. Although when she is completely broken down, he'll get bored and may move on to another victim.

> *I found it difficult to talk about the emotional abuse as I felt as if I should have been stronger and seen it. How could an intelligent woman like me be so stupid!*

Men from all walks of life can also find themselves under the total control of a female partner.

It's not just the victim who suffers. The ripple effect goes out to their children and the whole wider family, whose lives become dominated by the situation.

Shame

Neither men nor women find it easy to say they've been abused, as the shame they feel is so great.

> *I kept the truth about my desperately unhappy marriage a secret from everyone through shame and partly because I didn't know that what he was doing to me was illegal or even had a name. I thought it was all*

my fault. He had brainwashed me so thoroughly over the years that I ended up believing I should be grateful that he was supporting me and tolerating me at all. I had no family, no money, no career and nowhere else to go. I had thought ours was just a really shit marriage and that I should just get on with it. I had made my wedding vows with complete sincerity and a determination to see things through no matter what.

Please don't blame yourself for being taken in by a narcissist; remember, it's always about him, not you! He's a master manipulator and there's no shame in having been taken in by one. I have been too. And other family court professionals and judges are taken in and manipulated by them all the time.

But now the scales have fallen from your eyes, beating yourself up is just a waste of time; self-compassion and self-care are the order of the day so that you can reclaim yourself and your power, and focus on your future life.

Am I a narcissist?

No, no, no! If you're asking the question, and many survivors do, then you're most definitely not; the thought that they could be anything less than perfect would never even cross a narcissist's mind. Whereas you will be going over and over what you see as your own failures and inadequacies.

You may have behaved in ways you're not proud of while negotiating life with a narcissist, such as lying to him to protect yourself or your children from further abuse, or lying to others to protect yourself from shame or pressure, or manipulating your narcissist to protect yourself or your children. This makes you a survivor, not a narcissist.

The narcissist may have told you, or others, that you're a narcissist. Once again, this is projection by the narcissist.

Co-dependency

In Greek mythology, the mountain nymph Echo fell in love with Narcissus but was doomed only ever to repeat (i.e. echo) his last words. An 'echoist's' identity is very tied up with the narcissist, whom she admires, echoes and becomes dependent upon. They are at opposite ends of the spectrum: over-givers and over-takers. To some extent the narcissist and the co-dependent (over-giver) complement each other as the narcissist wants to be admired and feel important, and the co-dependent wants to feel needed.

Co-dependents pretend nothing is wrong; they cover up for the narcissist, clean up his mess and apologise for him, enabling him to carry on the same way. Many narcissists struggle to manage their own lives and depend on someone else to solve their problems rather than changing their own behaviour, which is, after all, the source of many of their issues.

The problem is that the co-dependent's identity can become so intertwined with the narcissist that she struggles to speak about herself and remains focused on his issues.

This works for the abusive parent and against the protective parent in court proceedings as the dynamic of drama and chaos continues, characterised by the narcissist's explosive, erratic moods and her desire to 'fix' or placate him. Even if she is able to focus on her own case, she often doesn't have a strong enough voice to put it across.

From submitting the petition to receiving the decree absolute, my divorce took over seven and half years. I had many moments of asking myself whether I was dealing with a total narcissist. I started reading about it and recognised myself and my ex in what I read. I recognised being treated like a function, a thing, only valuable as much as I served his needs. Things would get pretty hostile as soon as I did or said something that challenged his self-image. I began wondering: 'What if I am a narcissist as well? Surely, I would not think I was one even if I was.' It took me to a very dark place. I was feeling disempowered and hopeless. I did not like how I felt about myself or how I treated my ex when I was swimming in this narcissism soup.

Through my research, I came across the concept of co-dependency, and I recognised myself in that as well. I realised how from the very beginning of our relationship, I was not aware of what I wanted or needed. I was so focused on his happiness that I lost myself. I was abandoning myself over and over again without having the slightest clue that I was doing it.

Shifting my focus from learning to deal with a narcissist to transforming my co-dependent ways was a huge turning point for me. I was so excited to focus my attention back on me, to something I could work with and heal on a deep level. I knew that this healing would ripple into all my relationships and lead to a calmer, happier, more content life.

I have two daughters. Even though I know I modelled to them co-dependent ways of being and relating, it is not too late to change that. How I show up today matters. So I keep taking the time to ask myself: 'What do I need?' and act on that.

My current partner is a compassionate, deeply caring, all-around decent man. Still, he is not a mind reader! If I want or need something, I have got to tell him. That does not come easy to me. I am learning to take time to connect with myself, to get clear on how I feel, what I want, what is important to me. I am learning to take risks and be more open and vulnerable in communicating with him. Even though it has been over nine years since I left my ex, I still notice that there is a part of me that expects to be put down, blamed, and criticised if I open up. Sometimes I still find myself surprised and deeply moved when I am met with understanding and empathy, when I feel heard, and my opinion is considered. Even though it is scary and some days are better than others, it is so worth it. I don't want my co-dependent ways to sabotage this relationship.

When it comes to my ex, his comments or behaviour can still sometimes throw me off-kilter and zap all life out of me. But it happens way less often, feels a lot less intense and passes much quicker than in the past. Instead of losing myself in the drama of 'How on earth can he treat me like this?' I focus on being there for me. There is more emotional space between us. I feel safer, more at peace with it all.

When the relationship is over, the protective parent's dependency can move from their partner to the children, who they cling to for dear life, believing they can't survive without them. This may be due to the survivor suffering from PTSD or because they've been so worn down over time through the ongoing cycles of devaluing and discarding that they have a huge dependency on anyone who validates them, including their children.

Self-care, self-love and self-validation are the best ways out of co-dependency. These won't come naturally but, one step at a time, you can make your way to healthier relationships.

Ostriches, overwhelm and sinking to rock bottom

*Digging up old emails, this is really hard, it's like mud that
I cannot wash off.*

If you've spent years walking on eggshells around a narcissist, pandering to his every whim and trying to protect your children from the worst of his excesses, you may have thought life without him would be all peace and light. And hopefully it will be, in time, but dealing with the narcissist could be even more challenging once you're separated. If you're in the family court you could be there for a year or three, maybe more, so make yourself as comfortable as you can in the meantime.

I've noticed how often my clients bury their head in the sand, not that I can blame them. Just when they should be recovering and healing from years of abuse, even more is demanded of them by both the narcissist and the court. Just thinking about a 28-page Form E (the financial statement required for a financial settlement, see Chapter 12) is enough to make those of us who aren't accountants behave like an ostrich, and the nightmare of children proceedings would make anyone run for the hills. When it all gets too much, it's tempting to let other people make the decisions for you and just go along with whatever your social worker, solicitor, other professionals or even your ex suggests. But giving your power away like this, at the very time you want to be reclaiming it, is only going to sink you further into the sand.

Being immobilised by overwhelm is a common and understandable reaction, but paralysis and procrastination can be damaging for your case and maybe even for your children; when you've shut down you can't protect them or be completely there for them. The first thing to do is to be able to recognise when you've gone into overwhelm. You've probably spent years watching and analysing the narcissist's moods and emotions, and now it's time to focus your detective's eye on your own reactions. The sooner you can recognise the overwhelm, the sooner you can get out of it and take responsibility as the adult you are. Sometimes you'll notice you're putting off a big task, like your Form E, other times you'll just have so much to do that you can't think where to start.

If you're in the family court, I can tell you now that the paperwork alone will be overwhelming, but forewarned is forearmed. Make a plan now of what you'll do at times when you feel overwhelmed – when you feel you can do nothing except put your head under the duvet. Make a short list of three things you should do at these times, and put this list somewhere you can easily find it in the event of an overwhelm emergency – on a card on your bedside table, on a Post-it note on the fridge, in the front of your notebook, or on your phone. You may need to have it written down in more than one place.

What three things should you put on your list? Item one should be an act of self-care. Looking after yourself is critical, so work out what will best help you when you feel overwhelmed – is it to sit quietly and drink a cup of tea, phone a friend, go for a walk, have a hot bath … or something else?

Item number two should be preparing for action. Here, you should make a list of all the things you have to do. I recommend doing this across three columns: column one is for urgent tasks (as in, things with an urgent deadline); column two is for tasks that are important to you (in terms of achieving your goals – more on this coming up in Chapter 5); and column three is things that are both urgent and important to you. Finding someone to pick up your child tomorrow may be on your urgent list, while your Form E (Chapter 12) may be on your important list. Finishing your position statement (see Chapter 10) for your court hearing tomorrow would be both urgent and important. When you've made your list, check that everything on it is urgent or important for you, not for anyone else, however much you might normally want to help them out. Then prioritise the actions on each of your three lists by writing numbers against them.

Number three on your overwhelm list can be to spend 15 minutes doing or starting the top priority item that you identified in the previous step.

If you try these steps whenever you feel overwhelmed and find they're not working for you, just tear up that bit of paper and keep making yourself a new overwhelm list until you find one that works for you.

Occasionally it's more than overwhelm and survivors sink to rock bottom. Working, battling against a narcissist and going through the family court can all be full-time jobs and that's before you've even thought about looking after the children. Sometimes it's just too big a load for one person. But remember that if you do sink to rock bottom, the only way from there is up. Meanwhile, call in the cavalry – and every favour you're owed. Don't be afraid to tell friends or family how you feel and ask them to look after the children while you just sleep and take care of you for a day or two. If you've been isolated by the narcissist, call your local domestic abuse agency and ask what help they can offer you. If you're really desperate, call the Samaritans. And do all you can to prevent the narcissist getting wind of your desperation; in my experience survivors of narcissistic abuse are incredibly strong and resilient and you're likely to be back on your feet before he can notice anything's amiss.

Keep putting one foot in front of the other, take one step at a time, and you'll get there.

PTSD (post-traumatic stress disorder)

I experience almost constant flashbacks,
insomnia and exhaustion.
I am furious to have been taken in by him and by my gullibility.
But my missing papers, his lies and the lack of clarity
are the biggest causes of stress. It is almost like a form of
information OCD.
As my emotional world is in chaos, I think I am attempting
to reassert some semblance of order through
paperwork and bank balances to self-medicate.

It's not just soldiers who suffer this debilitating disorder; it's common among people – including children – who've been abused. It's not so much about what was done to you, as what it did to you, because we all react differently to events in our lives depending on what we've experienced before. A traumatic situation triggers the fight, flight or freeze response in our body and normally our pounding heart and sweaty palms return to normal when the frightening event is over. But with PTSD, you can remain in a hyper-vigilant state and be startled easily, have angry outbursts and be unable to sleep. And when you're living with a narcissist you may be in a permanent state of 'red alert', always trying to comply with his 'rules' and not set off his anger.

Anything that reminds you of the original event(s), even hearing your ex's voice, can trigger a flashback and you can feel as though you're back in the original situation. This can, understandably, immobilise you. You may also dissociate (take yourself mentally outside your body), which means you feel numb, detached or disconnected, disorientated and confused.

None of these are helpful things to happen to you when you're in the family court, and especially if you're giving evidence. If you can't maintain eye contact you may look shifty; if you zone out you look as though you're not concentrating and the judge might think you're not taking it seriously; if you can't breathe you won't speak loudly enough for the judge to hear you; if you can't remember everything, or even if you can you certainly can't keep it in the right order, it looks as if you're not telling the truth. It's not surprising that judges prefer the evidence of the charming and eloquent narcissists, whose credible stories are so much easier to follow. I talk more about giving evidence in Chapter 14.

Stockholm syndrome/trauma bonding

You could shake her. He has got into her head and taken it over.

Stockholm syndrome is where a hostage develops a bond with their captor. It's named after the 1973 failed bank robbery in Stockholm, where the hostages refused to leave their captors, refused to give evidence against them in court and even raised money for their defence.

Being in a relationship with a narcissist can be a bit like being in a cult where you're slowly brainwashed until you become their slave, conditioned to doing whatever's demanded of you, and not complaining about being humiliated and browbeaten. It becomes your new normal, and you're no longer able to see how very abnormal it is. It's 'boiled frog syndrome', essentially. If you throw a frog into boiling water it'll jump straight out again, but if you put it into tepid water over a low heat and very slowly bring it to the boil it won't notice how hot it's getting until it's too late.

If you find yourself frequently defending your partner, or trying to explain the inexplicable, you may be trauma bonded. Breaking the bond involves accepting that the charming narcissist who you fell in love with was an illusion, a ghost who doesn't really exist. It's hard to go back to reality, to learn to live without this make-believe person. And as with any other addiction, it includes refusing to return to the addictive substance, even when the narcissist is trying to hoover you back in.

The age-old 'Why didn't you leave?' question

Because all my life I was told I should stay, that leaving hurts kids, that the institution of marriage is more important than the humans who live in it, that divorce is bad, that unless I was being beaten I had no reason to leave.

On average, it takes a victim seven attempts to leave an abusive relationship – which makes even Scary Spice Mel B's efforts rather average!

As I've said previously, whilst you shouldn't describe your ex as a 'narcissist' in court, you will want to describe their behaviour and actions during the relationship. You may therefore be asked during your court proceedings, with implied or even overt criticism, why you didn't leave sooner. Such a question demonstrates that the person asking doesn't understand domestic abuse or coercive control and, whilst it's not your job to educate them, this lack of training is a big part of why things are going so badly wrong in the family courts.

Some of the reasons people stay are because they:

- Take their marriage vows very seriously and don't want to give up.
- Remember the good times and think if they try hard enough they'll come back.

  If I could make him who he is in my head, I would go back to him.

- Thought if they gave the narcissist enough love or stability, their need to abuse and control would disappear.

- Have 'normalised' the abuse and convinced themselves it's not that bad.
- Are too frightened to leave and they know the time of separation is the most dangerous for women.
- Have been convinced by the abuser that they don't deserve to escape and/or they wouldn't survive without them.
- Are so isolated, conditioned and controlled that they can no longer act independently.
- Are co-dependent or trauma bonded.

Sally Challen's barrister is reported to have said, 'The thing I've struggled with when I've talked to Sally is that she has said all along, "I still love him and I miss him so much."' And this from a woman who killed her husband because he was so abusive. The report in the Guardian newspaper went on to say, 'Perhaps this more than anything shows how complete Richard Challen's hold was. Not one family member, friend or neighbour the Guardian reporter spoke to had anything positive to say about him. It seems the only person grieving him is his devoted wife – serving life for his murder.'

Trauma bonding is a form of addiction, which is why it's so hard to leave the abuser. The relationship's a roller coaster ride of highs and lows and you're constantly chasing the highs. He'll leave you sitting at home for two days and then getting a text from him, even an abusive one, can be a high. He keeps you bonded by making you fearful, lying to you, keeping you 'off-balance' and, when necessary, using a watered-down version of his original love bombing.

I can't get him out of my head

That's the last thing he wants you to do! But it's an important thing for you to work towards as you can't move on while he's still camping out in your head. And if he's not paying rent for living there, it's time to evict him. Which may be easier said than done, as he's spent a long time getting you to think only about him. You know it's over and you want to break free but you're still obsessed with him.

You may still be struggling to make sense of the things he's done and said to you. But you can't make sense of a narcissist; they gaslight, they lie for no apparent reason, they use word salad, they say one thing and do another. If you try and make sense of them you'll simply scramble your poor brain. The narcissist doesn't operate in the same way as the rest of us if he has a personality *disorder*.

Look up 'disorder' in the dictionary: mess, disorganisation, chaos, confusion, clutter, jumble, shambles. Does that sound like him?

If you have a child with a narcissist, going 'no contact' isn't an option. But although he'll have to be in your life, he doesn't have to be permanently in your head.

It's time to stop giving him headspace; just say 'stop' every time he comes into your head, and think of something you'd like instead. Rather than spending all your time trying to understand him, focus on understanding yourself and how you react to things.

Think about what you do after you put the rubbish out: do you go out to the dustbin every day to check how it's doing?

The double whammy – or why children of narcissists often choose narcissistic partners

My mother was a queen narcissist,
so I learned at the feet of the best, or should that be the worst?

As a child, you believe the environment you grow up in is normal, and that your parents behave the way everyone else does. By the time you're old enough to realise that most people don't say or do those things, the damage is done and you're open to being seduced by partners with similar personality traits. They feel familiar and safe. You know just how to handle them and it's easy to fall into co-dependency with them.

If you had a narcissistic parent, you may be even harder on yourself for falling into the same pattern that shaped your childhood. Cut yourself some slack here. Instead of focusing on something that isn't your fault (your childhood) focus on supporting your own children as best you can, and giving them the emotional tools to have fulfilling relationships as adults. Read about how to support your children in Chapter 6.

The realisation that my ex-husband is a narcissist was hard enough but uncovering and beginning to reveal the stark truth to myself that my mother is also a narc has been a brutal 'double whammy', as I like to call it.
I always knew something wasn't right growing up. I felt uneasy, uncomfortable. I never felt I really belonged. There was perceived affection. We had a house, a car, nice holidays – it all appeared and presented itself

to the outside world as a 'nice, normal' family. Inside, family life was very different and dysfunctional. Her role of the 'perfect' mother was never questioned. I was not permitted to show emotion. I was an emotionally sensitive child and therefore I clearly reminded my mother of her own failings. She saw her own insecurities, perceived weaknesses and flaws in me and emotionally rejected me for it. She mocked me for being emotionally sensitive, she couldn't bear it and I took the blame she felt for her own insecurities and unhappiness.

I was a good child – you had to be with a mother like mine. I was scared of her, I now realise. All I wanted to do was to please her (and my father) but they blamed me for things. If something went wrong it was always made out to be me – they mocked me as I tried to defend myself but their presence and how it made me feel only made me look and feel more guilty. I never lost that label of being a liar, out of control, a failure, and as a teenager I gave up hope of ever changing that and lived up to it to a certain extent. I was fulfilling the image and the disappointment. It engulfed me. She couldn't bear it – my self-sabotaging behaviour was a reflection on her and the flying monkeys would swoop in to tell me how much I was hurting her and upsetting her.

I cannot recall a secure attachment (one of being held and comforted) with my mother. Everything was always on her terms. There was a coldness (and silence) at times which was not portrayed to other people. On one occasion I remember crying and she yelled 'Why are you crying?' I replied 'Because I love you' and she snapped back 'Oh don't be so stupid'. She was cruel at times with silent treatment, manipulation, love bombing, gaslighting, criticism. I was often met with comments like 'You have no right to cry', 'You've had a good upbringing' and 'You have no reason to be the way you are'.

My mother controlled us with food. I was never fat but my frame is bigger than my mother's as she was super skinny. She couldn't handle me being on the bigger side. I was poked in the belly often by her friends and told 'Why can't you be as slim as your mummy?' Treats were rationed and if you didn't eat the dinner she had made, you were shouted out and then given the silent treatment. She really didn't like anything that didn't go her way. She would then cry and play the victim about how she had just tried to cook a nice meal, and my father would rush to her side and console her. I was on a permanent diet. The damaging effects of this control has impacted on my disordered eating that I still struggle with today.

I had been conditioned all my life, controlled, locked in and knew no different, so it was hardly surprising that I married like for like. I didn't know there was another way and I was easy prey. My ex-husband seemed so sorted and uncomplicated when I met him. I was impressed by what he said and what he did (clearly love bombing I realise now). It later transpired that his job was not as high-powered as he had originally said, which should have been a red flag. Over the years we were together he would ever so subtly put me down, criticise, play the victim, the persecutor, all further compounding the worthlessness I felt as a result of my childhood and of course I knew no different. He was well and truly in control of me on so many levels, as was my mother.

My mother and my ex-husband detested each other from the start. It was a power struggle, a struggle of control for themselves and one of control over me. Who could be the master puppeteer?

There were definitely three people in the marriage.

Once I told my mother that my ex-husband was leaving me, this was a good moment for her and time to swoop in and gain even more control. She could despise him even more and revel in the fact that she had always hated him and how she always knew what he was like. I don't recall her ever saying 'How are you?' in all this, but I now realise she wouldn't do this as it's all about her.

I didn't see it at the start but now I see she was revelling in it. It was the crowning glory to think she had control over me – the child can be put back in her place. I massively overshared with her. I thought the care was genuine.

She was way too involved during the court process with my ex. She couldn't keep away and would then relay to her flying monkeys how much this was affecting her and how much she was doing and wasn't she wonderful. I went on my own to a court hearing one time and she was fuming about not coming. I had the silent treatment for days after that and felt the disapproval.

In other people's eyes – people who don't understand – she was there for me when I needed her, but it was all about her. It has always been about her and how much this has affected her. I have never felt whole in her presence, only anxious. I would feel exhausted having been with her, questioning myself, with a terrible sick, knotted feeling in my stomach. This was a toxic relationship. I no longer live in the same country as my mother, and have zero communication with her.

My mother would tell me my ex-husband had captured my true self and how I lived in fear of him. I heard this so many times and I believed it. What I see now, though, is complete projection. The truth of the matter is yes, I was scared of him, but I was scared of her too. She captured my true self as it was never permitted to grow. It was hers. But, since moving abroad, I have been working relentlessly with a therapist to find my true self, and I am journeying to be whole, present and free.

What I have learned, in terms of strategies to help others:

- Close your boundary. Know who your trusted friends are and speak/offload to them. You definitely need a support network.

- Do not over share with your narcissistic mother/father. Limit the communication to the essentials of what they need to know. They may *up the ante because they recognise the change but be firm and hold the boundary. Do things on your terms.*

- *Never think they will change – even if they are being pleasant. I thought this many times about my ex and my mother, but a leopard never changes their spots and, crucially, they can't. They will never change. We have to change how we manage them.*

What's normal anyway?

You've lived with the lies, the gaslighting, the blame and the threats for so long that you can't now remember what normal was anyway. But if you've got children, it's important that you don't normalise abusive behaviour. It's easy for mothers in this situation to consider things that happen to be normal, or just outside normal, when a stranger would be horrified by it. Find a trusted sister or friend who's a 'normal' mother to run things by and get a reality check. That way, you can deal more appropriately with the situations the narcissist creates.

CHAPTER 5:
HOW TO DEAL
WITH A NARCISSIST

It's a bit like sleeping lions.
You stay calm and pretend you're asleep and the narcissist
does all he can to provoke you into reacting.
Who wins is a battle of strength and wills.

To succeed in any dealings with a narcissist you'll need to toughen up and play him at his own game, by having a better strategy and tactics than he does. You have the advantage: you know how he operates and you have more emotional intelligence than he has. Let's explore how to use that knowledge and emotional intelligence, and deal more effectively with your narcissist.

In addition to the following tips, there's guidance on how to deal with the narcissist's tactics in court in Chapter 14.

First things first, plan your separation

Fools rush in where angels fear to tread.

I must stress again that your divorce is not going to be anything like a 'normal' divorce, so it's crucial to prepare well. Get yourself an attractive notebook – one that you enjoy picking up and writing in – and use it to make your plan, record your goals and set out your strategies.

If you are doing the leaving, or asking for a divorce, you're declaring war on the narcissist. And wars aren't won without a watertight battle plan so take your time to think it all through and prepare thoroughly before you make a move.

Think, how is your ex going to react?

If you've threatened to leave before, the narcissist won't believe you now. And even if you haven't, they probably still won't believe you; how could you possibly want to leave this most wonderful person, the best thing that's ever happened to you? Of course you don't really mean it, is what they'll probably think. But if they do think you mean it, they'll see this as a threat to the great source of narcissistic 'supply' that you are for them, and your rejection of them as a huge threat to their big (but fragile) ego. They're likely to respond with either narcissistic rage or a big love bombing/hoovering episode (see Chapter 1). Sometimes both; some people receive hundreds of messages a day, some telling them how much the narcissist loves them, others relating all the dreadful things he's about to do to them.

Some narcissists will play the victim, and even threaten suicide, in an attempt to get you to stay. They'll do whatever it takes to keep the power and control they have over you. If they start to feel you pulling away, they may become even more controlling, following you and stalking you more than ever before. Be careful that he's not behind you, or putting spyware on your phone. (It's always a good idea to set a passcode or change the existing passcode on your phone, and potentially even restore the device to factory settings to remove any spyware he may have put on it.)

Once they accept that you mean it, they'll probably tell everyone – including you – that it is they who are leaving you, not the other way around, as that would be too big and shameful a narcissistic injury for them to bear.

Their abusive behaviour will escalate, which is why it's important to think this bit through first. You know your own narcissist – how are they likely to respond? And more importantly, how will you respond to any or all of their tactics. Will you be able to withstand the manipulations of the pathological narcissist? If not, what help do you need to be able to leave?

Assemble your 'army'

Divorce is difficult for everyone, and if you're leaving a narcissist it's more than doubly difficult, so you'll want double the support that most people need. This must be part of your plan. Your 'army', which will ideally be in place before you leave, may include:

- A friend who can hold your feet to the fire when the narcissist intensifies their behaviour and you waver in your intention to leave.
- A support worker at your local domestic abuse agency, or a qualified IDVA (independent domestic violence advisor).
- A support group of people who've been through or are going through the same as you – there are plenty to be found online (see Resources at the end of the book).

- Friends/family/neighbours who can pick up and look after your children when the narcissist creates an emergency or drama, or you have to go to appointments or court hearings.

- A therapist or coach – one that specialises in abuse and trauma – who can help to build you up for the fight ahead, set boundaries, stay calm, stop reacting to the narcissist's power games and reclaim your own power. Again, check out Resources for some suggestions.

- A contact at your children's school who can look out for them and let you know any changes in their behaviour.

- Your GP to record any physical abuse and/or emotional effects of the trauma you have suffered, and to prescribe medication if needed to get you through this.

- A solicitor if you don't want to do correspondence yourself (see Chapter 9). They can also advise you on your likely financial entitlement in order to give you more confidence in leaving – and indeed, on whether you should be the one to leave the home (more on this coming up next).

- A barrister (Chapter 9) or McKenzie Friend (Chapter 10) for court hearings.

- A financial advisor if you need advice on the shared assets and how much you'll need to be able to survive or, hopefully, thrive.

Although the narcissist may well have convinced you that you can't survive without him, in fact the opposite is true (because the narcissist is always talking about himself). He's far more fragile and vulnerable than he's ever let you see and could well panic and feel out of control without you to prop up and mop up his life. Other people may begin to see what only you have witnessed until now and eventually tire of his rages and demands on them, so if you can stay calm and observe (and take notes) from a distance, you'll be able to use his behaviour to your advantage. More on this coming up later.

The time of separation is the most dangerous for women. You must expect to be punished for your crime of leaving him and/or not living up to his expectations during the relationship. Sometimes the narcissist's aim is to destroy their former partner. All the more reason to have a strong support network around you.

Should you leave the family home?

It's usually not advisable to leave your home without somewhere else fairly permanent to go, as it could be difficult for you to get back in there. But if you're in danger and there's no other way, then you can leave and apply for an occupation order (Chapter 13) as soon as possible to be able to return.

If you are going to leave and believe you might be in danger, it would be better to move out and leave a note, rather than say you're going in advance. If you have children, try and leave them with someone else rather than at school, in case your ex gets wind of your move and tries to take them out of school; he'll have parental responsibility so the school couldn't refuse to let him take them.

In the note that you leave him, be sure to spell out that you're going because of his abuse, which is so frightening for both you and your children. Say you'll never stop him seeing his children and you'll call in the next day or two so he can speak to them. And keep a copy/photo of your note.

What else should you do?

Get all your important documents out of the house before you leave: passports, birth certificates, bank statements, personal information, etc. Leave them with a trusted family member or friend, or in a locked drawer at work.

Collect all the evidence you can before you leave. Record as many conversations and arguments as you can, keep emails, notes, etc. There's more on gathering evidence in Chapter 14.

Make a budget, and close your joint bank or other joint accounts as soon as you can after leaving.

Make your separation plan, then take it one step at a time.

Deciding your goals and building a strategy

When you're leaving a narcissist, not only do you need to plan your separation like a military operation, you also need to create a strategy – and stick to it. This is essential if you want to avoid being chewed up and spat out by the master manipulator. After all, his aim is to tip you off-balance and constantly keep you on the run so you don't have time to figure out what he's doing. You can counter this by having your own goals and strategy.

What are your goals?

Your plan starts with your goals. So what is it you're really aiming for from this divorce? Forget about winning. Aiming to win against a narcissist is not a good goal because they have to win at all costs and they're ruthless. Winning is in their DNA, but it's probably not in yours so you'll have lost before you even start. Worse still, the family court professionals (including the judge) very often side with the abusive parent. So trying to win is an almost impossible goal and setting yourself up for failure.

Many survivors go into court proceedings wanting to expose the narcissist for what they really are. I get it, I really do, but I have to warn you that it's another unrealistic goal when you're going through family court proceedings. It does happen, but only rarely, and even when it does the narcissist brushes it off with his usual excuses and refusal to take any responsibility.

It's not possible either to make him see reason or that his behaviour is wrong or immoral. He's built differently to the rest of us and simply doesn't care about the things that upset other people. The more you try to get the narcissist to do the right thing – even for his own children – the more he'll do the wrong thing. Because getting narcissistic supply from you, in the form of your upset or anger, is more important to him than not damaging his children.

Getting the court proceedings over with as soon as possible is another goal of most of my clients. Unfortunately it's another unrealistic one. Dragging out the court proceedings is another way the narcissist will get 'supply' from you as he knows you want it to be finished and to get on with your new life without him.

Now we know what you shouldn't be aiming for, let's come up with some more realistic objectives. Achievable goals when divorcing a narcissist include:

- To keep your children safe.
- To empower your children to the best of your ability.
- To protect and empower yourself.
- To gain freedom and a peaceful life for yourself.
- To obtain a 'lives with' order (i.e. that the children live with you).
- To ensure his contact is supervised/has no overnights/is the minimum possible.
- To obtain a financial agreement or order you can live with (rather than what's fair or what you're entitled to).
- To save your sanity.
- To spend as little as possible on legal fees.

Start by making a list of all your goals for your separation/divorce/court proceedings – simple bullet points like the list above will do. Then take each goal in turn and write as much as you can about it. For example, if one of your goals is to have a peaceful life, what exactly does your peaceful life look like?

Who and what is in it and how will you feel when you've got it? If you don't have well defined goals, you've nothing to aim for, which means you'll spend your time just trying to defend his allegations and stop him getting what he wants.

Working out how you'll achieve your goals

Once you've got your detailed list of goals (which is essentially your plan for your future life), you can then work out how you're going to achieve what you want. This chapter gives you plenty of practical strategies for dealing with a narcissist and getting what you want (such as 'shutty shutty' and using reverse psychology – more on these coming up), and you'll find many more ideas to add to your strategy throughout this book. Here are some other general strategies that you may find useful:

- Pick your battles. You can't fight them all, so it's best to prioritise and let some things go. Sometimes it helps to give the narcissist something he wants and to let him feel he won that round.

- Use your head, not your heart. You know this man and his patterns of behaviour won't have changed (although they may have become more extreme) so think about how he reacts in various situations and predict what he's likely to do next.

- Keep making notes of his lies, continually gather evidence and keep records of his behaviour. It may later prove useful in demonstrating a pattern of behaviour. See Chapter 14 for more on gathering evidence.

- Refuse to be shocked. You know what he does, and he knows how much it winds you up. If you stop looking frightened or infuriated you stop him feeling entertained, powerful and in control.

- Don't let him know what you really want – or he'll go out of his way to make sure you don't get it. Read more about how to negotiate with a narcissist (as best you can) in Chapter 8.

- Protest (i.e. write to him or his solicitor) every time he's a day late serving anything, or failing to produce something in the court proceedings. Keep a list from the outset of what he's delayed and what he's failed to provide, and eventually you'll be able to show the judge the pattern of his behaviour – and hopefully get it shut down.

- Play the long game. For example, sometimes a man will fight tooth and nail to take the children away from their mother – but he doesn't really want them himself, he just wants to hurt her. He can't actually cope with them and it breaks down after a few months and the children return home. So, painful as it is, it can sometimes be more effective to give in than to fight.

- Remember that, however impossible your situation may feel, narcissists do sometimes break down, collapse and lose everything. (Remember Donald Trump?)
- Dig into the research on domestic abuse and the effects on mothers and children (see Chapter 16 for more on useful research).
- Toughen up and take control. Accept that the proceedings are probably going to go on for years rather than months, so work out what you need to sustain you through this, and how you can use the time productively. Don't wait for it all to be over to move on with your own life. Take back control and don't just live in limbo waiting to see what he's going to do next.

Failing to plan is planning to fail so take the time you need to create a bullet proof plan for your future life, and a strategy to get you there. Then read it through every night or every morning (or both) so that your brain remembers what it's supposed to be working on. Your plan should remain solid but you may have to change your strategies as you see what works and what doesn't.

Now let's explore some of those practical strategies that will help you deal with your narcissist – without losing your mind.

Set (and keep) boundaries

A narcissist is a damaged individual, and whilst you may have spent a lot of time trying to mend him, unfortunately he can't be helped. He doesn't have a mental health problem that is amenable to treatment and support, but a personality that is disordered. His thoughts and behaviour can't be changed no matter how hard you try. As you've been giving him so much attention, he'll no doubt try to reel you back in during your separation and divorce by telling you how much he needs you or your help. This is precisely why you must keep strong boundaries. Don't believe a word he says, and don't be gentle with him just because he tells you a bigger sob story than any you've heard before.

Narcissists specialise in violating boundaries, which they see as others trying to control them. You'll need to make it clear – through your words and actions – that you're no longer his victim and now operate in 'don't mess with me' mode. People treat us the way we allow them to treat us, so gently teaching others what we'll accept and what we won't is how we normally establish our boundaries.

But narcissistic people think only of themselves and their own wants and needs. They expect others to give in to them. They're not unlike wild animals; you're never going to tame them, but you can put a cage around them. You can tell them, and then show them, that you're not going to engage in further fights or arguments with them.

You'll want to be very clear where your boundaries are and to be much firmer about upholding them than you would be with other people. But it's not easy to be clear about your limits when you're in distress and turmoil, and he may be subtle in pushing your boundaries. What do you do if he's moved into a flat but says he needs to keep his motorbike in your garage? Or he's not allowed pets so you'll have to keep his tortoise but he wants to visit it every day? Or he insists on coming into the house every time he picks up the children? Or tells you his parents are coming to see the children next Sunday?

One way to work out what you should do is to think about reversing your roles. Do you have a key to his new flat so you can walk in at any time? If not, there's no reason why he should have a key to your home, even if it is still his house too. Would you feel you had a right to keep your things at his place, or would you respect his privacy? It may seem like hard work to make and keep your boundaries – and it will be to start with – but it's the only way to start clawing back your own life.

Decide what you'll do in advance if your boundary is ignored or violated. For example, if you've told your ex you'll no longer tolerate his insults and will end a phone call if he's rude to you again, you'll need to tell him when he's insulted you (as it may just trip off his tongue without him actually realising it) and end the call immediately. Every time he does it. To begin with, he may well escalate his threats and attacks so you'll need to weather the storm until he gets the message.

Or let's say he comes up with some sob story to explain why he needs to change the time or place for a handover. It may seem harmless and he may convince you that it's only fair, but if you agree you're on a slippery slope; he's persuaded you to break a boundary, whether it's yours or in a court order, and next time he'll be after a bigger breach. Because there will definitely be a next time, since he won the last round (and for him it's all about winning). So always stick to orders or agreements. You can say something like, 'The court order says/we agreed/we always meet in Sainsbury's car park and we'll be there at 10am on Saturday.' Don't say 'no' – that's an unbearable word for a narcissist – just keep repeating what you will do until he can hear it. Or give him a (fairly meaningless) choice, such as, 'We'll see you in Sainsbury's car park at 10am or 10.30am. Which do you prefer?' Though don't agree to him returning the children later in exchange.

Another way to create healthy boundaries is to restrict your communication with your ex to written communication only – preferably via a specific family communication app like Our Family Wizard, or failing that via email. Always keep a record of these communications in case you need them in future. WhatsApp and text messages aren't so easy to use in evidence – they have to be screenshot, they don't always show the date or time, and they take up a lot of space in exhibits to court statements – so stick to the family apps or email where possible. But if you do use texts and WhatsApp, screenshot messages and save them elsewhere as a backup.

Educate yourself

Knowledge is power so research all you can about narcissistic abuse, how to heal from it, and how to leave and divorce a narcissist. (There's a list of helpful books and websites in the Resources section at the end of this book. Please read as much as you can of the ones you feel drawn to.) Understanding the narcissist is the first step towards your healing. It will also help you to recognise the techniques they use against you so you can respond differently in future.

Other useful ways to educate yourself include:

- Find out how many of the things he does, such as stalking you, are criminal offences. (Your local domestic abuse service can help with this – or head to Google.)

- Read and learn as much as you can about the court proceedings you're involved in – it's far less scary if you understand what's going on.

- Ask yourself, what are the things that most frighten you about your situation? For a lot of people it's the debts or mortgage repayments, and their credit ratings. Narcissists don't care about debts, or mortgage repayments, but they know you do. So they'll mess around with payments, and take mortgage holidays you won't agree to, just so they can enjoy seeing you getting into a tizzy. In other words, they're extracting narcissistic supply from you.

- Before you spiral into fear, ask yourself: 'what's the worst that will happen if ….' and if you don't know the answer, find out. Otherwise your head is just full of fear and panic, meaning you're not in any state to make the big decisions that are required of you in dealing with court proceedings. Once you have concrete information, you can decide what to do about it.

You can also re-educate your brain by using a gratitude journal. At the end of every day write down five things you're grateful for. They don't have to be big things, but you do have to notice them. They can be as small as being able to drink a cup of tea in peace, or your child giving you a big smile. However small they are, they will add up and soon make you feel a lot better. And reading your gratitude diary on a bad day will help to bring a smile to your face and encourage you to carry on.

Protect yourself

I am sure that is the danger,
that I react when worn down and depleted.

You may think you know the depths your narcissist can sink to but if you're just starting in the family court I have to warn you: you ain't seen nothing yet. It's a good song, but not so much fun to live through. You'll want to do all you can to protect yourself from what's to come. Here are a few suggestions:

- A narcissist is likely to harass you by reporting you to the police and/or social services for every little scratch or bruise they see on your child, as well as for things that haven't even happened. If there's a social worker already involved with your family, consider whether you need to protect yourself by getting in first and report every smallest mark. This will be especially helpful if the social worker doesn't understand or recognise the coercive control or abuse you're suffering – you can explain that you're only telling them because you know he'll be on the phone to them about it tomorrow. Even if he isn't, they'll eventually come to appreciate your fear of his control and abuse and hopefully start to see things differently. And of course keep dated notes and photos of all the little marks so that when he tells the court you threw your child to the ground and she split her hand open you can produce a dated picture of the little scratch from when she took her hamster out of its cage.

- Recognise that the nice behaviour and the abusive behaviour are both conscious decisions made by your ex, and let go of your guilt. When they make threats of suicide, taking you back to court, etc. don't react emotionally, however bad you feel. Just tell them that's their choice and you've nothing to say about it. (Or maybe even that you wouldn't dream of trying to control them by telling them what to do!)

- Always respond from your head, not your heart. And if he's not asking you a direct question, hopefully your head will tell you not to respond at all. There's more on communicating with your ex later in the chapter.

- Remember it's not about you! You don't take it personally when your two-year-old has a tantrum, so respond in the same way when your narcissist can't control himself, or can't communicate more effectively than a toddler. Be the grown-up when dealing with juveniles of any age.

- Write a list of all the ways your ex controls you and next to each one put what you can do differently the next time.

- Don't trust the system, i.e. the organisations that are supposed to protect you and your children (particularly the family courts, social services, Cafcass and the police). That said, you won't help yourself by being overly suspicious of professionals you have to work with – just be wary and aware.

Know your own narcissist

It's time to make an objective study of your narcissist and know who he is. They all seem to have attended the same drama school and behave in remarkably similar ways but they do have individual variations. You may have worked out that his behaviour is predictable although you may have been too busy reacting to it to notice the patterns. Either way, being able to predict what he will do next is invaluable for your battle plan. And if he's likely to take you to court over the children, being able to show the patterns of his behaviour is what's going to help you. This is why gathering evidence is essential (Chapter 14). But in order to gather evidence, you must first observe.

Does he create drama and distraction, or just wallow in 'poor me' victimhood? Or both? In which order? Is there a period of calm before the storm? Does he think and plan ahead, work out the consequences of his actions, or does he just live for the day? Does he pick fights with you? When does he do that – before people come to visit, or before you go out? Does he do it to wind you up and make you look bad while he can just smile calmly? Work out what his strategies are.

Anticipate how he'll behave and don't be surprised when he behaves like a narcissist! Work out what you can do that works with him, not what should work because it would with everyone else. Finding what does work may be a process of trial and error as, whilst they all operate in very similar ways, some will be more motivated by one thing (like money) while others are more motivated by another (such as controlling you). Doing the detective work and understanding what makes him tick enables you to take back some of your power.

You'll want a good understanding of what makes you tick too. Then you have an advantage as you know about both of you, whereas he only thinks about himself. Of course he knows what winds you up, and how you'll react to him, but he doesn't really know who you are. Plus, you have the advantage because he has no idea that his behaviour doesn't serve him well.

Rather than seeking it, some narcissists are cowards when it comes to confrontation and don't cope well with it. If yours is one of these, he may cave in before a final hearing, even at the door of the court. Or you may be able to take the upper hand by threatening proceedings, or saying you're looking forward to the next hearing and having a judge make a decision.

Borderlines and some covert narcissists may respond better if you validate their feelings as they're so frightened of being abandoned. It's a case of trial and error, and the more scientific you can be about it, the sooner you'll succeed in working out the best way of communicating with your narcissist.

Protect your devices and technology

A controlling person will think nothing of putting a tracking device on your phone and cameras in the house. He's probably into your email too.

Don't take any chances. Set up a new email which doesn't contain your name (e.g. Winning Woman, imawinner@gmail.com) so there's no way he can guess it. Use this for all legal communications and anything else you wouldn't want him to see. I believe that Proton mail may be more secure than other emails but please don't take tech advice from me! Check it out for yourself. Make sure your new email isn't linked to any other account.

If you can use your old email address just for him, get a friend to monitor it for you if you find his messages triggering.

I would also recommend that you sever any iCloud accounts or cloud-based software if it is, or could be, connected to any of your ex's devices; you don't want any documents you save on your laptop to be uploading straight to his phone. Change any shared passwords, or any that your ex may be able to guess that you use. I would also change any that he might not be able to guess, just in case. In short, change them all. Be sure to carry out a thorough check of all your online activity (including social media) to ensure your ex has no access.

A frequent form of control is for the narcissist to take out the phone contract for his partner so, although she may think it's nice that he pays for it, he can see who she's calling. You may need to get a new phone and a new account depending on your situation. Some survivors just have a cheap pay-as-you-go phone to call and text their ex on (which can then be switched off), and use their smart phone for everyone else.

Get off social media

Unfortunately you really should go off the radar completely when it comes to social media. Anything you post can be used against you in court proceedings. His flying monkeys who are on it will give him information from your posts even if he's not on it himself – and his monitoring of your activity won't stop when the court proceedings are over. Ideally, then, you would delete your social media accounts altogether, but if you can't bear to do that then at least don't post on them. If you really must use social media, set up a new fake account (with the maximum privacy settings) that your ex won't be able to find.

If he's on social media, you or a friend on your behalf should be monitoring his accounts and taking screen shots of anything that could be of use to you in the future.

Do grey rock and 'shutty shutty'

The idea of doing grey rock is to get the narcissist to look elsewhere for their supply instead of feeding on your emotional responses to them. This means not reacting to anything he says or does that he knows will get you riled up, such as lying, being rude to you, bringing the children home late, feeding them junk food or letting them stay up until 11pm.

If you think about a big lump of grey rock you'll realise that it's *very boring*, which is just how you need to be with someone who is trying to provoke you into giving them a reaction. How much drama can you get from a grey rock? No matter what you throw at a rock, or how hard you throw it, it will give you nothing back. If you hit it hard with your bare hand, it's you who'll get hurt. How long could you shout at a grey rock without getting bored and going away? That's what you're aiming for, boring the narcissist into giving up on you and leaving you alone. He feeds on your emotional reactions, so you need to starve him out of your orbit. You want him to lose interest in you and find another victim.

Every time your narcissistic ex contacts you, he wants an emotional reaction. Your aim is to deprive him of the drama he craves. So when you receive a message from him, your first task is to ask yourself if you really need to reply. I know it's hard for a polite person to ignore a question that's asked of them, but it does get easier with practice.

A good question to ask yourself is, 'What will happen if I don't reply?' Unless the answer is 'My child will suffer harm' or 'He'll drive 100 miles and we won't be here' or 'I'll be in breach of the court order', don't reply. Because every time you acknowledge his messages, you'll get more of the same. If you're worried about the court saying you need to communicate better, make sure you have copies of three or four examples of his communications to hand to show the judge or your ex's barrister why you don't.

If you really have to give an answer then 'yes', 'no', 'maybe' or 'thanks for your message' are your basic responses. If you need to say more, make sure you keep it as short as you possibly can and that there's no emotion in what you say; stick to the facts, and don't try to defend yourself or point out his errors. There's nothing you can say that will convince him that what he says to you isn't true – because for him that's not the object of the exercise anyway – so just focus on what's best for your child. Don't make small talk, don't ask him questions, and keep your new life to yourself.

To begin with, the narcissist will be annoyed and may well up the ante by doing things he knows will annoy you in order to provoke a response. He may return the children late, or even later than usual, and however anxious this may make you, it's important not to show it or to react.

Don't dignify him with your energy or emotion. Just remember who he is – an anti-social manipulating actor – and who you are: an unresponsive grey rock. It'll take a while, as well as patience and self-control, to re-programme your brain to respond differently, so be patient with yourself whilst you're a grey-rocker-in-training.

Author Lisa Romano calls doing grey rock 'shutty shutty', which is an excellent mantra to keep repeating to yourself as a reminder not to engage with him. It may be your natural reaction to fight back if he tries to insult or hurt you, but if 'shutty shutty' is the first thing that comes into your head it can save you from taking his bait. You can't win a fight with him because you want such different things: you want a quiet life without him in it, while he wants to provoke and punish you, and get supply for himself. Don't give him what he wants, but go for what you want. His love of confrontation is part of who he is, but it's not in your nature so you're not competing on an even playing field. You cannot win, in other words. So shutty shutty and walk away. (Or even better, shutty shutty and write it down on your evidence log, see Chapter 14.) He'll keep coming back as long as he knows he can get supply from you, so don't feed the monster.

When the narcissist takes you to court to get more time with his children, that's not usually what he really wants. He wants to get at you. (Or to pay less in child maintenance.) So do all you can to pretend you're not anxious and alarmed, just bored.

How to communicate with a narcissist

It's really best not to. Going 'no contact' is the best-case scenario, but if you have children together this probably isn't an option. Keep calm and keep to your own agenda. Ignore his rudeness or abuse, which is designed to upset or anger you and has always worked in the past. Be aware that when you ignore his behaviour, it may escalate for a while to get a rise out of you. Remember, shutty shutty is the order of the day. Keep all communication to the absolute essentials.

Let's explore some strategies for communicating with your narcissist.

Don't speak to him verbally if you can possibly avoid it

Get it all in writing (via email or a parenting app) instead. There are several reasons for this:

- If he later denies what he's said, you've got no proof to put before the court, or even him.
- However hard you try not to react to his lies and accusations, he knows how to push your buttons and your amygdala goes into fight, flight or freeze before you even realise what's happened – ultimately meaning your response is doomed.
- You won't get an answer to your question or the issue you want resolved. He'll either give you a reply that sounds as if he's answered but turns out to be word salad or he'll throw more questions back at you, probably on a totally different topic. You can go round and round like this for as long as you like, and he'll enjoy every minute of it.

Don't take the bait of his insults or accusations

Keep your focus on the issue you are trying to resolve in this communication and refuse his invitation to give him more narcissistic supply and side-track you from your intention.

Don't say sorry

We apologise when we've done something wrong and accept responsibility for our mistakes. This is normal, decent, human behaviour and helps to make the world go round. But it doesn't work with narcissists. In their eyes, you're either all right or all wrong and any apology can be used against you later. So when you say, 'I'm sorry, I misread the letter, I thought it was next week', they hear 'I'm totally incompetent, I can't even read plain English, I get everything wrong and can't be trusted not to mess up even the simplest things' and you'll get an immediate response telling you this. Instead you can say, 'I'm sad that I missed sports day' or 'I regret that I missed that appointment' or 'I did forget the meeting', which shuts down the conversation.

Don't show any emotion to the narcissist

It's what they feed on. If they're so desperate for your attention that you feel you have to say something, you can acknowledge them by saying 'I can see you're upset' or 'That must be difficult' but say it matter-of-factly with no emotion or sympathy. You may have to scream and shout or cry, or beat your pillow after you've had an interaction with them, but while you're there, act like a sleuth, watching and reporting the facts.

Don't get emotionally engaged

You're not going to convince a narcissist he's wrong so don't even try. He'll never say, 'You're right, I was the one who did that to you'. If he does say he's wrong, you can be sure he's saying it to manipulate you or someone else.

Don't use the children to pass messages between you

It may seem like the easiest way as the message is likely to be about them anyway, but it's really unfair to put that stress on to a child who may fear the other parent's reaction – even yours, if they think it's likely to upset you. If your ex tries to use the children, send a written message saying you won't respond to any messages sent that way, and then make sure you keep that boundary.

Don't verbally attack the narcissist unless you've first carefully calculated the effect this will have

If you tell him he's a narcissist, a loser, a failure or that his kids hate him, you'll cause him a narcissistic injury as that's more than his fragile ego can cope with. And you or your child are likely to be the victim of his ensuing narcissistic rage. If you're able to whisper such destructive words on your way into court so that he explodes with anger in front of the judge and exposes his true colours then so much the better. Though you'll be sure to pay the price in the days or weeks to come, and if there's any chance that it'll be the children rather than you who might pay that price, you won't want to antagonise your ex.

Do practice your responses

Practice, practice, practice – both in your head and by doing role play with a friend or coach – until you're able to look totally unconcerned and able to not react when he tells you what's happened, or is about to happen, to one of your children. He wants to shock you, but if you can just say 'I see' or 'Uh huh' or even 'What's your point?' he doesn't get the emotional reaction he wants. He might then ask if you heard what he said and you can just reply, 'I heard what you said. Is that all?' Your stomach may be churning but as long as you're outwardly calm and sound very bored, this tactic will eventually work. Practice makes perfect.

He may up the ante in the meantime. To start with, he'll struggle to process the fact that his scare tactics haven't worked to rile you like they always have, so he'll keep trying for a while. You don't need the advanced acting skills the narcissist has – you only have to perfect the one, very bored, expression and reaction. Think of things he could come up with and your possible bland responses. Make a list of them, learn them and practice saying them in front of a mirror or with a friend. He'll do all he can to provoke you into reacting but eventually he'll get bored with trying and move on to a more entertaining victim.

Do be picky about what you reply to

As I've said, when he attacks you in writing, it's best not to reply at all. But if the message also contains a question that you have to answer, simply start your reply with an emotionless 'I deny all your allegations' or 'Your attempt to show me in a negative light is noted and I don't agree with your interpretation of events', and then answer the question. That's it. Work out a standard response that you're comfortable with, then copy and paste it in response to every diatribe from him.

Don't waste your time and energy thinking up new replies.

The same applies to letters from his solicitors. Are they full of lies and accusations? If so, does it even matter? Look at your list of goals for these proceedings – is defending yourself from his lies on it? I hope not, because that's an unachievable aim and you're setting yourself up for failure. So don't be drawn in. Simply dismiss the two pages of lies and accusations with the trusty 'Your allegations are denied' and move on to answer the question(s) in the letter that absolutely have to be answered. If there are none, there's no need to reply to the letter just because it comes on solicitors' headed notepaper. Read more about dealing with his solicitor's letters in Chapter 10.

Do delay your replies wherever possible

No matter how hard your ex pushes your buttons, don't reply the same day unless the message is urgent. So ask yourself before you hit reply, 'Is this message really urgent?' If you receive it at 3pm and it's about picking your child up at 4pm, it's clearly urgent. If it's about a parents' evening in two weeks' time, it's not urgent. (Though, for the narcissist everything's urgent, and he expects you to drop everything and do what he wants immediately. Because your immediate attention is his narcissistic supply.) Unless it's really urgent – your urgent not his urgent – don't reply the same day. Sleep on it instead. In fact, the longer you can leave it before you reply the better.

After you've slept on it, put your detective's hat on and see if you can work out what the message is really asking, if anything. Print it out, then take a red pen and delete all the insults, accusations and statements of fiction so that you can see the actual issue or question that you need to answer. Draft your answer then sleep on it again. Then go back and halve the number of words you wrote before you finally send it. (Likewise, keep your letters to his solicitors as short as you possibly can; the less you say the less they can use against you later.)

Do remember that anything you write could end up before a judge

So before you press 'send' on any message, read it through again and ask yourself if you'd be happy for a judge to see what you've written. It's best to strike a balance between using the grey rock method and looking polite and helpful; so use his name at the start, say please and thank you and even 'have a good day', 'take care' or whatever you might normally say.

If you can, it's best to use a co-parenting app like *Our Family Wizard* or *AppClose* so all your communications are in one place, which is helpful if you need to put them into court as evidence later. It also means you can look at it when you want and don't have him in your inbox all the time. Plus, *Our Family Wizard* has a tone monitor and will tell you if you're about to say something too rude.

What about when you need to initiate contact with your ex?

Your ex will always have parental responsibility and, if your child lives with you, you'll be obliged to keep him informed of important events in your child's life. Again, keep this brief and emotionless.

If you had to take your child to the doctor and it was more than a sniffle, just tell him what the diagnosis was and what the treatment is. If he's having little contact with his child, you may have a court order telling you what information you have to give him maybe every month or every three months. Just give the facts as briefly as you can. You can make yourself a template with headings such as health, education, hobbies and then cut and paste each time you have to send one. It doesn't have to be very long at all, just a few lines, make it as easy for yourself as you can.

> I was told by my very expensive solicitor, that all communication I have with my ex I should treat like I am writing a business communication, i.e. ZERO emotion. I have written many emotional emails in answer to his horrid messages over the years but have never sent them. Keeping the finances and contact issues as separate emails, knowing I don't need to respond to every point he makes and leaving my emotions out of all my communication has been my saviour in all this and following this advice has kept me sane.

If you need more help with your communication tactics, Tina Swithin's *The Narc Decoder* is a brilliant book which will help you translate his emails and write a reply. You'll also find more pointers in the chapter on negotiating with a narcissist (Chapter 8).

How to talk to yourself

Even more important than how you speak to the narcissist is how you talk to yourself. After years of having him filling your head you'll have trouble knowing which of your thoughts are really your own, but the detective in you will be able to catch the offending notions. What are the words going round and round in your head? There's likely to be one phrase that runs on a loop, so keep listening until you can catch it. It could be something like 'This can't be happening', 'I'm so stupid/worthless/useless/ugly', 'I can't believe he's done this' or 'I can't cope with this anymore'.

All these thoughts are disempowering and it's how he's kept you small. Changing the script will help you to reclaim your power, boost your mood and take you from victim to survivor. Turn the words you've detected into their positive opposite, for example: 'This has happened and I can deal with it/this too will pass', 'I'm clever/valuable/capable/beautiful ...', or 'I can cope with whatever I need to'. Make sure they're words that sit well with you as you'll be repeating them often.

Every time you catch the offending thought in your head, shout 'stop' and push both hands out in front of you as if you're pushing the thought away. (Best to do this in your head if there's anyone else around or you'll be giving him proof of his incantation that you're crazy!) Then immediately replace the thought with your positive mantra.

By the time you finish this book you'll have a few mantras to keep repeating to yourself. Useful mantras to remember are:

- 'Shutty shutty, write it down.' Or 'Shutty shutty, walk away.'
- I am calm and detached.
- I'm in control.
- This will work.
- Attack, don't defend (more on this coming up later).
- Evidence, evidence, evidence.

The idea is to reprogramme your brain. His brainwashing has created unhealthy neural pathways in it, like muddy tyre tracks over a lawn. The tracks are now so well worn that any little thing can trigger the negative thought so fast you're not even aware of it flashing through your brain, but it's still doing damage. When you stop these thoughts for long enough, the grass will grow back and stop the thought flashing through at such speed. You then replace the thoughts with your new healthy mantras and create pretty tracks of your own choosing. Repeat your mantras to yourself during every waking moment, and just before you go to sleep. Put them on Post-it notes on your mirrors, your car dashboard, your screensavers, your purse, your fridge ... anywhere and everywhere so they start to replace your ex and his imposter thoughts for you.

You can never stop your brain thinking – it's what brains do. But you can stop imagining the worst, and you can stop worrying about him. He's not ill, he won't commit suicide or come to any other harm he might suggest in his efforts to manipulate you. He's a narcissist and he looks after himself very well. So put your brain to better use by giving it positive and productive things to do. The best way to do that is to ask yourself good questions; your brain will keep turning things over and come up with answers for you. The best question to ask yourself is: 'Will that work?' rather than 'Is that the right thing to do?' or 'Will I be in trouble if I do that?' Other good questions are 'How can I make this work?', 'What's the best way to ....?', 'What can I do to ....?' and 'How can I best protect my children?'

Another useful tip to help keep him out of your head and diminish his importance is to change the name you use for him; instead of thinking of him as Keith, use 'k' instead. Use that too when you're writing about him, though never when you're writing to him!

If he's sounding off at you, instead of reacting to him, make a game of it in your head; look at him as though he's a two-year-old having a tantrum on the floor, and say to yourself 'There he goes again'. Get your inner detective to count how many times he does it and make a note when you get home.

Use reverse psychology

I've said that you shouldn't give the narcissist any more information than you have to, and keep your communications to facts only. That said, when you're looking for a specific outcome, you can use reverse psychology – and throw some extra information his way – to achieve your goal.

Whatever you want, the narcissist will do all he can to make sure you don't get it. So don't tell him what you really want – tell him something else! You want to keep the house? Tell him you're after his pension. You're desperate to keep out of court? Call his bluff: tell him you think it's best if a judge listens to what your children want and decides for you, so would he please apply as you can't afford it or don't have time.

If he thinks you're keen to go to court, he'll start to worry about what evidence you've got against him. You don't want him to have so much time with the children? Ask him to have them for extra time. Tell him you want a night out with the girls or a weekend away with a 'friend'. He won't demean himself by acting as your babysitter and if you can hint that there's another man in your life he'll make sure you have the children 24/7 to stop you in your tracks. He'll be beside himself with jealousy. (But never give him more time, more hours or more nights in a row, than he already has with the children.)

Bottom line: only tell him something if it serves *your* purpose, and never tell him what you really want.

You might also want to try a bit of flattery, when it serves your purpose. A narcissist won't do or give anything unless there's something in it for them, so if you want something from him you can try manipulating him by using flattery ('You're so brilliant at mending things. Could you fix Jimmy's bike for him?') He's bound to fall for it. This is of course giving him a little narcissistic supply, which you're normally trying to avoid, but it's fine if you can deliberately trade it for something you want, rather than allowing him to extract narcissistic supply from you with nothing in return.

Read more about negotiating with the narcissist in Chapter 8.

Stay focused

I said before that you need to plan your future life, create a strategy for achieving it, and then look at that plan/strategy every single day. This will help you to stay focused amidst the noise and chaos created by the narcissist. After all, when you're bombarded with a constant diatribe of abuse and demands for attention, it's easy to lose focus.

The master manipulator will do all they can to draw you in again, to get you angry or upset, and/or to continue to control you. This is where your laser sharp focus is required, so that you can stay on topic and maintain your boundaries. Don't argue, explain, discuss or defend yourself. Stick to the facts and if necessary repeat the same thing again and again until you're blue in the face.

Before any communication with the narcissist, be clear in your mind what you want to achieve from it, and don't be diverted or fall into one of his traps. Keep looking at your plan and strategy. Stay focused on what you do want, and how you're going to get there, and take it one step at a time.

Family court can be overwhelming, making it difficult to focus. It's sometimes hard to know where to start when there's so much to do and so little time, headspace or energy left; it's tempting to just dissolve into a heap of powerless panic. Don't lose focus here, either. It's essential to prioritise, and, just as with your strategy, take it one step at a time. Revisit the three steps for dealing with overwhelm from Chapter 4, i.e. make a list of what you have to do and prioritise the tasks according to what's urgent, what's important to you, and what's both urgent and important.

Get professional mental health support

By the time you leave a narcissist, you're likely to be in poor shape mentally and emotionally, if not physically as well. You need de-programming, like people coming out of a cult. You'll want to get stronger and build yourself up before you embark on the battle of your life. Narcissists are predators and if they sense any weakness in you they won't hesitate to exploit it mercilessly.

Your job is to protect your child, and you must toughen up to be able to do this. The narcissist can charm the police, social workers, teachers and therapists into believing him and taking unfair and unwarranted action against you.

> I know it sounds unbelievable but I really don't know how it all happened. I lost my children, my home, my work. I was left with nothing. And when I went to the police for help (my ex kept climbing in through my window), I ended up in the Crown Court, prosecuted for attempting to pervert the course of justice.

So who can you turn to for help? Circle back to the 'plan your separation' section earlier in this chapter for a list of people who can help you through not just the separation, but also the court proceedings and building your new life.

The therapist may well be the most important person on that list because if you're falling apart you can't do anything else. But do choose your therapist carefully – i.e. make sure they have experience in dealing with trauma and abuse – or they can do you more harm than good. Sadly, most therapists aren't trained in dealing with narcissistic abuse. Some will blame and shame you, and tell you to put it behind you and move on, instead of validating your experience and helping you to come to terms with the awful relationship.

Talking therapy isn't always the best as it can embed the trauma; in some cases, EMDR (eye movement desensitisation and reprocessing) can be more effective and a lot quicker. Though I'd suggest you may need some form of ongoing professional therapy or coaching right through your court proceedings.

You may be able to access therapy through your GP, although there are likely to be long wait times for this. Incidentally, when you go to your GP, you need to say that your notes must record why you went, not just what your symptoms/ problems are. Otherwise, if you have to produce your medical records in court, perhaps because your ex is alleging that you have mental health problems and are unstable, the records will just show the mental health problems, but not that they were caused by him. If the GP hasn't already got a record of your abuse, I'd suggest you write out beforehand exactly what you want them to put on your notes – for example, 'For x years x months, I suffered a controlling and abusive relationship and now ...' Keep re-writing until it's short and concise enough that you can sit there while they type it into your notes (best book a double appointment!). The wording should be something you'd be happy to see used in court if necessary. If your GP refuses, you'll just have to get up and leave, but if you don't go to your GP when you need help it means the narcissist is still controlling your life.

If you cannot access therapy via your GP, and you can't afford private therapy, then support groups may be a good option. There is also *The Freedom Programme* (see Resources). It's a free domestic abuse programme designed to help you understand and make sense of what's happened to you, as well as how your children may be affected. It's important for you to understand all the behaviours that are abusive and the effect they have, so that you spot whether they're being transferred to your child once your ex can't get at you anymore.

In addition to therapy, support groups and *The Freedom Programme*, I recommend the following actions to boost your mental health:

- An assertiveness training course could help you to hold your own with your ex, with lawyers and in court, and generally rebuild your confidence.
- Meditation or mindfulness may help you to remain composed and reassuring for your child on days when your ex is sounding off.
- Prioritise self-care. Choose just one thing to do for yourself every day, even if it's just sitting down with a cup of tea and a magazine for 10 minutes. When that one thing has become a habit, you can add another. Be as kind to yourself as you are to your children.

Remember, there's light at the end of the tunnel, and success and happiness are your best revenge. The narcissist is not a happy person and one thing that makes him feel better is to make you even more miserable than he is. That's his goal. What's more, if you become happy and successful in your life, that proves that he was the problem in your relationship (not you as he insists), and that's the last thing he wants anyone to think. So get the help you need to work on your success and happiness.

Don't tell him he's lying

He already knows that! Don't tell him you don't believe him, even when his lies are blatant. Just say something like, 'You can believe that if you like' or 'I accept that's what you think'. Then shutty shutty, and write it down to use at an appropriate time.

Ignore, too, his manipulations of the truth. Stick to your own truth and agree to disagree: 'I understand that's your point of view'. If you're saying this verbally, be careful of your tone of voice. It's important not to sound sarcastic, angry or upset but to come over like a boring grey rock with no emotion. 'Whatever' with a shrug of your shoulders can be a good one to try too.

Don't try to reason with him in the hope that he will relate to you and stop his abuse of you and/or his children

He's not rational, he has his own code of conduct, and even if he was interested in relating to you on your terms, he's simply not capable of it. Instead, he dehumanises his victims so that he doesn't feel any guilt.

Don't over-share

Everything you tell a narcissist can be used against you at a future time, so don't give long stories or explain the ins and outs. That's what you did in the past, when he was your intimate partner. Now you're separated and the dynamics have changed, which means you must deal with him differently. Keep to the absolute essentials. Imagine it's your bank manager you're talking to; would you explain to him why the children had corn flakes instead of a boiled egg for breakfast, or are wearing odd socks?

Don't defend or justify yourself or explain

That's what you did in the past, even when there was nothing to defend. And there's still nothing to prove or defend because it's not about you, it's about your ex's disordered personality. Sometimes a denial is advisable so that your silence can't be seen as acceptance of the allegations. In that case, a simple 'That's not true' or 'Your allegations are denied' is enough. Don't give more than enough as there's always the potential for it to backfire on you.

Don't ignore your ex's exes and new partner

When your narcissistic ex gets a new partner, you're likely to feel either relieved or hurt, maybe even jealous. But when you're dealing with a narcissist it's important to act from your head, not from your heart, so that you can get one step ahead and be ready to outsmart them.

I know this advice won't go down well, but I'll say it anyway: if you have children with an abusive or controlling ex please do all you can to befriend their new partner. Or if not befriend, at least be on speaking terms. Your ex will do all they can to 'divide and conquer', to ensure you hate each other. The last thing they want is the two of you comparing notes and blowing their cover.

There are two main reasons to befriend the new partner. Firstly, the narcissist is most likely to have targeted another lovely empathetic person similar to you. This may not be immediately obvious as your ex will no doubt be making the most of the love bombing phase to manipulate the new person in their life into hating you, with their lies about the dreadful things you're supposed to have done. But if your children are spending regular time with their narcissistic parent, it should be reassuring for you to know that there is a less disordered person present who will hopefully look out for them. If you can have some dialogue with the new partner, then that has to be good for your children – and if you can talk to them instead of your ex, that has to be good for you.

Secondly, if you're in court proceedings, you may be able to use the new relationship to help you if there's any evidence that all is not well (though it's likely to be longer before he starts abusing her because, for now, she's helping him against you). Your predecessor(s) may also be able to help you – you may want to reconsider all your ex told you about them, and get in touch with them, if you're not already.

Of course it's hard enough to get your own abuse recognised by the family court, let alone someone else's, but the case of R v P (Children: Similar Fact Evidence) 2020 could be helpful. This case is extreme in many ways, not least the court's mismanagement of it; there had been at least 15 different judges involved, and this was the sixth time it had been listed for a fact finding hearing.

The father (F – the mother and father are often referred to as M and F in court reports) applied for contact with his children, aged five and two, whom he had not seen since he separated from their mother. Her allegations of F's coercive and controlling behaviour included:

- He insisted on her abandoning her studies.
- He mispresented his name, occupation and financial position to her parents.
- He sent messages to her family purporting to be from her.
- He isolated and alienated her from her close family and friends.
- He made baseless allegations to public bodies, including the police, against her family.
- He required her to move constantly, to isolate her and to avoid them being found by her family and public bodies – to the extent that her parents hired a private detective to locate her and their grandchildren.
- He shouted at the older child.
- His behaviour led to a wholesale change in the mother's demeanour and character.

Three months after the mother left F, he began a relationship with Mrs D. She lived in London with her 11- and 9-year-old boys, who saw their father regularly.

A year later, the police advised a Welsh local authority to contact the London local authority dealing with this case. They reported their concerns about the D children and their mother's relationship with F. Mrs D had moved with F and her children to Wales and all contact between her children and their father had stopped. As a result, the court transferred residence of the children from their mother to their father. The Welsh local authority had concluded that F had behaved in a coercive and controlling way towards Mrs D and thought the information was likely to be relevant to the enquiries of the London local authority.

The mother of F's children said the Welsh report was relevant because it was so similar to her own allegations in that:

- Mrs D left her job as a primary school teacher within months of meeting F and the school was sufficiently concerned to make a referral to adult and children social services.
- Mrs D quickly became estranged from close family relationships and friends.
- Mrs D lost the care of her much-loved children and appeared not to have made efforts to keep in contact with them.
- F had made baseless accusations to public bodies, including the police, against Mrs D's family, claiming harassment by them.

- F and Mrs D had repeatedly moved around (including with the D children) to avoid detection by family and public bodies, leading to Mrs D's parents hiring private detectives to try to locate her and their grandchildren.

- F had repeatedly shouted at one of the D children (this was videoed by a concerned neighbour).

- F mispresented himself to Mrs D and her parents including in respect of his name, occupation and financial position.

- Mrs D underwent a rapid and wholesale change in her demeanour.

The mother in this case therefore argued that the Welsh report should be included with the evidence in her own proceedings against F. The judge disagreed and, as so often happens, took the side of the abusive parent saying she didn't see how F could have a fair trial if the report was admitted. The judge was also highly critical of the mother's solicitors.

Fortunately, the mother had a good barrister for her appeal. She argued that the judge was wrong to exclude this report as F's relationship with Mrs D and her children showed a strikingly similar pattern of behaviour to that alleged by the mother. The barrister pointed out that it is often difficult for a parent to prove that the other party's behaviour has been coercive and controlling because that sort of behaviour is a pattern rather than an event.

The appeal judges found the original judge was wrong to prioritise fairness to F, when exclusion of such significant evidence would be unfair to the mother, and they allowed her appeal. The case was transferred to the High Court for the fact finding hearing to go ahead with all of the mother's evidence included.

Whilst it's unlikely your case will be as extreme as this, your ex's previous partners could be helpful to you – not least in deciding how you talk to the new partner. Narcissists tend not to learn from their mistakes or change their behaviour, so if you can remember what they told you about their previous partner, you can predict what they will say about you to their next one. For instance, if you can say, 'I expect X has told you that I'm a crazy, selfish gold-digger' they will be struck by the exact words and more likely to think twice before dismissing you, even if they don't instantly believe you. You may at least be able to stop the narcissist recruiting them as a flying monkey.

Of course it's possible that you acted as a flying monkey at the start of your relationship with the narcissist, in which case you may need to eat humble pie and apologise to their previous partner. Nevertheless, they may still be willing to help you – just think about how you might react in their position. Even if they don't want to help you, they may consider giving evidence for you in order to help your children. What have you got to lose by asking?

Attack, don't defend

When it comes to the legal proceedings, in my experience you may sometimes need to fight fire with fire. For the empathetic people who find this difficult, I recommend a visit to the zoo – go and watch how mama bear defends her cubs if anyone goes near them.

Unless you can stand up to him, your ex and his lawyers are going to eat you for breakfast. That's not to say you need to defend yourself against his many allegations and accusations (which, after all, are just a distraction technique to deflect attention from his own behaviour). Defending yourself doesn't work and it's usually not even necessary – it's up to him to provide the evidence for his allegations, not for you to prove a negative. Instead, you need to fight fire with fire and go on the attack.

Of course, it may be totally against your nature to fight (whereas he loves the drama of a fight). But, sadly, when you're in the family court you're already in an adversarial system. The court sets you up to fight each other. (This is one of the four major problems with our family court identified by the Harm Report – see Chapter 16 – and although I hope it may be changed one day, it probably won't be before your children are adults.)

That said, standing up to him instead of placating him as you've always done may antagonise him, so do be careful as to when, where and how you challenge him. This is why you need to know your own narcissist. As I've said before, you need to pick your battles carefully.

Here are some useful strategies for getting into an 'attack, don't defend' mindset:

- Visualise yourself in a duel with your ex. There he is, coming at you with his sword flailing. Are you really going to stand there passively refusing to fight, using your sword to lean on like a walking stick to stop you shaking with fear? If you wave your sword furiously back at him, you've at least got a chance he won't annihilate you instantly. But as he's bigger and stronger than you, you'll have a much better chance if you can act strategically, such as stepping aside just as he's about to strike you, preferably with your leg out so he trips over and lands flat on his face! Then you can then either stab him in the back, or run away. Or both.

- Ask your coach or therapist for help. Coaching or therapy can help you to change your mindset so you can stand up to him and react differently to how you have in the past – differently enough that he can feel the change in you, that you've moved from defending yourself to attacking, and that he can no longer mess with you. Being on the offensive will be an alien feeling to you, like walking in someone else's shoes, but eventually those shoes will become comfortable. Believe you can get what you want, and you're more likely to achieve it.
- Forget what others may think of you and focus only on your goals. The protective parent is often so worried about what the judge will think of them, about whether they should go to mediation so they'll be seen as doing the right thing, about not putting a foot wrong, that they lose sight of their own ultimate goals for the proceedings.

What about practical action you can take to go on the attack? Let's explore some useful strategies that may work for you.

Act like him

It's undeniably hard to win against a narcissist in court – winning shouldn't be your goal anyway – so probably the best advice I can give you is to act more like him and less like yourself. Be demanding, not defensive. Be just as ruthless as he is, and don't hesitate to expose his whole ugly truth if he won't settle and keeps escalating his lies. Get some drama lessons ... or just watch and learn from him. Remember, he's a big bully and really scared inside; he knows you could be more powerful than he is but he certainly doesn't want you to know that or to think you could outsmart him.

Manipulate the manipulator (if possible a little more ethically than he does)

Now, don't be tempted to lie about something you could ever be caught out on. However, no one can ever prove what you were or weren't thinking at any given time, so don't let the fact that you've absolutely no intention of doing something stop you from telling him or his lawyers that you're considering it. Use your own smoke and mirrors.

You might, for example, say you're considering telling his family or his employer what he's done (what he's actually done, that is – I'm not suggesting you sink to his level and make up allegations of abuse), or that you're thinking of moving away, or stopping doing or paying for something that he's dependent on, or making another application to the court. This could be said in a letter to his solicitor, in an email, or potentially even in a position statement to the court – all of which avoid verbal contact with your ex. You might also try saying that you know he's got hidden assets – make an educated guess at what he might have put where, you've got nothing to lose. If he's said or done something to your children that you can't actually prove, don't let that stop you making the allegation. Turn the tables. Interrupt his pattern, get him on the back foot, running round in circles defending your allegations and trying to stop you doing things instead of you being the one who's off-balance. Then you can start to change the power dynamic and turn the ship around.

Ask yourself the right questions

Instead of asking yourself 'Is this the right thing to do?' ask 'What would he do in this position?' or 'Will it work to give the correct information?' Do what's right for you and your child, rather than what's normally the right thing to do. What you're dealing with is so far from normal that the normal rules just don't work.

Don't be afraid of involving the police

Don't just tell him you're going to report his latest abuse or harassment to the police – do it so that you have an official record. Once you've made a few reports about him following you or sending you incessant texts, ask the police how many incidents they require before they'll prosecute him for harassment.

Don't be surprised if the behaviour of his lawyers, or the social worker, is mirroring that of the narcissist.

You won't be able to report them to the police, but now that you're a detective, rather than a victim, you can note it all down in the same way as you would for your narcissist (see gathering evidence in Chapter 14). You should be able to use it in your children proceedings.

Don't be afraid of going back to court

Of course I know what dreadful decisions are made in children proceedings, but I also know the only way with these abusers is to play the long game. Eventually he will get complacent or just too cocky and trip himself up, at which point others may finally see him for who he really is. Instead of dreading every court hearing, try to see them as being another stepping stone on the road to you achieving what you want. That way, you take back a little control.

And if he's not complying with court orders or directions, complain instantly. If you don't, he's just walking all over you all over again. Threaten him with applying for orders for costs, just like his lawyers probably do to you.

Ask yourself where you want to be in five years' time

Will you feel proud of yourself for playing by all the rules and not risking upsetting the judge or other professionals (who are, after all, people you'll never see again)? Or will you regret not having gone on the attack, and done all you could to protect yourself and your children? I'm afraid it's a choice you have to make, sooner rather than later. Your ex will be building his case all the time. Can you afford to sit by and not do the same?

CHAPTER 6:

PARENTING YOUR CHILDREN – HOW CHILDREN ARE AFFECTED BY A NARCISSISTIC PARENT AND WHAT YOU CAN DO ABOUT IT

For the protective parent, their children are always their priority and may cause them to question whether they are doing the right thing in divorcing the children's other parent. And you're right to question this seriously as you'll have to balance the harm the children experience from the impact of the abuse if you stay in the relationship, against the harm the children may suffer during their time with the abuser when you're unable to protect them like you can when you're together.

> *My ex is controlling me through the children, and Cafcass are letting him and enabling it. I've not been able to stop crying all night after court today. They just ignore the abuse and enable perpetrators to continue. There is no point in leaving at all. It's worse now than it was when I was with him.*

Some mothers do regret leaving as whilst they were in the relationship the father had little interest in his children and she was able to protect them from the worst of his abuse. But after separation he suddenly becomes dad of the year and wants a lot of time alone with the children, if not 50/50 residence, and the children have to cope with his abuse on their own.

If you have any doubts as to whether you're doing the right thing, please talk it over with a professional – IDVA, health visitor, counsellor, or even me (diana@dealingwithdivorce.co.uk) – before you leave. If necessary, talk to more than one professional.

On the following pages is Sarah's story, the daughter of Carol, who I talked about in the introduction.

A child's life with a narcissistic father: Sarah's story

The social worker's report

The papers Sarah sent me included a Section 37 report, which is only ordered when the court is considering whether a care or supervision order may be required, so the judge must have been pretty worried about Julian (11) and Sarah (nine). Unfortunately social services back then appear to have been no better than they are now (although my memory is that they generally were).

The children were interviewed at home, which would not have helped them to be truthful about the situation. Julian explained that there was hostility and continual arguments between his parents, but said he had never witnessed any violence between them. He was slightly critical of his mother but said he was very close to his father, although he loved both of his parents.

Sarah told the social worker that she loved her mother, but not as much as her father, and she strongly felt her mother should not shout at her father. She blamed her mother for the many arguments and admitted hitting her mother, which she explained as disobedience due to the arguments.

Strangely, it does not appear that Jay, the children's father, was interviewed by the social worker – usually the narcissistic parent is quickly able to manipulate the professional to their point of view, but in this case it seems that Jay had been able to get the children to do this for him. Jay also failed to attend a childcare conference, despite saying he would be there.

The social worker concluded that the children were not suffering or likely to suffer significant harm and the main concern was 'the very difficult and complex relationship the parents have with each other'. Clearly the term 'parental conflict' had not been coined by then but, as now, the abuse was not recognised.

The report goes on to say that 'the children have presented as bright, confident and show no indications of serious distress. Both children have thrived despite the acrimonious and difficult parental relationship'.

The family was referred for family therapy but, needless to say, that did not work well or last long.

The children's lies

Sarah says that as adults she and her brother can testify to Jay's abuse of their mother, and of them as children. I was struck by the fact that both children had lied to the social worker and, when I asked Sarah about this, she told me they didn't conspire to lie. Yet both falsely claimed their father was not abusive. Sarah said, 'I know I didn't trust adults and Dad made it clear that Mum was saying things against him that he didn't agree with, and that we'd have to talk to someone. It is impossible to trust adults when your parent is manipulative so their presence felt alien. I wanted to say what would make them go away.'

The children were frightened of their father's temper and had experienced his violence to their mother, yet they told the social worker how wonderful he was. They also lied at school about what was and wasn't happening at home, and both schools gave the social worker glowing reports of the children. We think of children acting out and expect that people will be able to tell by their bad behaviour if they have a problem, but many children stay under the radar by behaving impeccably. The only clue in the school report was that Sarah's concentration was poor.

Sarah explains, 'Because my brother and I were both above average students, when school slipped we were still above average or the work was acceptable enough for them to believe the problem was with our attention and not with our home life. I felt the failures were mine so, when questioned, my response was about how I should be doing better at school, not an explanation of a troubling home life. I'd make a lot of jokes to try and disarm and deflect conversations but I rarely talked about myself or my experiences.'

It would appear that the judge favoured the children's version over their mother's and did not award Carol custody. She therefore remained living in the house with Jay as she would have lost her children if she had left but, unsurprisingly, she fell into a state of depression.

Sarah says, 'The social worker's report is shameful. I would hope they wouldn't make judgements based on our report as children, but that's what happened.'

Alienating the children from their mother

Sarah remembers Jay being physically and verbally abusive, and experienced Jay abusing Carol. Eventually, both children too became physically and verbally abusive to their mother and started acting out to win their father's approval. Carol highlighted an incident where Julian even hit her with a stick.

Sarah says, 'I know Dad did everything he could to control and manipulate my mum and he taught me as a child to be abusive to her. I found a home video where I'm recording her while I bullied her and called her names. It's just horrible to think about how that was normalised and the hardest part is not being able to ask for her forgiveness. My mum was a wonderful person who did everything for us as children. She filled us with love and was a kind, caring person. Once she got sick, everything fell to pieces and Dad tried to pick up the slack, but his idea of spending time with us was taking us to his hobbies like his tennis club or having us wait in the car while he went to the pub; he didn't care about doing things we wanted to do or getting to know us.'

Children do what their parents show and tell them. Moreover, children with an abusive parent adapt their behaviour in order to survive. Sarah and Julian had to work out how to protect themselves from their father, and abusing their mother would have been a way of getting a lot of brownie *points with him, thus making themselves safer for a while. No matter how terribly they behave, it's never the fault of the child in these situations.*

Favouring one child over the other

A narcissist will almost always favour one child: the golden child. In this case it was Julian and Sarah was the scapegoat. It's not always consistent, though, and the children may swap roles from time to time, or even frequently. Sarah has told me that she has eventually done better professionally than her brother and Jay now favours her. Both roles are damaging for a child, albeit in slightly different ways.

Sarah would have been desperate for her father's approval as she would have known her brother was his favourite, and children go to amazing lengths to gain a parent's approval, which is another explanation for her abuse of her mother.

When Sarah was a few years older, Jay often fought with his daughter, regularly threatening to throw her out of the home if she didn't abide by his rules. Julian never tried to protect his sister because their father created a culture of abuse. Fortunately Julian didn't abuse his sister, though, which does sometimes happen.

Using the children against their mother

Jay got Sarah to steal her mother's papers for him. These included her personal letters and printed statement, which she gave to her father prior to the court case so he could use them against Carol.

Jay manipulated his children by reading Carol's statement out loud to them while accusing her of lying. To win their favour in the lead up to the court case he also spoiled the children with numerous gifts, convincing them that their mum was trying to split up the family.

In her letters, Carol writes that Sarah is acting out against her, has started stealing personal items without asking, and is being physically and verbally abusive; she would threaten and then run away from her mother in public places, causing her no end of stress.

The effect of narcissistic abuse and coercive control on the children

Sarah says, 'I had so many questions growing up and it was hard to understand what was going on. We learned as children not to be vulnerable because he would attack us, so our conversations became surface level. We'd show up and eat dinner but avoid conversations that risked us getting hurt. My dad created a culture of fear and we had to live out his narrative. He used his relationships to distance everyone from my mum when she needed support the most and so we had no support network from family or friends either. The first time I felt safe was when I was moved out of home and I was allowed to just be myself for the first time.'

Four or five years after the court proceedings, when she was 14 or 15 years old, Sarah was moved out of the family home by social services after she had started self-harming and threatening suicide. On another occasion, the police were called because Sarah stayed out late and Jay reported her missing. After the police left, Jay hit Sarah. She reported it to her school counsellor who moved her out of the home, and for several months she stayed with a school friend's family who lived across the road.

Sarah says, 'My dad was very aware of how to push our buttons without going over the line. He'd pull my hair or grab my face and wake us up in the middle of the night to tidy the house because he was angry it wasn't clean. I was grateful when he crossed the line because I could then use it as leverage to leave the house.

I had a social worker, psychiatrist and counsellor and I wasn't able to talk to any of them about Dad because when you grow up without vulnerability it's an impossible concept. You're asking a child to suddenly operate in a way they never have before. It sounds conflicting but I didn't know I deserved better or that Dad's behaviour was as big a problem, but I was also trying to escape from it.

I enjoyed time outside of the house so I wouldn't come home, then he'd try and exert more control and I'd avoid him. I wouldn't fight, I just became more aloof to avoid his temper and less communicative but I was rebelling in a way. I left home at 16 because he said I had to abide by his rules or I'd be out so I made my peace with leaving. I didn't have my own bedroom because Mum was sharing with me, so the situation wasn't appropriate for a growing teenager. Not having my own room at home felt like I didn't have much to leave.'

Sarah moved out of the family home permanently and dropped out of school before finishing her GCSEs. She chose to become homeless rather than continue to suffer her father's abusive and threatening behaviour and lived for a number of years in poverty in a squat with people with social and drug problems. She had a string of unhealthy relationships; she was sexually assaulted by a 42-year-old man and was then in a relationship with a 40-year-old and got pregnant. When Jay found out, he told Sarah to get an abortion, which she did, but he gave her no support. Eventually a friend's mother realised Sarah's situation and invited her to stay at her house, where she slept on the sofa.

And when the children grow up …

Sarah has had a lot of counselling and now sees that 'I had been absorbing my dad's anger for a long time and projecting. I stopped after I started therapy and realised the anger I was holding on to wasn't mine.'

Nevertheless she says, 'It's been hard writing out the truth because I didn't want to admit weakness. I just told myself I could deal with anything because I had such a hard childhood.

I struggled in work when I eventually got on my own two feet and now I'm a manager I realised that I couldn't communicate appreciation. By default I'm wired to believe all faults are mine because I was never enough, so I went to therapy and that's when I realised the damage he'd caused. It took 36 years for me to understand this. I also realised that I'm motivated by fear of not doing enough, or by a sense of duty, and I struggled to recognise that I had needs and to be able to prioritise myself over others. I ended up attending a 12-week group therapy class, which gave me lots of tools for revisiting my trauma and recognising the impact of them day to day.

A couple of Christmas's ago I went home after a breakup and had been crying. I chose not to talk to my father about it but he came and sat down next to me and asked whether I was crying because of my breakup, which I confirmed. He just laughed and said, "You're not one to stay with people" and got up and left. He had a hard childhood so we became great at rationalising our experiences: Dad had a hard life; things could be worse, etc. It stunted our emotional expression.

I spent many years bringing the wrong people into my life; I was attracted to people who were unsafe emotionally because that's what I grew up with. Now I know how not to bring those people into my life but I'm timid about dating.

I took every chance I could in life because I wasn't given any as a child. I now work for a Fortune 100 company; I'm a "woman in tech" managing a team of strategic product managers. I educated myself outside of school and worked tirelessly for my future. I'm proud I managed to build financial and emotional stability to feel safe enough to revisit my past. There's a part of me that realises I lived out his dreams and not mine, because I eventually became the "golden child". But I'm this despite his actions, not because of them. The next phase of the journey is getting to know the side of myself that wasn't nurtured so I can live a full life.

Julian has not had any help because he is worried that, as we had such a terrible time as children, it would break him if he went to therapy. He still does endless things for our father, only to be criticised for not doing enough, and he's wired to operate out of a sense of duty.'

The effects of growing up in an abusive household are lifelong. Neither Sarah nor Julian have married or had children. Sarah learned that parental alienation makes it harder to be a parent because it's likely she would struggle to attach with her children due to her experience growing up.

Sarah's description of her and her brother's lives sound to me as though they have suffered very significant harm. But so long as social workers, Cafcass and other family court professionals continue to dismiss abuse and coercive control like this as 'parental conflict', children will continue to suffer and have their lives wrecked.

Understanding the short- and long-term effects on children

My daughter went to live with her father when she was 13. The bubbly, happy, cheeky teenager that came back 12 months later had started self-harming, had an eating disorder and told me she had even tried drinking bleach because she didn't 'want to live anymore'. The one thing that stands out that she said was 'Why doesn't he like me?'

Once you've come to realise that your ex is abusive and narcissistic you may struggle to accept that your child still loves them. More often than not they will, because we're hard-wired to love our parents. It's very hard for a child to admit that her father doesn't have her best interests at heart, and she's more likely to blame herself and keep trying to win his approval.

Please don't underestimate both the short- and long-term effects on your children of having a narcissistic parent. These may include your child:

- Not being able to identify or trust their own feelings.
- Being valued for what they do (for their parent) or what they achieve (reflected glory) rather than who they are.
- Being there for the parent, rather than their parent being there for them.
- Being criticised and judged instead of loved and accepted, so will always feel 'not good enough'.
- Becoming aggressive or violent themselves.
- Growing up to be either narcissistic themselves, or co-dependent, and suffering C-PTSD (complex trauma), depression, or anxiety. Self-harm, suicidal thoughts and substance abuse are other common outcomes.
- Having major problems with trust and intimacy as an adult.

Even babies are not oblivious to abuse; they are acutely aware of their surroundings, particularly the emotional state of their primary caregiver. Children too young to speak can still understand, and even if they don't understand the words, they can certainly pick up on the tone they're said in as well as how they land with the other parent. They can pick up on fear and a tense atmosphere. Children need to be protected from abuse, no matter how old they are.

Children who experience domestic abuse all react differently. One child may be acutely aware of the abuse, and may take on the role of family protector. Their sibling may refuse to acknowledge it at all, even if physical violence occurs right in front of them. Another child may identify with the abusive parent and start imitating their behaviour. It's vitally important to nip any such behaviour in the bud and make it clear it won't be tolerated; if left unchecked it can result in the child replacing the perpetrator as the violent oppressor in the family. I give more tips for supporting your children and managing their reactions later in the chapter.

A child may agree to go to their other parent even when they really don't want to because they don't want to hurt their feelings. Or they may go because it's normal to have a deep need to be loved and accepted by both parents and they are still seeking and craving that from the narcissist. And they may go because they have fun with 'dad of the year' who lets them do more adult things that mum would never allow. Whatever their reason, children adapt and learn to cope with their time with a challenging parent, but it's still disconcerting when I hear from a client how many nights their child has said they can manage with the other parent. And I'm always left wondering how such young children know so precisely what they can manage. Maybe they would also know, if asked, what would make it easier or a happier time for them.

If residence is in issue you may be shocked to learn your child has said they want to live with their narcissistic father, but they may feel that's safer than antagonising him or that to be part of his 'in-crowd' is essential to their survival.

Understanding the narcissistic parent's attitude to their children

5-year-old to older sister:
'If you come to Daddy's and say nice things to him,
he won't shout at you.'

Men who abuse the mother of their own children are not good fathers, no matter how loud and how often the family courts say otherwise.

The separated narcissistic parent will want a lot of time with his children, not because he loves them but for one or more of the following reasons:

- They're his.
- They're his new source of supply with their admiration of him.
- He knows it's not what you want and he always wants that.
- He hopes taking them away from you will destroy you.

- Your reactions to his bad parenting will be a good source of supply for him.
- He can get them to spy on you for him.
- He can still control them even if he can't control you anymore.
- He can use them to do the housework and mundane tasks you used to do for him.
- He wants to prove to the rest of the world that he's father of the year.
- He wants to show off his clever, beautiful children.

Narcissists see other people in their circle as their property, or people there to serve them, rather than as separate human beings. This includes his children, who he views as mere extensions of himself, and who save him having to look in the mirror. Older children may well understand that when their father is putting pressure on them to spend more time with him it means he's not okay and wants them to take care of his needs. Younger children faced with a father who will not wait to increase contact at their pace may be more distressed and less compliant as they will have no comprehension of the demand being made of them.

The narcissist's children's appearance, behaviour, choices, friends, and activities are all a reflection of himself and he expects his children to be as 'perfect' as he considers himself to be. In fact, they are his ultimate 'supply'; not only do they look like him, they look up to him, admire him and accept his authority and control without question. And he's more admired by others for having such good-looking, well-behaved and intelligent children.

As his children are extensions of him they're not allowed independent thoughts or ideas and he'll question every decision they make if it's not in line with his rules or values. Sometimes they're not even allowed their own clothes; many narcissistic parents strip their children as soon as they arrive, or even before, and change them into the clothes they've bought for them. Other narcissists send the children home again in clothes that are too small or worn out and refuse to return the clothes the mother's bought, forcing her to buy more. They may not be able to take birthday or Christmas presents home with them.

The children know they have to do what Daddy says,
you don't upset him.

His children may say that he seems as though he's listening to them but what they say doesn't go in, it just bounces off him. This makes the children doubt themselves, feel downtrodden, stressed and confused. The narcissist may drop subtle, or not so subtle, hints about the other parent's faults to the children which will make them feel very uncomfortable. Or he may 'gang up' with them against their mother, telling them he's on their side and will make sure she doesn't punish them. The children feel their loyalties are divided but it's safer for them to go along with dad's ideas.

Although the narcissist may have terrific pride in his children, he can't enjoy them as normal parents do. He needs constant admiration and supply and doesn't react well if all the attention is on his adorable children rather than him. This can be a particular problem on birthdays or Christmas when he can't feel the love and joy others do, or take pleasure in seeing his children happy, so he'll do what he can to sabotage your plans and upset your day.

He never took much notice of the children, let alone did his share of looking after them when you were together, but suddenly he's acting like the best dad ever. This is the first, and crucial, thing you need to point out to a social worker or to Cafcass, as otherwise the children's reluctance to see him will be blamed on their difficulties in dealing with the separation, or the 'parental conflict', rather than on the fact he didn't have a relationship with them before.

Once the court proceedings are over, the big fatherly act may cease and even if he's not abusing them, you may be shocked by his neglect of his own children. They may come home half-dressed, or with dirty nappies hanging off them. They may be hungry and not stop eating for two days after. Or filthy, not having been washed for a week. Or even sick or injured. Take photos (preferably without the children knowing) and write it all down. Every single time. You have to be able to show a pattern of behaviour, not just an isolated incident, or even two. Read more about gathering evidence in Chapter 14.

If you have a new relationship, the jealousy of the narcissist may know no bounds and he may attack your new partner or make false allegations of child abuse against him. And he'll use your children as spies even more than usual if he wants information about your new life.

The golden child and the scapegoat

As we saw with the case of Sarah and Julian, the narcissist will often favour one child over another, and will create problems between them in order to 'divide and conquer' so they don't compare notes or gang up on him.

The golden child will be the 'easiest', most compliant child, or the one who idolises her father. She'll be better treated with rewards and favours and may be praised to the hilt but she doesn't receive unconditional love – she has to strive to keep being perfect and may be emotionally abused. She sees how her scapegoat siblings are treated and works hard to ensure that doesn't happen to her. She learns what's needed from her and never feels good enough even though she may be envied by her siblings.

The scapegoat is the 'problem child' who can never do anything right in the narcissistic parent's eyes and will be compared unfavourably with the golden child. They will be the victim of most of the narcissist's emotional or even physical abuse and be blamed for everything that goes wrong.

Then there is the 'lost child', who is unimportant and invisible to the narcissist, and may be neglected rather than abused. He'll keep a low profile, spending most of his time in his room playing computer games, or he may become anorexic, or self-harm.

The 'mascot child' or clown tries to diffuse and deflect the abuse or tension with humour or giggles.

These roles don't necessarily remain fixed given the narcissist's love of chaos and confusion; a child may be golden one day and scapegoated the next. Both of these children are at risk of either becoming narcissistic themselves as adults, or they may have hugely damaged self-esteem and confidence, and ultimately go on to attract narcissists as partners for themselves.

When you believe your children may be in danger

Claire Throssell has been vocal about how her two children, aged 12 and 9, were murdered by their father when he set fire to their home. He was a bully, the boys were scared of him and they didn't want to see him. But the court had ordered five hours of unsupervised contact despite Claire's concerns.

The court makes orders, and of course they have to be taken very seriously; but the mother knows best. The judge has not lived with your children 24/7 and however many reports the court may have about them, they cannot know them, or their parents, like you do. So mothers must listen to their intuition and their bodies. Claire recounted how, when the boys' father had said he understood why fathers do that, she went cold. That was her warning. But she still let her children go, partly because of the court order and partly she said because she wanted to give him the chance to become a better father. Whilst the sentiment was admirable, it was not realistic, as any leopard would confirm. A parent needs to prove, perhaps by attending a parenting course and having supervised contact for a while, that they can be a better parent before they have unsupervised contact with vulnerable children. That's not to blame Claire; if Claire had refused to let her children go, the father would have taken her back to court, and may have found another time and another way to commit the atrocity he intended.

This is an extreme example. Out of 500–550 homicides a year, an average of only three will be family annihilations. There are, however, many cases of continuing physical and emotional abuse of children – by mothers as well as fathers – that don't result in such tragedy but are still hugely damaging to children. In these cases, contact may also need to be stopped, by simply not sending the children for contact anymore and/or going back to court.

The courts work on the presumption that contact with both parents is in the best interests of children. Judges have to decide if a mother's fears are justified or if they're just seeking to stop contact as revenge on their ex; it is very difficult to spot the people who are a real risk. Parents with genuine fears must stand up and fight for their children. And if they're not able to do that because they've been so worn down by the behaviour of their partner that they've lost their confidence, they need to get the support necessary to help them protect their children.

Taking children abroad and child abduction

One question I hear from parents is,

'Can my ex stop me taking our children abroad?'

The short answer to this question is usually 'yes'. When a divorce or separation is difficult, children's holidays abroad with one parent can be contentious, although one would always hope a parent would not want to deprive their children of a holiday or travel experience. It's always reasonable to expect the other parent to provide details of a planned holiday including flight/travel details, address/type of accommodation and who else will be travelling with your children.

Both parents have parental responsibility (unless they are not married and the father is not on the birth certificate) so you each need the agreement of the other to take the children abroad. It's wise to take with you a signed letter from the other parent giving their consent. There's a Home Office template for such a letter (link in Resources section), although you may not need all the detail – just amend it to suit your own circumstances.

Such a letter is not a legal requirement in this country but border controls around the world are getting stricter due to the increasing numbers of children being abducted. So if you're stopped it will be much easier if you have such a letter, and you might also need it if, for instance, your child required medical attention abroad.

You may also need documents such as your and/or your children's birth certificates, or your marriage or divorce certificate to prove you're related to the children if you have a different surname. You also need to check on the entry requirements of the destination you are travelling to as some countries, such as the US and South Africa, require more formal proof that your children have the right to enter the country without the other parent. And some countries have different age limits for when a child is considered an adult. You should also check with the airline you are travelling with in case they have different requirements.

If grandparents are taking children abroad, they will need a letter signed by both parents.

If you're unable to reach agreement about a holiday abroad, mediation is the best way to resolve it. If you still can't agree, you'll need to ask the mediator to sign a C100 form so that you can apply to the court for a specific issue order allowing you to take your children on holiday.

If you have a court order saying that the children live with you, you're entitled to take your children abroad for up to 28 days without your ex's permission – but do make sure you take the court order with you. Your ex would still need your permission in the usual way, unless it is a joint 'lives with' order. If you have concerns about giving your ex permission to take the children abroad, you can refuse (providing the court hasn't ordered that he can take them). He'll then have to apply to the court for a specific issue order to be able to take them. You can always apply for a prohibited steps order to stop him.

Occasionally parents want to move abroad after a divorce, particularly if their family live in another country and they need their support as a single parent. If you want to do this, you need either the written agreement of your ex, or a court order allowing you to remove your children from the jurisdiction (i.e. England and Wales). The court would need to be satisfied that the move is in the best interests of your children.

Please don't be tempted to take your children abroad without the written agreement of your ex or a court order; it's not beyond a narcissist to say you've abducted your child and this is a serious criminal offence for which parents are given lengthy prison sentences these days. The maximum sentence is seven years but will usually be between 18 months and 5 years depending on the seriousness of the case and the effect on the child.

Forget co-parenting – try parallel parenting

*My first thoughts are I can't and don't want to see a family therapist
and discuss how I am going to co-parent with the ex.*
It will be more humane for the ex to hire someone and kill me instead.

You can't co-parent with a narcissist any more than you can negotiate with one.
Unfortunately you're likely to come under pressure from social workers, Cafcass
and the judge to speak to/co-operate with/work with your abuser as they don't
seem able to join the dots and see, despite all the evidence you've given them,
that this just isn't possible. The narcissist doesn't care about his child and isn't
capable of co-parenting; he counter-parents and controls, leaving the protective
parent to navigate the chaos and pick up the pieces.

Like a virus, a pattern of behaviour doesn't stop, it just mutates to the new
situation. He knows your children are your Achilles heel and he's going to exploit
that, but you can change your behaviour by not reacting as he expects you to,
which will eventually shift the balance of power.

What does parallel parenting mean in practice?

Parallel parenting is the answer in this situation. This means you have as little
interaction with the narcissistic parent as possible. It's hard work, far from ideal
and certainly not the best for children, but it saves both arguments and your
sanity. It's like walking down the same road on opposite pavements; 'normal'
parents would keep crossing the road to check in with each other about how
their kids are doing, and to work out problems and make decisions together.
You, on the other hand, must make sure you don't get pulled or lured to the other
side of the road, while keeping a strong boundary to stop your ex encroaching
on your pavement.

This means seeing each other as little as possible, usually by doing
exchanges at school or handovers through a third party or in a public place
such as a supermarket car park. It means separate parents' evenings at school.
It means you have no control over what he does in his parenting time, though
that won't stop him trying to control yours. It means communicating in just one
way, preferably in an app such as *Our Family Wizard* or *AppClose*, but otherwise
by email. Insist on only communicating in the way you choose. If you refuse to
answer messages delivered in other ways he'll eventually toe the line.

If you possibly can, make a detailed parenting plan with your ex at the earliest opportunity. You may be able to do this in mediation or through solicitors, or maybe just emailing it backwards and forwards between you if you've got some leverage over him that will incentivise him to do it. Cafcass and other organisations have parenting plans online that you can use and adapt to suit your children and situation.

Then you can just insist he keeps to the plan when he tries to change things – because he will inevitably try to push the boundaries and disrupt your life. He'll be late picking the children up so as to make you late for work, or late returning them so they're late for bed and have their routine disrupted. (And of course so you'll worry about them, and whether he's ever going to return them.) Don't let this take you by surprise! Anticipate that he'll do these things, plan your life around it and whatever you do, don't let him see you're angry, upset or have had your plans disrupted.

But do record every little event – both in your own daily log, and on the app you communicate with the narcissist on, or by email. Just detail the late or other behaviour, explain how it affected the children and ask him not to be late (or whatever) again so as not to undermine his future contact with the children or upset them again. Insist again that he stick to the agreed parenting plan or court order.

Unfortunately, all this means you can't change the arrangements either and your children will be the ones who miss out, for instance, when a birthday party falls on 'his' weekend. There's simply no room for flexibility with a narcissist; if you give him an inch he'll take three miles. It can also come back to bite you in court proceedings because, if he wore you down and you agreed to one overnight stay on a special occasion (or in an emergency), or a holiday abroad, the judge may tell you that you didn't have a problem then so they will allow him extra time now.

Making parental decisions with your ex

Your ex will always have parental responsibility and if your child lives with you, you'll be obliged to keep him informed of important events in their life. If you have a 'lives with' order you can make all the day-to-day decisions but if your child is going to change school or have medical treatment, for instance, you'll have to consult your ex first. With a 'normal' ex you'd be able to talk through the pros and cons, maybe visit potential new schools together, and come to an agreement. You can't do that with a narcissist, who will counter-parent, not co-parent.

If you can think ahead and use reverse psychology, you're more likely to get what you want. If you favour the Green School, give him all the reasons why you think the Blue School is best for Johnny. When he insists on the Green School you can reluctantly and eventually 'back down' and 'give in' to him. If you want your child to have medical treatment, tell him all the reasons you don't agree with the doctor and ask for his opinion. When he tells you how stupid and wrong you are, you can agree he's right and get him to sign the form.

This is why it's so important to get a 'lives with' order if you're in court proceedings – read more about child arrangement orders in Chapter 14. (That said, I'm usually reluctant to suggest you should go to court *just* for a 'lives with' order, as it often backfires and gives the abusive parent more time with the children. But if you are already going through child proceedings in court, you'll want to push for a 'lives with' order.) This order means you have to consult your ex on big decisions, but consult does not mean agree. You may consult a solicitor or a doctor, but that doesn't mean you have to do as they advise. Similarly you don't have to do what your ex wants, but you do have to let them know what's happening.

If you don't have a 'lives with' order, you don't, in theory, have the final say – though in practice, if the children are living mainly with you, you probably do.

This is another reason why it's so important to have counselling or coaching so that you're strong enough to resist the efforts of your ex to continue to control you. Then you can politely tell him that's what you're going to do and if he really feels that strongly about it he can apply to the court for a prohibited steps order (to stop you doing something) or a specific issue order for the court to decide on the school or holiday, or whether your child has medical treatment.

Private school fees are often an ongoing way of your ex continuing to control you with frequent refusals or threats not to pay. You may have always assumed that your child would be privately educated and there may be more than enough money for it. But do consider carefully whether it's really worth years of that sort of stress and disempowerment, or whether you might be better moving into the catchment area of a good state school. You could of course try reverse psychology and insist you don't want your child to go to the private school any more, and then every time the fees are due get in first and say it's time to take them out of that school!

The smaller everyday things will more often be an issue. Remember that the narcissist is not interested in doing the right thing for his children (unless it happens to suit him on any particular occasion). And the more that you give him helpful advice and try to get him to do the right thing, the more he'll continue to do the wrong thing – because he just loves to see how it winds you up and to receive the narcissistic supply you continue to give him. So 'shutty shutty' is the best thing you can do; he'll stop bothering to deliberately do the wrong thing once he sees it has no effect on you.

I successfully argued against 50:50, though we had 60:40. We were originally forced by the court to work to his shift pattern, which meant I had five nights, then he had three. It has honestly been a nightmare. He constantly forgot all their things, he would then make us be home at certain times to wait for him to drop their stuff off, only for him to be too tired or forget. He preferred to drop their stuff off at 5am outside my house (on his way to work), though he would sit there for a bit outside as well at that time. The kids were so anxious because it would be stuff like school shoes, winter coats, lunch boxes. When he did return stuff it would be in dribs and drabs, and family court just saw it as him trying his best, which is ridiculous. The man is an engineer – he can manage the stuff that's important to him.

I was constantly broke, despite the fact I have a well-paid role, because I had to keep going to the shops to buy new shoes or coats, as he would also forget to return any spares. He was ordered to give six months' notice of any changes, but would give two weeks; that meant I had to pay for all childcare I had booked in but now didn't need (he only had them when he wasn't working so childcare was all my financial responsibility), and I would have to now rearrange two semesters of teaching, student meetings, supervisions, research time, grant meetings, participant interviews, etc., as with such late notice childcare was booked up for the days I needed.

The kids and my life had to be completely micromanaged, to the minute in some cases, to ensure they still got to do their activities. He would religiously take them to martial arts because he would train after them, but hardly ever take our daughter to her dance classes or even attend her competitions, so I would pay for all these classes for her to not attend. He only ever did any homework when we were going through family court, didn't home-school them in the pandemic, despite not working when he had them, so all that responsibility has fallen on me. He never booked them doctors' appointments, dentists, opticians, but would message me things like 'X has broken his tooth, book him an appointment' – he would rather leave our child with a broken tooth for three days than book him an appointment himself because he felt that was my job.

He expected to be informed and updated on every single little thing. He wouldn't bother to get information from the school, I was expected to manage it all and report back to him. Yet he would do as he pleased, move house when he wanted, with whomever he wanted, change their religion, and sign them up for activities every day of the week knowing I had to work. Our lives were completely and utterly at his mercy and he could disrupt them as he pleased with his demands.

Even being close to 50:50 residence is a living hell when your ex is controlling and entitled. I know from court that he honestly does not see anything wrong with the way he has conducted himself – as far as he is concerned everyone should work around his work because it's his work. If he needs everyone to change, they should just do it. If he forgets their stuff, well he'll drop it off when convenient for him. I'm the mother so it's my job to work around him and them.

Oh and little things like changing their address at the opticians for no reason, so we stopped getting reminders (his reasoning: 'well they are with me almost half'), and changing emergency contacts to his girlfriend. Yet when our daughter ended up in hospital he refused to collect our son from school stating he already had plans and it was my day so my responsibility to sort it. There was no co-parenting. It was simply like I was a nanny he paid a tiny amount to each month to do the hard parenting and look after them until he was available.

Supporting your children and coping with his bad parenting

Yes, children adapt. Children in war zones adapt!

He may feed the children junk food, or even things they're allergic to, and let them stay up until midnight watching horror films .... but there's nothing you can do. Remember, you can't co-parent with a narcissist. And the courts will only dismiss it as 'different parenting styles' and say he's entitled to do whatever he likes in his parenting time. This is really hard for a good parent to have to sit by and watch.

Focus on what you can do

While you can't do anything about how your ex chooses to parent, there are plenty of things you can do when the children are with you:

- If he returns the children in a sorry state – such as late, tired or high on junk food – don't ring him up and shout at him, or write to him about his parental failings; he'll be delighted by your outrage and will treat the children worse still next time in order to get an even bigger reaction from him. He's not a capable parent and you can't teach him or make him into one any more than you can teach a two-year-old maths. All you can do is lower your expectations, shutty shutty, write it down and act bored. It's certainly not easy, but practice makes perfect.

- Compensate in your time with the children. Feed them healthy food, and get them to bed on time. Don't be tempted to let your boundaries slip because the children have got used to running riot with him. They might think it fun, and he's undoubtedly told them his way is better, but children depend on firm boundaries for their security and they really need to feel safe and held in at least one of their two homes.

- Don't ignore or dismiss your children's comments about their other parent's poor or hurtful behaviour. They need to know it's not okay. Ask how they feel about what's happened and validate their feelings, for example by saying, 'You look sad when you're telling me that and it must have been very hurtful', 'You sound angry about that and I can understand why you felt that way', 'What you saw was really scary. You're safe now and do you have any questions?' Have a conversation about how people behave (without denigrating the narcissist himself, just his behaviour) and ask your children what they think is the right thing to say or do in the situation they describe. What would their friends' parents do? What have they seen you do? Empower your children to think critically for themselves, rather than them having you in one ear and him in the other, leaving them utterly confused.

- Teach them how to set boundaries for themselves, something they'll never learn from a narcissist. A closed door is a tangible example of a boundary to explain to a child – it's a boundary that stops a parent from walking into their bedroom without knocking.

- You can teach your children problem-solving skills and how to cope with things when you're not there, earlier than you might normally.

- Keep telling them how much you love them and believe in them.

- As one seven-year-old said to his mother on return from his father's: 'One of you is lying and I don't know which it is.' When your ex has lied to your child, ask how they feel about it. You can suggest that they might be confused and ask what they think, whether they think you normally lie to them and what other people would say about this issue. (See also parental alienation, Chapter 7.)

- All their emotional intelligence and empathy has to be learned from you as the narcissist has none, so teach your children empathy and how to be emotionally literate. Ask them how they feel about things that happen, good and bad, at school and everywhere else, not just when they see their father. Ask them what makes them feel safe, and when don't they feel safe. Use emojis and pictures, comment on people on TV and ask your children how they think they're feeling. If they can recognise and name how they feel, they'll be better able to explain to a social worker or Cafcass why they don't want to see their father (if it comes to that), and you'll be less likely to be accused of coaching them.

- With younger children you can watch how they're playing with dolls or toys, or what they're drawing, and make emotional comments, such as, 'That doll's all on her own and looks sad, what would make her feel better?' or 'Oh no, they're fighting, that's scary.'

- Help them to understand that we all like different things (e.g. she likes red, you like blue) and feel differently about the same things (e.g. you love rain, he really doesn't like it) and that's quite normal and okay. Then they'll come to understand they don't have to like/feel the same as their father, and that they're not responsible for other people's feelings. Also that people can be disappointed, and survive.

- Be very careful about what you say in front of your children. It's easy to assume they're not listening when you're on the phone, or talking to a friend or relative in the house. But if they know you're upset or that there's a problem, they are more than likely to be eavesdropping. If they hear you talking negatively about their father they may adopt your views rather than forming their own; they will know you don't like him and they may tell Cafcass, even inadvertently, but it will go against you. It also makes it difficult for them to talk to you about their father if they know you don't like him and don't want to upset you. And it can be scary and unsettling for a child to hear your conversation and know you're upset or anxious but not fully understand why.

- Look after yourself. I know it's worrying when your children are away with him but you want to keep up your strength and be able to give them your full attention when they're back. Relax and have fun (and/or some therapy) when you have this time for yourself so that you can be a fully present and healthy parent with the energy to compensate for the narcissist's poor parenting.

- Keep a log of everything. When your child comes back hungry because the narcissist forgot to feed them, make a note. When it happens again, make another note. Keep doing this until you've got enough notes to show a pattern of neglect and take it back to court (see more on evidence in Chapter 14). And bide your time, because sooner or later your child will say they don't want to see their father, and he'll then take you back to court and accuse you of alienating them. You'll be able to produce your long log of events and emails showing how his behaviour has affected the children and how you've encouraged them to go and done all the right things.

- It's always best to let your child's school know what's happening at home and to ask them to let you know of any unusual behaviour. Most schools will have a counsellor or someone looking after the wellbeing of children so do ask for the appropriate help for your child.

When it comes to supporting my children, my main priority throughout has been to remain that steady and predictable person for them. I try to imagine how difficult and confusing it must be to move between the two worlds that are so different. I am there to offer my listening ears, a hug and a calm space through good and difficult times. Even when they act out, keep secrets or lie to me because their dad asked them to. He recently gave our youngest a phone and told her to keep it a secret from me. She was very scared I'd get very angry when I found it as she knew she wasn't to have a phone for another year. I get how difficult it was for her as it was a massive iPhone but I think it was a relief for her not to have to continue to lie to me. I know it's not their fault but their lies to me are difficult to cope with.

I think of my parenting as tending to my little allotment. I put all of my focus on what is within the fence around it. It also helps me remember and respect that my children have their own relationships with their dad, which is very different from mine.

Another thing has been emerging over time – I am more open and honest with my children about what it is like for me when something happens. They pick up on it anyway so I think it's best to be open about it. It has been nine years since we separated, our daughters are pre-teen and teen, and they can understand more of the complexity of my relationship with their dad. I want them to know why I keep my distance at times or why I set certain boundaries. It is a gradual process. We are growing together through this. I am connecting with my truth bit by bit, and they are growing up and are ready to receive it and make their own sense of what is happening. I hope that by sharing some of my experiences with them and inviting them to do the same as and when they are ready, I can break through the secrets, the lies, glossing things over without creating more damage.

What should I say to my child?

Occasionally a parent is told – by a social worker, Cafcass or even the court – not to talk to their child about what's going on with the court proceedings. The narcissist will tell his child all about the court proceedings, which of course will worry and upset her, but he's desperate to get her on to his side. So you may both be told not to talk to a child about the court proceedings – which is fine, except the narcissist won't keep to that even though he's agreed to it in court. And if your child is worried because of what she's been told, it wouldn't be fair not to reassure her. Children are human beings, not mushrooms to be kept in the dark, and after all, this is all about them.

Children hate feeling excluded and find it scary when they know something's wrong but no one will talk to them about it – their imaginations will come up with far worse than the reality of the situation, so don't let anyone tell you what you can or can't say to your own child if they need facts or reassurance. And never be tempted to shut them down if they ask difficult questions or tell you something worrying or upsetting has happened. If you tell them it's okay, or it doesn't matter, when clearly it's not okay, or it does matter to them, you're giving them the message that their feelings are wrong, or don't matter, and that they can't confide in you.

Children do come out with things that can stun you into silence so have some ready-made questions memorised in your head for such occasions – things like 'That's interesting, tell me more' or 'Oh dear, I'm sorry to hear that. How did you feel when that happened?' Get them to keep talking until you can recover yourself enough to comment appropriately!

A good question to ask your child at an appropriate time when they've shared something worrying might be how safe they feel with their father and perhaps compare it with how safe they feel with other people, or at school.

Sometimes a child will just shut down and tell you nothing. That doesn't stop you from talking to him; he'll be listening and soaking it all up even if he won't look at you and appears to be focused on something else.

You need to be careful what you tell your child as you're likely to be accused of coaching them whether you've done so or not. You can encourage your child to tell the truth if they have an interview with Cafcass or a social worker. And that if they're too scared to tell the truth, they can at least say that.

How much do you tell your children when you want to protect them from the truth about an abusive parent? What you say and how you explain things depends on the age of your children and your particular circumstances. You could say that their dad isn't a bad person, but he's done some bad things or made some mistakes. Or maybe that he does things other people wouldn't do, or he makes choices most of us wouldn't make. When they're older, or if you're sure they wouldn't repeat it to him, you could try saying that his brain doesn't work in quite the same way as most people's. Or even that his brain confuses what's true and what's not true but that your child should trust their own brain because it knows what the truth is even if their father's doesn't.

Be wary of telling your child that a narcissistic parent loves them. You've no idea how he feels, or even what his idea of love is. And if he's abused your child it could be confusing to tell them he loves them, or they could think you're saying this is normal behaviour between people who love each other. Keep to your ex's behaviour, what's acceptable and what's not, and leave your children to come to their own conclusions about whether they're loved or not.

> 'Why is he doing this to me, Mummy? Why does he hate me?' When my ex refused consent for my 10-year-old daughter to attend one of the best state schools in London, she was off school for three days. All her friends had got in and she couldn't bear facing them and having to tell them she hadn't and her father was the reason.

When your child starts acting out

If your child starts behaving aggressively or violently it's important to take immediate steps to deal with it and stop it getting out of hand. You can explain to your child that their behaviour will not be tolerated in your house, and in a tone of voice that will signal that you really mean it. Also that when people hurt other people, it's usually because they've been hurt themselves so you're wondering what's made them so upset and angry. Ask them what they need that they're not getting at the moment and what would be a better way of getting rid of their anger in future. Don't expect any answers at the time but maybe some days later your child will feel ready to talk. Keep giving them lots of hugs however horrible their behaviour; remember, it's not their fault.

You may feel you need help with this, but social workers and Cafcass are rarely the best people to ask and are more likely to use it against you than to offer you any help. Victim blaming is horribly common, as is putting it all down to the 'parental conflict'. If you can't access a school counsellor you may be able to get help privately from a child psychologist or a play therapist. Your ex will have parental responsibility so, in theory, you can't send your child to anyone without his consent. He may agree if he thinks he can manipulate the therapist and blame you, but won't if he thinks his behaviour might be rumbled.

Consider the possibility that your child is simply not getting the attention they need; the narcissistic parent thinks only of themselves, and you may be traumatised by the abuse and distracted by court proceedings and chaos. If that's the case, is there a grandparent or other friend or relative who can give your child some undivided attention? When you are with your child let them feel that you're totally present with them and not on your phone or reading emails, however distracting or distressing the court proceedings may be.

You'll want to keep firm boundaries and keep to a routine as much as possible as these help a child to feel secure and know that your home feels predictable and safe. It may be fun to run riot at Dad's house and stay up half the night, but it's actually scary for a child not to know that there's a real adult in charge if something untoward were to happen.

Never question your child about what they've done at their other parent's; it only puts them in a difficult position as they know you hate each other. But you can tell them you've been thinking about them while they've been away and that you still love them even when they're not here. It may help to tell them before they go what you'll be doing while they're away and what you'll be doing together when they come back as it's hard for a child to keep switching between two very different houses and rules. Knowing exactly what they'll come home to can make the transition easier for them. It'll be a question of trial and error to see what works for your child.

Be sure to make detailed notes of your child's behaviour in a daily log, as well as what happened in the days before and days after. Over time, you'll be able to see if a pattern emerges.

When a child doesn't see their father

This will no doubt be a huge relief to you, but it's still a situation you have to manage as you never know when he might make an application to see his children.

Somehow you have to be able to portray their father in a neutral way so you can't be accused of alienating them. If your children are young and don't remember him, you don't want them to idealise him and be desperate to see the father they've built up to be a hero in their mind. Once they're at school and realise the other children have fathers and they don't, they'll start to be curious and ask questions. You don't want them to know that you hate him, or they may feel fearful of asking you questions about him. You can ask whether they remember him so they know it's okay to talk and ask about him. It's also a good idea to give them photos of him and his family, which you can put in a little book they can look at any time if you can't bear to have him in a frame or on the wall.

It's also advisable to make notes now about any incidents of abuse (of you or the children), examples of neglect or bad parenting, and anything else that may be relevant – because if he applies to the court in five years' time you'll struggle to remember all that happened or the dates of any incidents. And if you were together for any time after the birth of his child be sure to note how involved he was, how much time he spent with them, how he prioritised them and what his attitude was

CHAPTER 7:
DEALING WITH PARENTAL ALIENATION

Narcissists are frequently jealous, and they will be envious of your relationship with the children, and may try to turn your children against you as that's their ultimate weapon to hurt and destroy you. Parental alienation is the worst element of abuse by a narcissist who wants to destroy their ex and they will completely alienate their child if they can. On the other hand, some borderlines and covert narcissists want to continue the fight and keep control of their ex by continuing to use the child as a weapon so they won't turn them *completely* against you.

Parental alienation is a big – and contentious – topic and I can only scratch the surface here. The term Parental Alienation Syndrome was first coined by Dr Richard Gardner, a controversial American child psychiatrist, back in the 1970s. Almost 50 years on we still can't agree on what it is or what to do about it, but here's my take on it. (Please note that parents in these situations are normally referred to as the 'alienating parent' and the 'target parent', whereas I prefer the terms 'abusive parent' or 'brainwashing parent' and the 'protective parent'.)

What is it?

Parental alienation is the brainwashing of a child by one parent, which turns them completely against their other parent. It's child abuse. Like snake poison, brainwashing works quickly and a loving child can turn, almost overnight, into an unrecognisably rude and aggressive one who now hates you.

Alienating a child from their parent robs the child of their sense of self, and the love of their other parent. The child also comes to realise that the love they have from one parent is dependent upon their rejection and vilification of the other.

As well as having immediate effects on things such as school performance and their self-esteem, it means that the child will, later in life, be much more susceptible to mental health problems, delinquency, drug and alcohol abuse, difficult relationships, etc.

The child is placed in an impossible position. At some level they will know that there is no truth in what the brainwashing parent is telling them about the protective parent. But they are hearing it so loudly and so often that in the end it's easier for them to believe it, to go along with the lies, and ally themselves completely with the one parent to avoid all the conflicting emotions of dealing with the two of them.

What it isn't

Some parents do an excellent job of alienating their children all by themselves, without the other parent needing to say or do anything. They are usually abusive – either to their child, or to their child's other parent, and sometimes to both – but instead of looking at their own behaviour, they accuse the innocent parent of turning the child against them. In other words, they make false allegations of parental alienation.

Whilst the parents were together, the protective parent will have insulated the child from much of the abusive behaviour of the other parent, and the child will probably have kept out of their way as much as possible. But once the parents are separated, the abusive parent will demand as much contact as possible with the child … who will not want to go, and may protest vehemently and vote with their feet. But this is not parental alienation, however much the abuser shouts that it is.

Other children struggle terribly with their parents' separation and some really can't cope with the transition between their parents and the two homes. Some suffer from separation anxiety. These children will behave differently to usual and may appear withdrawn, or say they don't want to see their other parent. But they are not being alienated – they just need help and a lot of reassurance to come through this huge change in their lives. Or they may need the dynamics between their parents to change. But again, this is not parental alienation.

Who does it?

Angry parents who want revenge, and parents who have a personality disorder. Often, such parents had a poor or absent relationship with at least one of their own parents.

Let's start with the angry parent. Occasionally a parent may be so angry with their ex about something they've done (or not done) that they are unable to separate that from their parenting. Sometimes a parent can be so wrapped up in their child's life that they've lost their own identity and feel threatened by their child's relationship with the other parent, so they try to destroy it. Or they are just so insecure themselves that the fear of the child preferring the other parent takes over.

More usually, however, alienation is done by a parent who has a personality disorder (usually undiagnosed), such as borderline personality disorder, paranoia, or narcissistic personality disorder. There will always be at least an element of narcissism as these people have no empathy for anyone, even their own children who they are damaging so badly by alienating them from their protective parent.

When the narcissist accuses the protective parent of alienation

If he's not able to alienate the children from their mother, the narcissist will often accuse her of alienating them from him. This is his strategy to distract everyone from the real reason the mother doesn't want him to see his children, or why the children themselves refuse to go, i.e. because he has abused her and/or the children. It's another smoke and mirrors tactic because while you're busy defending his allegation you're not getting people to look at and deal with the real issue – his abuse. And sometimes the narcissist both accuses the other parent of alienating, while at the same time turning the children against that parent.

If you talk about his abuse you're likely to be labelled as hostile, or accused of coaching the children to hate their father. And if you stop them having contact or can't persuade the children to see their father, you'll again be accused of coaching, or of emotional abuse. His allegation of parental alienation will be taken so seriously by the court that it'll usually trump anything he might have done, and the danger is that residence of the children will be transferred to him.

This is currently a huge problem in the family court but forewarned is forearmed. You'll need to get one step ahead. The aim of the court will be to ensure he has as much time as possible with his children, so do all you can to make it look as if you're promoting his contact, not obstructing it:

- If he's not seeing the children, you could potentially get a family member or friend to supervise some contact with him.

- You could set up phone or video calls between the children and their father.
- You could get the children to write to him.
- You could send him pictures or videos of the children.
- You could ask him (in writing) to send photos of himself and his family to help you to talk to/remind your children of him. Several of my clients have done this but few, if any, have ever received a photo; this is good evidence to refute his allegations of alienation.
- And if he sends messages asking to see the children don't ever say 'no'. Give him a large helping of word salad so it looks as though you could be being helpful even if it's not quite clear! Be unfailingly polite and just a little friendly.
- Make sure you keep him informed of what's happening in the children's lives. He has parental responsibility and is entitled to know (major things, not what they had for breakfast), and if you fail to tell him he'll use it against you as evidence of parental alienation.

Bottom line: do whatever you can so that the court can't be persuaded you're trying to airbrush him out of your children's lives.

What do family courts do about parental alienation?

The worst case scenario is the narcissistic and manipulative parent persuading the professionals (social workers, Cafcass, lawyers) and the court that residence of the child should be transferred to them. And once the child is living with them 24/7 it doesn't take long for the brainwashing to be complete, and for the child not to want, or feel able to have, any further contact with the protective parent. If there is no court order defining future contact with the protective parent (because it is deemed best to leave it up to the child who has made their view so clear), the child may not see that parent again or, if they do, it won't be in any meaningful way.

Often the court will label the case as being 'high conflict' and judge both parents as equally responsible for what is happening. I have a little sympathy for this as it's very hard to see who is the protective parent and who is the abusive one when both are fighting equally hard – one to protect their child, the other to destroy the other parent. But drawing the line down the middle does nothing to help the psychologically abused child, or the alienated parent.

Although the courts have a culture of 'contact at all costs', this seems to apply to fathers more than mothers (although I know fathers don't agree). If residence is transferred from a protective mother to an abusive father, the mother is likely only to get supervised, if any, contact. Whereas the contact of an abusive father is only occasionally supervised or restricted.

If a father hasn't seen his child for a long time, and allegations of abuse are made, the court may well order supervised contact at a contact centre but this is usually only intended to be a short term solution before moving contact out into the community.

Cafcass has an 'impact of parental conflict' tool which I was rather sceptical about, but I have seen it used well in a report. Up to a point. The family court advisor (FCA) saw right through the child's complaints against her mother and said that she 'describes one parent entirely negatively, the other entirely positively', which is typical in parental alienation, and mirrors the narcissist's black and white thinking. But nowhere did the advisor state that this was parental alienation and, worse still, she said the child is 'actually lucky to have two loving and capable parents'. I take issue with that; a loving and capable parent does not alienate his daughter from her mother however much he may hate the mother himself. The FCA also stated that the issue is parental conflict; it's not, it's parental alienation by a narcissistic parent. But since the tool she used has 'parental conflict' in the label, it's probably not surprising (and, indeed, is the reason why I was sceptical of the tool in the first place). So Cafcass still has a way to go in dealing with parental alienation though they do sometimes get it right.

> *I had a good Cafcass officer and Judge who saw through*
> *my ex's attempts to alienate me.*
> *They were also sympathetic to gay families and their rights.*

What often happens is that the court, being very short of time, takes at face value the brainwasher's allegations that the protective parent is harming the child, and deprives the child of an important and loving relationship.

What can you do about it?

Firstly, be kind to your child. I know it's hard not to retaliate when a child is being beastly, rude and obnoxious to you, but it's not their fault and they don't deserve even more abuse. They're as much a victim of the brainwasher as you are, and they're just a child.

My advice to clients who complain about their ex badmouthing them has always been not to do the same, however tempting. Which was fine, as far as it went. But since reading *Divorce Poison* by Dr Richard Warshak, I realise that my advice was woefully inadequate and that the other thing that you must not do is ... nothing. Don't ignore the brainwashing and hope it will go away. It won't.

Your child is being abused by their other parent. It is very unlikely that you are going to be able to stop them having contact with their parent, so you need to help them cope with it, just like you'd help them cope with bullying at school. Their reality is being distorted by the constant brainwashing and you want to counteract that and help them find the truth. They can't do this by themselves.

For example, if your child has been convinced that you are all bad, and their other parent is all good, you can help them to understand that we're all human. That means that even those of us who try to be good and kind and do the right thing will make mistakes sometimes. We might have lost our temper and shouted when we shouldn't have done, or forgotten an important date or event we should have remembered. But these incidents don't wipe out all the good and loving things we've done before; they just mean we're not perfect. If you can give examples of positive and negative things that both you and your ex have done, you can demonstrate that no one is all good or bad, and that it's okay and normal to have mixed feelings about people.

If your child has been told a lie, you need to deal with this. But encourage your child to think for themselves rather than just refuting what the abusive parent has told them as that's just going to entrench their position. So instead of reacting with 'He's wrong' or 'What really happened was ...' ask 'What do you think?' or 'Is [what you've been told about me] what you've seen for yourself in the past?' or 'Do you think that's how I normally behave?'

The brainwashing is often more subtle, though, but it still needs to be picked up on and dealt with. You can help your child by asking how they feel about what the brainwashing parent has said, and suggesting that it might make them feel confused, upset, etc.

A child can be brainwashed and alienated by constantly having the other parent in their ear even when they're not with them; as soon as they're old enough to have a phone, the narcissistic parent may be messaging and talking to them from dawn until after their bedtime. Your child won't want to turn their phone off and you'll be in trouble if you block him from their phone. One solution is to get a cheap burner or pay-as-you-go phone for your child to use exclusively with the abusive parent, so they can turn it off and not be constantly bombarded and/or feel pressured to reply.

If you think you're being alienated from your child I would highly recommend that you read *Divorce Poison* by Dr Richard Warshak. It gives lots of examples of the action you can take to prevent and deal with alienation. It's quite long but easy to read with lots of stories of parents and children who've been through this. However, it comes with my usual caveat for American books – any reference to what happens in court in the US does not apply here in the UK. 'Custody evaluators' translate as Cafcass – but only roughly.

If you're not sure if you're being alienated, here's a list of things your ex may do. Sometimes the protective parent may unwittingly do one or two of these as well, so do be wary of your own behaviour as well as your ex's:

- Constantly badmouth or belittle you to your child.
- Limit your contact with your child.
- Shift responsibility to your child to make decisions about the time they spend with you.
- Make it clear to your child that any mention of you is unwelcome.
- Create the impression that you dislike or do not love your child.
- Create a false belief that you are dangerous or unworthy.
- Interrupt or interfere with communication between you and your child.
- Withdraw love or express anger if the child does not comply.
- Force your child to choose between their parents.
- Confide in the child personal, adult information or tell them about the court proceedings.
- Force your child to reject you and your family.
- Ask your child to spy on you.
- Ask your child to keep secrets from you.
- Refer to you by your first name instead of Mum or Dad.
- Refer to their new partner as Mum or Dad and encourage the child to do the same.

- Withhold medical, school or social information from you and keep your name off the records.
- Cultivate the child's dependency on them.
- Undermine your authority.

You may be clear that your ex is alienating your children from you but it's very hard to get Cafcass or the courts to see it. Keep documenting the evidence, and keep going back to court and insisting that you keep in proper contact with your child. Read more about children proceedings in Chapter 14.

One of the tactics used by an alienating parent is to keep saying how he will promote contact with you if residence is transferred to him. Because he is easy to believe, and because the courts want to avoid children being alienated, and because you may not be promoting contact so readily, the courts are more inclined to transfer residence to him. And once he has them, it won't take him long to turn them totally against you and you'll be lucky to see them again; of course he'll be able to say he's encouraging them to go but they don't want to.

It's a fine line between protecting your children from further abuse, and protecting yourself from allegations of parental alienation.

CHAPTER 8:

NEGOTIATING WITH A NARCISSIST – MEDIATION, COLLABORATIVE LAW AND SOLICITOR NEGOTIATION

When you're splitting up, there are many aspects of separating your joint life that have to be negotiated, from who keeps the house and eggcups to how much time you each spend with the children and who pays for their mobile phones.

Can you ever really negotiate with a narcissist?

The ways most people negotiate their separation are:

- Around the kitchen table
- Mediation
- Collaborative law
- Solicitor negotiation

Although I discuss these options in this chapter, be aware that it's almost impossible to get any of these to work with a narcissist as it's their way or the highway. You know the saying 'Never negotiate with terrorists'? The same thing goes for narcissists. That's because negotiation involves give and take, but the narcissist will only take, or bully you into his way of thinking. They can't get narcissistic supply from meeting in the middle, so they have no incentive to come to an agreement.

You may already have tried couples counselling and found it didn't work. That was because you didn't have a relationship problem – your partner has a personality problem, and no doubt made everything your fault and took responsibility for nothing. He certainly didn't make any changes in his behaviour.

If you have to negotiate with a narcissist, always give him a choice – even if it's only over whether you do a handover in Tesco or Sainsbury's car park. Try not to say 'no' outright if you can help it. Otherwise he may feel backed into a corner and lash out at you, or stonewall you. Instead give him a choice between two fairly meaningless options (both of which are acceptable to you).

When it comes to negotiating bigger issues:

- Always ask for way more than you really need or want.

- Never tell him what you really want. Instead, dress it up in a bit of word salad and immerse it somewhere in your offer. If he knows what really matters to you he'll go all out to make sure you don't get it.

- If you do get what you want, be sure to continue your story that you didn't want it at all and say how unhappy you are with what you've ended up with. He has to win, even if you know you really have!

- Never be tempted to accept a favour the narcissist may offer you, however generous or helpful it may seem to be, as it will come back to bite you somewhere down the line. There are always strings attached and they're likely to be used to string you up.

- Consider carefully everything he asks you to produce during your negotiations and take legal advice if necessary. Is what he's asking for really necessary to be able to reach a settlement, or is it just another way to control you?

- Never give him more information than you absolutely have to; you've nothing to gain and potentially plenty to lose. You can always ignore the first request for information and see how hard he pushes for it. Sometimes you just need to wait and see what he does next to fill your silence. It's really important that you're able to hold your nerve during negotiations and not jump through hoops every time he asks you to – because, the more he sees he's able to continue to control you, the longer he'll carry on doing it. On the other hand, you do need to ask him to produce proof of all his claims, since he's the pathological liar.

- And finally, keep in mind that if you're more desperate to settle the case than your ex is, he has more power than you going into the negotiation, and will certainly take advantage of that. You can take away that fear by working out your Plan B (as in, 'What will I do if the worst case scenario happens?') and the ways in which your Plan B could negatively impact your ex. You can use those factors as leverage in your negotiations.

Let's explore the various options for negotiating with the narcissist.

Traditional mediation

He will probably adopt the role of 'the kindly gentleman of reason'
at the end of his tether, dealing with an over-emotional,
suspicious, hysteric who is imagining all sorts of nonsense.
All the standard 'gaslighting' techniques.

The general rule is that you cannot mediate with a narcissist. It's usually a complete waste of your time, money and emotional energy. After all, the aim of mediation is to reach an outcome that both parties can live with, and this requires negotiation – something that's rarely part of a narcissist's skill set. If he wants to go to mediation, it's typically because he thinks he can bully you into agreeing to what he wants rather than go to court – usually because he's been advised he's unlikely to win in court, or because he doesn't want to spend his highly prized money on lawyers' fees, or because it's his only opportunity now to be in the same room as you and continue his abuse/control of you (and get narcissistic supply from you).

All too often, the narcissist will manipulate the mediator, who may not be up to the task. In defence of mediators, most people who go to mediation genuinely want help to settle their differences as quickly as possible and move on. Most mediators have no training in personality disorders and no experience of working with victims of abuse as mediation is not usually recommended in these circumstances.

What's more, the narcissist will constantly move the goalposts, making it impossible for you ever to reach an agreement. He knows just what to say to rattle you and throw you off course so you can't think straight. He'll make you look like the crazy one while putting on his act of being the calm, rational, long-suffering yet concerned one. And even if you do reach an agreement, he may not stick to it in practice.

All things considered, I rarely see the point of going to mediation with a narcissist. If you do decide to go, it's important to be very clear as to your reasons for putting yourself through this. You may want to feel you've tried everything before you resort to court. Or you may go to mediation knowing that it won't work, but you want to be able to show that you tried. Whatever your reason, it's important to go into this process with your eyes open, expecting a bumpy ride. To have any chance of getting what you want, you'll need to:

- Choose the right mediator in the first place
- Be feeling strong
- Have a clear strategy to get what you want
- Arm yourself with the necessary ammunition

Let's look at each area in turn.

Choose the right mediator

Given what I've said about the narcissist manipulating the mediator, it's really important to choose your mediator carefully. If your narcissist is a misogynist with no respect for any woman, you may be better off with a male mediator. But if your ex is only disrespectful of you (not other women), a female mediator could be a better choice as long as she doesn't succumb to his charm and manipulations. Thinking about your ex's relationship with each of his parents may give you a clue as to who would be best.

You can find a mediator who is local to you through the National Family Mediation (NFM) website – although, since this was written during the COVID-19 pandemic, most mediators have switched to video meetings rather than in-person. Many solicitors are also trained as mediators and if you or your ex have a solicitor they are more likely to recommend another solicitor than an NFM mediator – but you don't have to accept their recommendation. (Bear in mind that solicitors are more expensive than NFM mediators but may be better for dealing with a financial settlement.) Alternatively, you can send me an email (*diana@dealingwithdivorce.co.uk*) to see if I can recommend a mediator.

You will have to pay for mediation, unless you are eligible for legal aid. At the time of writing, there is also a government voucher scheme providing £500 off the cost of mediation for eligible cases – google 'Family Mediation Voucher Scheme' to find out more.

Make sure you're feeling strong

You need to be able to keep your emotions in check during a mediation session, even though the narcissist knows which buttons to press to throw you off balance. If you get angry or upset, this gives him an immediate hit of narcissistic fuel, making him feel more powerful whilst you're left feeling depleted and deflated.

Succeeding in mediation requires more than keeping your emotions in check, though; it requires a shift in the power dynamic between the two of you.

Even if he's not hurling accusations at you with the same vitriol he uses behind closed doors, he'll still be doing all he can to keep you on the back foot. His aim is to keep your focus on defending yourself rather than you calling the shots to get what you want for yourself.

Not only do you want to feel strong, you'll also want to show that you feel strong. Use powerful body language such as steepling your hands and sitting up straight. Make eye contact and keep your voice firm. (A coach or therapist can give you the help you need to be able to do this.) He will pick up on these subtle changes and feel that there has been a shift in the balance of power.

Also keep in mind that mediation is confidential and whatever is shared there cannot be used in court, which may be frustrating for you if the narcissist confesses to any of his abusive behaviour or gives any other useful information. And just because he can't use anything that you've said in court, it won't stop the master manipulator using it against you in other ways, so prepare yourself mentally for this eventuality.

Have a clear strategy to get what you want

Part of feeling stronger is having a clear strategy to get what you want. Firstly, of course, you must be clear about what you really want, and what you could live with if you don't get exactly that.

If necessary, take legal advice before you start mediation so you know what you're entitled to, and so that you can start by asking for much more than that. And then you want to 'shutty shutty'. Keep your cards close to your chest. Never ask for what you really want. You want to keep the house? Tell him it's a big share of his pension you're after. Whinge and cry when you get the house, leaving him to celebrate his big 'win' in both keeping his pension and causing you more 'distress'. I know this will go against your nature (because you like to be open and honest) but remember that you're not dealing with a 'normal' person, so you need to act accordingly.

It's also necessary to figure out what your ex wants or needs. Knowing your own narcissist is the key here. He's a very different person to you, and he doesn't want what you want. What does he want? He wants to win, that's a given, and it's your job to make him think he has. Other than that, different things float different narcissists' boats, and you know what yours is most keen on – is it money, free time, power, control …?

If you're trying to agree arrangements for your children, for example, does he really want more time with them, or to pay less or no child maintenance?

Or does he just want more narcissistic supply by upsetting and worrying you? If you're not sure what he wants, try telling him you want to go out for a day or away for a weekend with friends and ask if he'd have the children for you – does he jump at the chance of extra time with them, or tell you he's not your babysitter? But again, don't give him more time than he already has eg if he's not having overnights don't offer him one just because you want to go away.

Bear in mind that the narcissist's sense of entitlement means he'll always expect to finish mediation with more than he's really entitled to – and just occasionally that's okay, if you can live with the outcome.

Arm yourself with the necessary ammunition

Again, this is where you need to know your narcissist. What have you got that he wants? What motivates him? What are his pain points? Where does he get his narcissistic supply? What supply will be more important for him to protect and keep now that he's no longer getting supply from making your life miserable?

Anticipate what he will say and prepare your arguments in advance. Then, during the session, you can point out the issues you do agree on and tell him that you anticipate what his argument is, and why it won't work. For example, you anticipate he'll say he should have the children half the time, but that won't work because he can't take them to school in the morning and also pick them up at the end of the day – his job means he can't do both.

Having all this figured out before you walk into the room gives you the best chance of reaching an agreement. And after each session you can review whether the narcissist is really invested in the process, or whether it's time for you to walk away.

Shuttle mediation

This is where you and your ex stay in separate rooms and the mediator 'shuttles' between you. Obviously this takes a lot longer and costs more as everything has to be repeated twice, but the bigger disadvantage is you miss your ex's emotional reaction and you don't know how much the mediator has 'sanitised' his responses before relaying them to you.

On the plus side, shuttle mediation does keep you safe and will hopefully avoid you being triggered and unable to respond appropriately. Since your ex is more likely to favour being in the room with you, it'll be up to you to work out whether shuttle mediation or traditional mediation is the best approach.

Collaborative law

This is where all the solicitor negotiations take place around a table – in meetings between both parties and their solicitors – rather than in writing. Under 'normal' circumstances, this is one of the best ways of agreeing a financial settlement and possibly arrangements for children too – it's more expensive than mediation, but much cheaper than going to court.

But you should be very wary of using this method with a narcissist. Yes, it avoids all the lies and false accusations that solicitors often just copy and paste from the narcissist's emails into their own correspondence, all of which can be very upsetting for you and drastically bump up everyone's costs. But if your narcissist is a charmer who's likely to influence and manipulate your solicitor as well as his, it's not going to work for you. Nor will it if the narcissist is just using the process to be in the same room as you again, or to string out negotiations he has no intention of ever concluding.

If the negotiations break down and you have to go to court, you are not allowed to use the same solicitors – so once again the narcissist will have succeeded in isolating you from part of your support system. You will therefore need to be very sure that it's going to work before agreeing to engage in the collaborative process.

Hybrid mediation

This is like shuttle mediation, in that a mediator shuttles between you and your ex in separate rooms – but you both have your solicitors with you. The disadvantages of collaborative law aren't there (particularly that your ex would try to manipulate your solicitor), plus you feel safe and supported during the negotiations. Even better, if an agreement is reached, the court documents can be drawn up by the solicitors there and then, for you both to sign at the end of the session – leaving the narcissist unable to 'change his mind' later. On balance, then, I believe hybrid mediation can be worth trying with a narcissist.

Solicitor negotiation

I feel so stupid for thinking I had nearly sorted the consent order.
It's soul destroying to be back in exactly the same place
I was in weeks and months ago.

Solicitors settle a large proportion of their cases by writing letters to the other party or their solicitor. They will try to do the same in your case, failing to understand that yours is not a normal divorce and cannot be settled in this way – it's simply not in the narcissist's interest. You have totally different aims and objectives here. Your aim is to get things sorted out and settled as quickly as you can so you can escape from your tormentor and build a new life. Meanwhile, his aims are to retain his power and control over you, to win, to punish and destroy you, and to keep you as a source of narcissistic supply.

The chances of reaching an agreement through solicitor negotiation are therefore minimal. Which is not to say that he won't string you and your solicitor along for months, or even years, writing back and forth arguing the toss about everything, all the while giving you the false hope that you may eventually be able to reach an agreement. One of his aims will be to make you run out of money and if he can do that before you even get to court that will feel like a big win to him.

Occasionally a narcissist will agree a financial settlement through solicitor negotiations (or mediation, or even directly with you) – maybe after stringing you along for months and months – if he wants something else even more than controlling and upsetting you. His possible incentives here might include:

- His debts are getting too hot to handle and he needs money sooner rather than later.
- He's a covert narcissist who doesn't like confrontation and wants to avoid giving evidence in a contested court hearing.
- He's got hidden assets (or maybe even more debts) that he wants to keep hidden.
- He knows he's going to come into more money soon and he wants to settle now so you don't get your hands on any of it.
- He's got a new partner who's pressurising him to settle, or he's trying to impress her by showing what a good guy he is being so generous to you.

Know your own narcissist so you can work out if you can use any of these as leverage and get him to settle without going to court.

If he threatens to issue court proceedings and doesn't do so, perhaps you can figure out why and use that to your advantage in negotiations. In addition, if he doesn't issue threatened proceedings, I would almost always advise you to issue proceedings straight away. That will either give him the incentive to settle before your first hearing and having to disclose his documents, or it will save you a lot of time and money in solicitors' letters if the reality is that he'll never settle without going to court.

CHAPTER 9:
GOING THROUGH
THE FAMILY COURT
– GENERAL CONSIDERATIONS

*Being in the family court is like living in a crazy upside-down world
where wrong is right and right is wrong.*

How did I end up here?

You say you don't want to fight. He also says he doesn't want to fight (you know he's lying but you still choose to believe him). So how have you ended up in court?

When you're divorcing a narcissist, you're more than likely to find yourself in court. If you've managed to distance yourself and keep firm boundaries, this may be the only way he can still get at you. As well as being intended to punish or destroy you, it will be an endless and fun way of getting narcissistic supply now that you are far less obliging in this regard.

It's a big game to him, but be in no doubt, he's playing to win. And he 'wins' every time he gets narcissistic supply from lying successfully, manipulating you or the professionals, making false accusations (against you as well as anyone and everyone else), using delaying tactics, and winning the judge over to his side whilst failing to comply with the orders of the court.

With all these 'wins' to play for, you can see why the narcissist would rather pay lawyers huge fees than settle out of court. Not only that, but if you ask a narcissist to agree to something, they feel as though they're being controlled, rather than doing the controlling. Perversely, handing over the decisions to a judge means the narcissist is relinquishing control, but of course they always believe that the judge will find in their favour and they will win. And more often than not they do. But if they don't, they can blame the judge for being stupid and getting it wrong, and play the victim.

This is why most narcissists are not afraid of going to court – unless they fear it's going to do too much damage to their bank balance. On the contrary, many narcissists (particularly overt narcissists) relish the drama of the courtroom, where their grandiose personality can take centre stage and they have a captive audience. They can also use the way the family court operates – i.e. that there is often more than one set of proceedings, as well as the divorce itself – to further abuse you. In other words, you may find yourself in court over the children, your financial settlement, an occupation order (for the right to live in a property), a prohibited steps order (to stop you doing something, such as moving away), a specific issue order (where the court decides something the parents can't agree on) and sometimes other proceedings too.

So if you win in children proceedings, the narcissist will take you back to court as soon as he can. And if he wins, he'll still take you back to court as soon as he can! He says he wants it to be over and he may act as if he does, but the drama, trauma and chaos of the proceedings go on and on.

Again, know your own narcissist; would he prefer to pay huge sums to lawyers in order not to pay you a penny, or is money more important to him than anything else – even controlling you – so he won't want to pay more in legal fees than he has to? Or is prolonging the court proceedings so you run out of money just part of his plan to destroy you?

Whichever way it is, the most important thing to him will be feeling that he's won. Winning is so important to all narcissists. Which is again why you must always ask in court for lots more than you actually want – when you get less, they think they've won, while you know you've either won or at least got the minimum you need.

How the family court works

The first thing to say is that our court system is adversarial – which means you're in a fight, whether you want to be or not (rest assured he wants to be). Lawyers and judges will try to tell you that the family court isn't adversarial, but take a look at your court papers and you'll see Jones -v- Jones. It's set up as a fight from the start. This is an important thing to keep in mind throughout the whole process.

But how does it work? Well, family law is civil, not criminal, law. The purpose of criminal law is for the state to prosecute and punish offenders for criminal behaviour, while the purpose of family law is to resolve disputes between private individuals – in the case of a divorcing couple, usually disputes about joint finances and care of the children. The family court will not punish people for what they've done in the past and is only interested in working out the best way forward. The only time the family court punishes people is when they break a court order and the other party applies for their committal to prison, but this is very rare indeed. The other way the family court can 'punish' you is by ordering you to pay the other party's costs, if they have won an application or if you have been found 'guilty' of litigation misconduct. However this rarely happens in children cases.

The family court makes 'orders', such as an order to sell the family home, or an order saying who the children will live with and how much time they will spend with the other parent. These orders set out the court's formal decision on the matter at hand – and there are (in theory at least) consequences if a court order isn't obeyed.

Before making these orders, the court will give 'directions' (instructions), such as to file and 'serve' (meaning to send to the court and other party) a statement or report. But of course the narcissist plays by his own rules so don't be surprised if he doesn't obey court orders or follow directions. He doesn't think they apply to him. You can ask for a 'penal notice' to be attached to an order so that if he still fails to comply he could be sent to prison for contempt of court – but it's a slow process and very rare indeed for anyone to be sent to prison. It might work, though, if your narcissist is someone in a position of some authority whose status or livelihood could be undermined by a prison sentence.

There are basically two types of family court hearing: 'directions hearings', also known as case management hearings, and 'contested hearings'. A directions hearing is to sort out procedural matters and decide what evidence needs to be obtained before the court makes a decision and a final order. A contested hearing is where people give evidence on oath, and/or both parties argue their positions, and then decisions are made by the court.

You may attend directions hearings and contested hearings in children, financial and injunction proceedings. You can usually tell which type of hearing it is, and whether or not you may have to give evidence, by looking at your Notice of Hearing, which will tell you how long the hearing will last. If it's 30 or 40 minutes, it's a directions hearing. If it's a couple of hours, half a day or more, it's a contested hearing. You may have a contested hearing, for instance, for interim contact or interim maintenance that is listed for a couple of hours, where you may have to give brief evidence.

Both children and financial proceedings have three basic hearings. However, your case may finish at any point before a final hearing if you and your ex reach an agreement. And there may be any number of additional hearings between your first and final hearings – because proceedings rarely run according to plan with a narcissist. The judge will decide on these additional hearings after hearing what each party says about them. The main hearings are indicated in **bold**:

In children proceedings, the different hearings you may attend are:

- **FHDRA** – first hearing and dispute resolution appointment. This is a directions hearing.
- **FFH** – fact finding hearing. This is a contested hearing where you will have to give evidence.
- **DRA** – dispute resolution appointment. This is a directions hearing and you may have one or more of these.
- **PTR** – pre-trial review hearing. This is a directions hearing to make sure everything is ready for a contested hearing.
- **Final hearing** – this may be a contested hearing where you will have to give evidence unless you and your ex can reach an agreement.

In financial proceedings the different hearings you may attend are:

- **FDA** – first directions appointment, which as the name suggests is a directions hearing.
- Interim maintenance, and/or legal services application – a contested hearing unless agreement can be reached.
- **FDR** – financial dispute resolution appointment. Confusingly, this is neither a contested hearing nor a directions hearing – although directions will be given at the end if agreement isn't reached. It's basically a hearing for the parties to negotiate an agreement with help from the judge.
- **PTR** – pre-trial review hearing. This is a directions hearing to make sure everything is ready for a contested hearing.
- **Final hearing** – both parties will give evidence and the judge will make a final order.

Read more about children proceedings in Chapter 14 and financial proceedings in Chapter 12.

The family courts are woefully under-resourced. There are not enough courtrooms, not enough staff, not enough judges, and not enough time. This means long delays between hearings, rushed decisions and mistakes being made.

And because it's an adversarial system, the court makes decisions only on the evidence presented to it – as opposed to an inquisitorial court system, which is concerned with investigating the facts of the case. The family court isn't interested in investigating the facts (unless it's a fact finding hearing), which can be a source of huge frustration for you – it only wants to reach a decision, based on the evidence presented. Furthermore, the judge won't ask to see specific evidence unless one party has requested it. (For example, one party may say they want an expert report or a valuation, and the other party may argue against obtaining that evidence – then the judge has to decide which party they agree with.) The whole process is based on what the parties can persuade the court to order, rather than the court investigating or seeking the truth.

In other words, the court is not proactive in any way and won't do anything unless you ask it to – usually by making an application and paying yet another fee. You would have to do this if, for instance, you wanted to appoint an expert (for example, to do an assessment of the family, or a pension report).

You would also have to apply for a penal notice to be attached to the order if your ex does not obey a court order or direction. Again, the court won't notice that your ex has done something they shouldn't have, or hasn't done something they should have; a judge looks at the file just before the hearing (if they have time), confirms the order is drawn up correctly after the hearing, and then no one looks at it again until the next hearing. If you want anything else to happen in the meantime, you have to send an application and a fee.

Here's another application that may prove useful to you: if you've moved house, or are in a refuge, you can apply to the court (on Form C8) to keep your contact details confidential. However, incidences of social workers, Cafcass, lawyers and even the court disclosing these details in error are shockingly common, so think carefully about what you do need to disclose and to whom. You may want to try giving the address of a relative, which is already known to the perpetrator, for your correspondence, or to set up a new email address just for the court proceedings.

Finally, I should say that I started writing this book before the COVID-19 crisis hit. When the UK went into lockdown, all family court hearings switched to remote hearings (i.e. by phone or video). By the time I finished this book, despite lockdown restrictions lifting, most of my hearings were still being conducted remotely. So you may find yourself attending some remote hearings, but don't worry – the same considerations and actions will apply, except that you'll need to ensure your position statement (see Chapter 10) is sent to the court a few days before, and to check at the start of the hearing that the judge has received it. Some hearings, such as a fact finding hearing, really shouldn't be held remotely as the judge cannot assess the witnesses well enough that way. You can always object and ask for a hearing in court if you think you'll be prejudiced in any way by a remote hearing.

The 'justice' myth

*I do want to expose his lies and cruelty though there is a pretty
hefty dose of latent revenge against my mother
smouldering away in there too.
I was never able to confront her in life.*

When I read that Aristotle's definition of justice was 'giving people what they deserve' my immediate thought was 'but that's not what they get in the family court'.

You don't get justice from the family court, you get a decision.

You may go to court expecting it will protect you and your children from further abuse. It will, if you're lucky enough to win that particular lottery.

I've got an amazing Cafcass officer who is currently fighting for my children's wishes to be heard and for the judge to understand the impact dv can have.

But the court may equally well help your ex to continue the abuse you've already suffered and make things worse, rather than better, for you and your children. The court operates on the assumption that a child needs both parents in their life and it's very hard to fight against this culture of 'contact at all costs', no matter how dreadfully a father has behaved. (There appear to be different rules for mothers, who are expected to be pretty well perfect.)

Also, our legal system allows an abusive parent to drag their victim back to court for many years. They will take you to court for contact with the children and if they get contact, they will take you back to court quite quickly to get more contact, or to complain you've not been allowing the contact. Then they'll take you back to court again, maybe for shared care. Once the case has finished, they'll be back applying for something else, over and over again. The more success they have with this tactic, the more times they will use the court to continue their control over your life.

The court does have the power to make an order barring a parent from making further applications (see Chapter 14) but this is rarely used. Even when it is, the order is often made against both parents, not just the one who keeps returning the case to court.

If you do manage to get truth or justice from the family court, you're one of the lucky ones. The sad fact is the judge has far too many cases in her list and wants you out of her courtroom as soon as possible. Judges are lawyers and they want to deal with cold facts, figures and logic, not emotions. Nevertheless, they don't always hold fact finding hearings when they should, either because they don't have time or because they don't think the abuse a parent or child has suffered is important, or relevant.

This is another problem: judges have far too little training in domestic abuse and no understanding of personality disorders. I believe a high percentage of children cases these days, at least those which aren't quickly settled, involve a parent with a personality disorder. Why on earth would two mentally healthy parents subject themselves to the awful experience of the family court if they didn't absolutely have to?

Victims of abuse go to court expecting – and deserving – their abuse to be recognised and measures taken to protect them and their children in the future. Whilst many do get the occupation and non-molestation orders they need (see Chapter 13), unfortunately it's a different story in children proceedings. Abuse is frequently not recognised and even when it is, it's often minimised, ignored or said to be 'in the past' and therefore not relevant. As a result, the protective parent is forced to put their child into potential or actual danger with the abusive parent and can do little to comfort frightened children.

So what can you do? Forewarned is forearmed, and you can revise your expectations. Accept that you're unlikely to get justice, or what you or your child deserves, and focus instead on getting the best possible outcome for your child. Refer back to your goals and strategy here (Chapter 5), and focus on what you can actually achieve, rather than what you deserve.

People are often surprised by decisions made – and not made – by the family court. People who lie in court are rarely even challenged, let alone sanctioned for it (again, the family court isn't necessarily interested in unearthing the facts, only reaching a decision). Many abusive partners may break court orders and directions, and the court turns a blind eye (unless you make an application to get the court to do something). Meanwhile, those who tell the truth and follow court orders to the letter feel outraged and that there is no justice.

Two cases in 2020 highlighted this. The first was the case of the Rev Gibbs, where a family court judge refused to send 60-year-old Mrs Gibbs to prison for contempt of court. For the last 20 years Mrs Gibbs had been making false allegations that her ex-husband emotionally and sexually abused their son (who was by then aged 33). Although her allegations had several times been found to be untrue, the Methodist minister had never seen either his son or his daughter again. Not content with this, Mrs Gibbs also set out to destroy the rest of his life, namely his ministry, and his reputation.

In 2017 Mrs Gibbs had begun an email campaign against her ex, sending abusive and lurid allegations to 50 or 60 people at a time, including journalists, MPs, the Methodist Church and the Supreme Court. The Reverend was taking her to court to stop her making these allegations, and he applied to the court to stop her from disclosing information about the court proceedings. Family court proceedings are held in private and no one is allowed to tell anyone else what happens there, or to disclose any of the documents (which is why such dreadful decisions keep being made about children, because so few people know what is really happening). However, contempt of court proceedings can lead to imprisonment and are held in open court, which is why this hearing was reported.

By 6.45 on the morning after the court order was made against her, requiring her to not disclose information about any of the court proceedings, Mrs Gibbs had sent over 100 more emails. She was sentenced to nine months' imprisonment for breaking the court order. Presumably she behaved herself inside as she only served four and a half months.

But the moment she was released, she started her email vendetta again. The court granted her ex-husband an order prohibiting her from making further allegations, but six months later she was arrested for breaching that order.

The judge then had to decide whether or not to send Mrs Gibbs back to prison. Reverend Gibbs's barrister argued that another period inside would give him some respite from her relentless email campaign as her allegations had a devastating impact on his life and ministry (though fortunately he had managed to hang on to his job).

The judge said there were two factors she had to consider: the authority of the court, and whether imprisonment would persuade Mrs Gibbs she should obey the court. Mrs Gibbs made it quite clear that she was going to go on sending her emails whatever the judge did, and that she was prepared to go to prison again rather than be silenced.

The judge decided she wasn't going to send Mrs Gibbs to prison again because a jail sentence wouldn't deter her. Instead, she took a very unusual course and wrote a summary of her decision vindicating the Reverend Gibbs, which she said he could distribute to all the recipients of the dreadful emails (although she felt by this time that no one would be taking any notice of them anyway). She also ordered Mrs Gibbs to sell her house in order to pay all the Reverend's legal costs.

Whilst I understand the judge's reasoning, I believe her decision sends the wrong message not only to the public, but also to all those going through the family court. My clients and many others often complain that nothing is even said, let alone done, about people breaking family court orders, which they very often do. And the message from this case seems to be that the worse you behave, the less likely you are to be punished for it, which can't be right.

And then there was MS v FS, another extraordinary case, though a very different one. Mr and Mrs S separated in 2010 or 2011 – they didn't even agree on that! In 2017 Mr S applied to the court for a divorce, presumably because he wanted to remarry. He was shocked to discover that not only had he already been divorced in February 2011, but the former matrimonial home had been transferred from joint names into his wife's sole name following a financial consent order made in June 2011.

Mr S applied to the court to set aside the decree absolute and the consent order. A handwriting expert gave evidence that some of the signatures on the various documents were not those of Mr S and the judge made a finding of fraud. He did not set aside the decree absolute, which was probably just as well as both parties had remarried by the time of the final hearing.

The judge also had to decide whether his judgement should be disclosed to the police, and Mrs S's professional regulatory body (she is an accountant). Mr S had to agree to this, as his information was contained in the papers too. Not surprisingly, Mr S did agree. However, the judge declined to make an order for disclosure to any third party, stating that the fraud only affected these two people and it was not necessary in the public interest to make disclosure of it. This would normally only be done in very serious cases, such as one which had led to the death of a child, or where a party who is a serving policeman was found to be corrupt, or a party who works with children was proved to be a paedophile. 'Given the number of skeletons which come out of cupboards in family proceedings,' the judge said, 'where would it end?'

Mrs S did not even apologise for her fraud, and you may think she got off lightly. She was however ordered to pay 80% of Mr S's costs. It's fairly unusual to be ordered to pay the other party's costs in financial proceedings and almost unheard of to have to pay such a big percentage of them. And it would have been 100% but for the fact that Mr S's lawyers messed up in their case preparation.

Men reading this may conclude that these two people got off lightly because they are women, but I wouldn't agree with that. After all, Mrs Gibbs had already served a fairly lengthy prison sentence. And I believe a judge would be even more unlikely to endanger a man's career than a woman's. The fact remains that people of both sexes get away with an awful lot in the family court so it's wise to assess your expectations when going there; if you go expecting justice for the other party's bad behaviour you're likely to be disappointed. An award of costs is the most you're likely to get, and then only in exceptional circumstances.

Please understand from the outset and remember throughout your proceedings: you don't get justice from the family court, you only get a decision.

How to conduct yourself in the family court

I was treated like a criminal.

It should be clear by now that protective parents are often treated badly by the family court. They can be disbelieved and disrespected as the narcissist talks the lawyers and the judge into his way of thinking. You must be prepared for this and not let your frustration, hurt and anger show.

Whatever type of hearing you find yourself in – contested or directions, financial or children – it's so important (and so difficult) to stay calm. The narcissist knows you, and knows exactly how to rattle you and get a reaction. For some reason many of my clients seem to believe that, despite the fact their abuser has done nothing but lie to them, he'll tell the truth in court. Believe me, he won't! He'll continue to tell only his truth. Since you know him, and that he's going to lie, that's not a reason to look shocked, upset or angry in court. It's time to develop and practice a poker face so you don't play into the narcissist's hands. Indeed, many narcissists allege that the mother of their child is 'crazy' or mentally ill, so it's vitally important that you don't give the judge any hint that he might be right.

This is why a therapist is so important, as they can help you to develop strategies to keep your emotions in check in court. If therapy isn't an option, you can practice staying in control by doing role play with a friend. Do whatever you need to do to ensure you don't lose it in court. And of course that includes having as little contact as possible with your ex so your brain and body have time to decompress and you can think rationally.

Whenever you're in court, here are some general tips on how to conduct yourself:

- Take a good supply of tissues, and breathe deeply! Yes, being in court is stressful, and sometimes people do break down (in which case, the court will usually give you a short break), but it's best to avoid giving your narcissist that amount of supply if you can.

- I've said it before but I'll say it again: never be tempted to label your ex as a narcissist, bipolar, alcoholic, drug addict or anything else in court, even if it's true. You will come over as being the crazy one with a problem.

- Be careful of your language – always say 'our' or 'the' children, never 'my' children.

- Be mindful of what you say and do, not just inside the actual courtroom but in and around the court building too. The court staff, in particular the ushers, have the ear of the judges so be sure to behave in a polite and dignified manner at all times (while keeping your fingers crossed that your ex has a big temper tantrum).

- Dress respectfully. There's no need to wear black or dress like it's a funeral (lawyers, on the other hand, are supposed to wear dark colours to avoid drawing attention to themselves). But you probably won't want to wear very bright colours or loud patterns. My advice is to wear something simple that makes you feel attractive and confident. If you're in children proceedings you can dress like a mum who's got her act together. For financial proceedings, dress as if you're going to an important business meeting (which is exactly what you are doing).

- If you're frightened of your ex, you or your solicitor should ask for 'special measures' beforehand (more on this coming up).

The above tips apply to any type of hearing. But there are some extra considerations for contested hearings, where you'll be giving evidence. I talk in detail about giving evidence – how to prepare, what to expect, etc. – in Chapter 14.

Asking for special measures

If you're a victim of domestic abuse and worried about the contact you may have with your abuser at court, you can ask for 'special measures' – preferably in advance of the hearing. These include using a different entrance to the court, having a separate waiting room and having a screen in court so you don't have to see your abuser or be intimidated by him. Some courts can provide a separate room for the survivor to listen in to the proceedings through a receiver and then give evidence behind a screen.

A screen is a visual reminder to the judge that you mean it when you say you were abused, though it also tells your ex that he can still affect you adversely. The other disadvantage is that you won't be able to see how he reacts to what's being said in court. You have to weigh up the pros and cons here to decide which special measures will work for you.

If both parties are represented, the judge can direct that parties do not attend directions hearings. A litigant in person can request not to attend in person but by telephone or a video link.

If you haven't asked the court for special measures, and are just worried about being in a confined space with your ex in a corridor or doorway as you go into the courtroom, you can tell the usher you don't feel safe and ask if they can get one of you into court first.

Funding your court proceedings

If your ex was financially controlling, you may be struggling to pay for a lawyer. Even if he wasn't, the aim of the narcissist is to cause as many delays and diversions as possible so that you run out of money before the end. So if you have limited funds you'll want to use them strategically, as you usually need legal help and representation more at the end than the beginning of the court proceedings. Money is always important to the narcissist, and a few won't want to spend theirs on lawyers (know your own narcissist!), but many don't care what this delicious drama leading to your destruction is going to cost them.

Avoid litigation loans at all costs

Just when I thought the family court couldn't get any worse, I received an email from Jenny warning me about litigation loans.

Jenny was interviewed by Winifred Robinson of *You and Yours* on Radio 4 in a feature about the specialist loans some solicitors pressure clients to take. The BBC decided not to reveal the names of the solicitors' firms being investigated by the Solicitors Regulation Authority because one of them was so aggressive about it, but I can tell you that they are all large, well-known, central London practices.

Jenny was clearly vulnerable, fleeing an abusive marriage and being the sole carer of three children, one of whom was disabled. Social services were involved and there had been three Multi Agency Risk Assessment Conferences. The solicitors were aware of all this at the outset and should have taken into account that Jenny's mind wouldn't have been on loans.

Jenny told me:

'I went to them to get divorce advice and they sold me a loan as if it was a normal and essential part of the divorce process. I did not ask for the loans, they really pushed me to take them. Their verbal estimate of costs was up to £50,000 maximum, but in writing they gave a maximum cost for the divorce of £100,000. They reassured me it would not come to that and said I would get back any funds not used at the end of the divorce. In the end my legal fees came to £350,000 and I also owe £150,000 in interest on this. The loan company is taking proceedings to force the sale of my home so they can be paid.

Going through my bills, the solicitors billed me for at least £8,000 each for selling and administering these loans. I was also charged by the loan company for 'administering the loan' on their side.

The solicitors told me to engage ADDITIONAL solicitors for public law children proceedings. They should have told me of their lack of knowledge in this area at the outset. Despite my then engaging another firm for this work, my solicitors ignored the advice they gave to press for non-molestation and occupation orders for my safety and the safety of the children.

The Judge at the final hearing said that they had added no value at all to my case. They had caused confusion, escalating costs, and spiralling debt. In his written judgement he said the sums secured against my home by the solicitors in litigation loans were "neither justified, nor justifiable".'

It's not only women who take these loans; Jenny knows of two wives whose husbands took loans. One found out accidentally; she couldn't understand why the judge kept saying there was no money left and it turned out it had all gone on her ex's legal fees via the litigation loan, secured on their home, which was jointly owned, without her knowledge or consent. In the other case, the wife was convinced her ex was having an affair with his solicitor as she couldn't understand why the solicitor was giving him all this money to pay for his fees. In fact, he had taken out a loan at 24% interest, on the advice of his solicitor, and it was secured against property in his wife's sole name!

If you need to borrow money for your divorce, please find a better way of doing it than a litigation loan. Sadly, once unscrupulous solicitors have access to this sort of loan they are likely to run up your costs until they've used it all.

It's always worth asking your bank for a loan, but usually they will only lend if they can be sure to get their money back. This is of course why the litigation lenders charge a higher rate of interest (they do risk not being repaid, although in many cases the loans are secured on the family home as a second charge so they can take possession if they are not paid). In my mind, there is no justification at all for these dreadfully high interest rates (up to 29%) – your bank may give you a secured loan for a quarter of the cost.

Family and friends will sometimes offer a loan to cover legal fees. The problem is they can be seen as 'soft' loans and the court will not take them into consideration in the final financial order. (Basically the court will see it as a gift, not a loan that you have to repay. So if you really do have to repay it, and it's not been taken into consideration by the court, you'll be worse off.) This is especially likely if the loan is from your parents, so if a more distant relative, or a friend, also offered help it may be better to accept that. And always have a written loan agreement drawn up and signed by both parties. You can find a template online and adapt it to fit your particular circumstances – for example, you can have a low or 0% rate of interest until the loan is due to be repaid at the end of your case, or when your property is sold, and a higher rate if it's not repaid within the time limit.

Another possibility if your spouse has money and you don't is to apply to the court for a Legal Services Payment Order (i.e. for him to pay your legal fees). These aren't easy orders to obtain but are definitely worth considering if you've no other option.

Remember to budget for court fees

The court charges a fee for every application you make – except for non-molestation and occupation orders. At the time of writing, the fee for a divorce is £550, but likely to go up to £592 later in 2021. The fee for a financial remedy order is £255, but it's only £50 for a consent order. Applications under the Children Act are £215 at the time of writing.

If you can't afford these fees you can apply to the court on Form EX160 or online for them to be waived or reduced.

What about legal aid?

Since 2012 only victims of domestic abuse are able to apply for legal aid. You have to have evidence of the abuse, and also be financially eligible, which means that very few people qualify for legal aid now. As a result, very few solicitors now offer legal aid and those who do tend to be exceedingly busy (and, because legal aid is so badly paid, they often aren't able to do a great job). On the plus side, legal aid does cover barristers' fees, so if you do qualify, it is worth having.

Solicitors and barristers – do you need one and how should you work with them?

Solicitors and barristers (counsel) are all lawyers – so when I use the term 'lawyers' I may be referring to either solicitors or barristers, or both. (Incidentally, judges are lawyers too as they were previously a barrister or solicitor.)

Lawyers are not psychiatrists, and they don't understand personality disorders. Training for them all is desperately needed as most are not currently able to recognise the abuse and suffering these disorders cause to children and parents. And unless they do, they can't handle your case properly. Therefore, there's a lot to consider when it comes to working with lawyers.

Do I even need a lawyer when I'm going through the family court?

I'm afraid I'm going to give you a typical lawyer's reply: it depends. Of course, some people can't afford a solicitor or barrister and have no choice but to self-represent (this is what's known as a 'litigant in person'). So, technically speaking, you don't have to have anyone represent you in court or in dealings with your ex and/or his solicitors. Turn to Chapter 10 for more on representing yourself.

But if you can afford to pay the fees, and can't afford the time to do all the letters, forms and statements yourself, you may want to instruct a solicitor to deal with the paperwork for you. If your narcissist ex is self-representing, your solicitor can be an invaluable buffer between the two of you, saving you from dealing directly with your ex's vitriol. If, however, your ex has a solicitor, he's effectively paying for the barrier between you (not to mention some of the legal work) – so, providing you have the time to deal with your side of the paperwork yourself, you may be happy to do your own paperwork and not pay for a solicitor.

What about the difference between a solicitor and a barrister? Well, solicitors are a bit like GPs, in that they give you initial advice and do all the paperwork. But if things get serious, your GP will refer you to a hospital consultant. Similarly, if you have to go to court, you'll probably need a barrister. (Some solicitors will represent clients in court – particularly if it's a straightforward directions hearing, or if they're located in far-flung parts of the country where there isn't much access to barristers – but, for the most part, this is usually done by a barrister.)

The good news is you can now instruct a barrister yourself by direct access, rather than having to go through a solicitor, which can save you a lot of money. I talk more about barristers later in the chapter.

In my opinion, it's more important for you to be represented in court by a barrister than to have a solicitor doing the paperwork. And it's more important to be represented by a barrister in contested hearings than in directions hearings. So if you need to prioritise your budget, that's how I would do it. The three hearings I would always recommend having a barrister for, if you possibly can, are the final hearing in financial remedy proceedings, a fact finding hearing in children proceedings and any appeal. When it comes to appeals, a barrister rather than a solicitor will advise you as to whether it's worth appealing, then draft all the documents and represent you at the hearing.

In other words, work out right at the start what your budget is for legal fees and how best to use that budget – and be sure to leave money aside to appeal. How much money are we talking about? As a very rough guide, if a case goes to a final hearing, a solicitor and barrister for children proceedings could cost between £20,000 and £80,000 or more – and that's for *each* proceeding (remember, the narcissist rarely stops at one application). For financial proceedings, in a straightforward case, the fees could be somewhere between £40,000 and £100,000. But the good news about financial proceedings is, when you get to the end, it really is the end. Based on these fees, you can see why many people choose to represent themselves (and why I've written this book with litigants in person in mind).

The wild variations in fees all depends on whether you have a solicitor in Wales or central London, how many court hearings you have, how complex your particular case is and how badly your ex behaves and delays. If you have a lot of assets, property abroad, businesses or trusts, your financial case will be far more complex and legal fees can run to several hundred thousand pounds.

Although I would generally recommend prioritising funding for a barrister where possible, I recognise that many people want to hire a solicitor to deal with the paperwork for them. So let's explore in more detail the process of choosing and working with a solicitor.

Choosing the right solicitor

You'll want to choose your solicitor carefully. It goes without saying that you need your legal team to be firmly on your side. So, if possible, choose a solicitor with experience of dealing with cases of abuse – or at the very least, difficult divorces.

Don't assume that someone who did a wonderful job for your friend who had an amicable divorce will be the right person for you, but if you know someone who had a difficult divorce they might be able to give you a good recommendation. Ask around or post the question on Mumsnet or other support groups. Always ask for the name of an individual solicitor, not a firm, which will have good and less good people.

You may be advised that it's important for you to have a solicitor you get on well with. I don't agree. Of course in an ideal world you would like them, but you're divorcing a narcissist and you can't get further from the ideal world than that. I worked with one client who had a solicitor with an appalling bedside manner but I couldn't fault his legal advice and concisely pertinent letters and documents, and he was cheaper than most. So she stayed with him and I gave her the support and guidance to manage all the peripheral issues, and to instruct the solicitor as necessary, which all helped to reduce her legal fees.

When you hire a solicitor, you're paying a professional a lot of money to do a specific job for you – not to be your friend; they need to remain objective and it's not helpful if they do become too emotionally involved. You want a battle-axe who can hold their own against your narcissist, not someone who's nice to have a cup of tea with. You can always work with a divorce coach or therapist alongside your solicitor to give you the emotional support you need as well as the clarity that will save you a lot of money in legal fees.

Don't be afraid to ring around and speak to a number of solicitors until you find the right one for you. When you talk to solicitors, be very clear as to what you need from a solicitor and don't be afraid to ask them lots of questions before you decide whether to instruct them. Good questions to ask at this stage are:

- What percentage of their cases settle and how many go to court?
- Of the ones that go to court, how many go to a final hearing?
- How many domestic abuse cases do they deal with? How will they protect you throughout the case?
- What experience have they had against a narcissist? What do they do differently in those cases?
- What are their strategies to contain your costs when the narcissist sends several letters a day and delays everything?
- How much is their hourly rate? A partner will charge a lot more than a very junior solicitor, or paralegal.

- Who will be doing the work on your case – will some of it be done by a junior? If so, will both solicitors be copied in to all your emails and will you be charged for them both to read them? You'll want to have the most experienced solicitor you can afford as they'll need both the confidence and the expertise to stand up to your ex. Plus, the more junior they are the less respect the narcissist will have for them.

Solicitors tend to specialise and you may need two different people if you're in court for both children and financial proceedings. Always choose a solicitor with the skill set you need. Some also specialise in high-net-worth clients – don't go to one of those if you're not hugely wealthy as you'll be at the bottom of their pile of work.

Most family law solicitors are members of Resolution, whose members agree to follow a code of practice that says they should work in a constructive and non-confrontational way. This is great and absolutely what solicitors should do in a 'normal' divorce, but it can be a big problem when you're divorcing a narcissist. Many solicitors will go through their usual procedures and write lots of letters trying to settle the case, as it won't occur to them that this is simply impossible. And you can spend thousands of pounds and waste a year of two of your life while they write their letters and the narcissist strings you both along. For some solicitors it's a matter of professional pride not to go to court and, if they do end up in court, they feel they've failed if the case goes to a final hearing. Keeping it out of court is not the right approach in every case – after all, the courts are there for a reason. These are all reasons to choose a solicitor with experience of dealing with narcissists and/or domestic abuse cases, or a solicitor who's a narcissist themself!

Some solicitors are only members of Resolution as they believe it will help them to get more work (not because they believe in the code of conduct). Such solicitors won't hesitate to issue court proceedings because they'll make more money that way. While this is definitely not the right solicitor for someone having a 'normal' divorce (because it makes a 'normal' divorce much more expensive than it needs to be) it could be just who you need for your divorce. Again, the questions above will help you assess a solicitor's attitude to going to court.

A solicitor will give you a costs estimate based on their usual success rate in settling cases, so be sure to ask for an estimate for if your case goes all the way to a final hearing.

How to get the best out of your solicitor

Hindsight is a wonderful thing.
And with that we can honestly say how much we bitterly regret all the
wasted time and money spent with our daughter's solicitor. It got us
absolutely nowhere except a huge hole in our finances.

Ultimately, solicitors are there to listen to you and then to advise you – not instruct you. You're free to accept or reject their advice. It's important to stay in control and not give away your power to your solicitor. In practice, this means don't be afraid to query the advice a solicitor gives you. Unfortunately many solicitors don't seem able to 'think outside of the box' – they just go through the set process and procedures and tell you that's how it's done, rather than considering there may be a better way in your particular case. Barristers may be more creative, strategic and solution oriented, which is yet another reason to perhaps prioritise hiring a barrister to represent you in court rather than a solicitor to do your paperwork and correspond with your ex.

Don't be afraid to tell your solicitor what you think your ex's next move might be, and how you think it's best to counter it. Most solicitors don't understand how a narcissist operates and, even if they have some idea, they don't know how your narcissist operates. You do, and your knowledge and intuition counts for as much as their legal advice. You're paying your solicitor to work for you, and sometimes you have to manage them and not let them take over. I know you're beaten down and exhausted and it's unbelievably tempting to let someone take it all over for you, but it's unlikely to work in your favour. At worst, it can be a total disaster.

My solicitor told me to be conciliatory, and don't mention the abuse. As the other side was saying I was alienating, my solicitor told me I was risking my daughter being given to him. And that his solicitor was too good to go against. In hindsight, I had terrible advice.

Unfortunately, many lawyers (that goes for solicitors and barristers) give bad advice in children cases where there's been abuse. Yes, they may tell you – quite correctly – that the courts have a culture of 'contact at all costs' and don't consider abuse of you or even the children a reason to deny the perpetrator contact. Unless he's beaten you black and blue, and sometimes even if has, or he's raped you or caused you serious injury, he'll still be assumed to be a good father and allowed to see his children without supervision. You may also be told – again quite correctly – that the courts sometimes transfer residence of the children to the abusive parent if the protective parent persists in their complaints of abuse. This is of course outrageous and abominable. But it's a fact, and one that lawyers are probably so used to that they're no longer shocked by it.

That said, I consider it bad advice not to even try to put all the abuse into evidence and ask for the protection of the court. It seems to me that often the only way to get the right result in our family courts is to keep on and on returning to court and repeating the story until finally someone listens. This dreadful culture needs to change. Fortunately we've now had the Harm Report (see Chapter 16), which I hope will begin to turn the tide – however slowly. In the meantime, your job is to protect your children as best you can, and not to accept advice that doesn't feel right to you.

Don't be afraid to instruct your solicitor not to reply to correspondence from your ex's solicitor without your explicit say so – not even to reply with the often sent 'We acknowledge receipt of your letter and are taking our client's instructions', which always seems like a complete waste of the client's money. Stay in control of your proceedings – and your costs – however tempting it may be to shut your eyes and let your solicitor deal with it all.

Finally, remember that most solicitors seem always to be very busy and won't be available to you 24/7. They'll always prioritise clients with an imminent court hearing and when you don't have one coming up you may have to wait a lot longer for them to deal with your queries or paperwork.

Working with barristers (counsel)

If you have a solicitor they will choose and instruct a barrister for you. If you're a litigant in person and you want to be represented in court, you'll have to find a barrister yourself. Most barristers now offer direct or public access, which means you don't have to go through a solicitor.

Barristers' profiles are all online – so look for one who specialises in your type of case. Where possible, it's always best if you can get a word-of-mouth recommendation, as you want someone who you know will fight for you. If you're struggling to get a recommendation from people you know, try asking support groups online, or you can always send me an email (diana@dealingwithdivorce. co.uk) letting me know which court you're in and I'll give you any suggestions I have. For a children case, particularly a fact finding hearing, you may be better off with a barrister who also does, or did, criminal work.

Barristers work from sets of chambers (barristers' offices) and, unlike solicitors, are all self-employed. This means that you and your ex could both have a barrister from the same chambers. In theory, this shouldn't be a problem. But who knows if they share a room and could overhear each other's phone conversations, or leave papers lying around that the other could see? On the other hand, they're more likely to talk to each other and could come up with some solutions. If you're not comfortable with a barrister from the same chambers as your ex's barrister, go elsewhere.

It's not uncommon for a client to feel their barrister is totally on their side, only for the barrister to have a complete change of attitude having spoken to the narcissist's counsel. The narcissist often does such a good manipulation job on his barrister that they in turn convince the other barrister the narcissist is right. Don't be afraid to ask your barrister what's been said to cause them to view your case so differently. And if you feel your barrister is no longer 100% on your side, get a new one before your next hearing. It's easier to change your barrister than your solicitor.

A barrister who won't fight for you, or who minimises the abuse or your concerns, is worse than no barrister. They don't know your case or children as well as you do, so you could do a better job yourself. Even barristers who are supposed to be there to fight for you will do anything to get the case settled and go home early. The judge wants to do the same so you may be under a lot of pressure to reach an agreement with your ex (not to mention being desperate to go home yourself). This is why it's so important for you to have a written goal for each hearing (which may be recorded on your position statement, see Chapter 10). Check whether the agreement proposed is in line with your goal, and if it isn't, insist on a proper hearing with the evidence being heard.

Sometimes barristers don't want to disagree with the judge because they have lots of cases in that court and not upsetting the judge is more important to them than doing a good job for one client. Shocking, but true.

The court time has been set aside, and you've paid for your barrister for the whole day(s) – yes, that's how it works – so don't agree at the door of the court to something that isn't in the best interests of you and your children, just because you don't want to give evidence. Giving evidence can, admittedly, be an awful experience but I've never heard anyone say they wish they'd just given in and agreed; most people want to feel they did everything possible, even if they didn't get what they want. But I do know of people who did give in and agree, and lived to regret it.

Like solicitors, barristers are busy and get booked up a long time in advance. If you're a litigant in person and not using a barrister for every hearing this can be a problem. You may not know until you receive the Cafcass report, for instance, whether or not you actually need a barrister for the next hearing. If the report is against you and you don't feel confident of the way forward, you may need to find a barrister at the last minute. However, sometimes cases settle and barristers are unexpectedly free; on the other hand, sometimes their cases don't finish when they expect them to and they may be unable to attend your hearing, even though you booked them months before. If this happens, don't panic. Barristers are used to picking up cases for each other at the last minute and should still be able to do a good job for you even if you have to ring around several chambers to find someone who's available.

Although you'll be paying a lot of money for your barrister, they're very busy and may not have enough time to thoroughly research and prepare your case. You can help them out by doing the research yourself – including the Harm Report, see Chapter 16 – and asking them to use what you find.

Finally, even when you have a barrister, always take a friend or relative with you to court hearings. They won't be allowed in court with you but you usually spend more time outside the courtroom than in it. Your barrister is likely to spend a lot of time away from you talking to your ex or his barrister, and it's not good for your nerves if you're left sitting on your own. More importantly, your friend can keep firmly in mind what you want to achieve, both at that hearing and overall, and can hold your feet to the fire when you're tempted to cave in. And if you're not sure what to do, they can be a valuable sounding board for you – a second opinion after your barrister's given theirs.

Judges and magistrates (and what to call them)

I want to swear but will reserve it until I am alone.
Women shouldn't have to put up with this kind of treatment.
It was totally biased and sexist and 100% mean.

There are a few levels of judges sitting in the family court. Your children case may well start before magistrates, also known as JPs (justices of the peace), which are the first tier. Magistrates are trained, but not legally qualified. Also, they're not paid – they're members of the local community who volunteer their time. They sit with a legal advisor (previously called justices' clerks) who is a solicitor or barrister who advises them on the law.

In a contested hearing, there should always be three magistrates, as two may not be able to agree. But in directions hearings, there are often only two magistrates – and some directions hearings are done by a legal advisor alone. If you're not represented by a barrister, or you're giving evidence and have to address the bench (i.e. the magistrates) you just speak to the chair – the one who's sitting in the middle, or the one who's doing all the talking – and call them 'sir' or 'madam'. You may also hear magistrates called 'your worships'.

Magistrates' courts are sometimes different courts in a different part of town (or even a different town) from the county courts, where the judges sit. More modern courts are often in a combined court centre.

At the next tier above magistrates are district judges. Financial remedy cases in divorce are always heard by a judge, who will probably be a district judge (DJ), or a deputy district judge (DDJ). You may also encounter a recorder who is a part-time circuit judge. All judges were previously solicitors or barristers – and a deputy is a part-time judge who is either still working elsewhere as a solicitor or barrister the rest of the time, or is a retired judge. Like magistrates, district judges are addressed as 'sir' or 'madam'.

If your case is more complex it may be heard by a circuit judge, which is the next tier up again. Formally known as His/Her Honour Judge (HHJ), you address circuit judges as 'your honour'. And then above that, if you're in the High Court, or Court of Appeal, the judges are addressed as 'my lord' or 'my lady'.

Many children cases start before magistrates but they're not lawyers and they probably don't have as much training in domestic abuse as the judges are supposed to have. So if your case is complex, with allegations of abuse, you should ask the magistrates to transfer it up to a judge. It's also possible, though very unusual, for a case to be transferred down.

I work as a McKenzie Friend, I see good and bad stories but they're not mine to share. My own journey through court was horrible, I had good and bad judges.

I started off with district judges, until one turned to me (Cafcass safeguarding letter stated no contact, Marac in place, scored at high risk of further violence) after the father asked if what had been said meant he would miss Christmas with the children "that's up to Miss X". I stated I would be following the recommendations in the safeguarding letter. " There is only a little bit of abuse here, these proceedings will end in contact, won't they Cafcass officer?" she said. "I couldn't possibly say until we have conducted an investigation." The Judge: "well I see no need why this should be with me, this can be dealt with by magistrates".

Anyway, luckily that Judge was very wrong. In my case it was the legal adviser who was an absolute star; he saw through my ex. He corrected magistrates, questioned and probed.

Cafcass didn't do a good job, but it wasn't bad either. I've seen Cafcass recognise an abuser and make it very clear in their reports. Then I see the meek ones like mine who almost seemed scared to call out a man. She held back from forming robust opinions. She had an opportunity to clarify a lot to the magistrates, but instead she remained neutral.

How your case goes depends very much upon the judges you get along the way. Unfortunately, the legal profession is an attractive one for narcissists and you may come across a personality disordered judge who is likely to favour your ex. But even the good judges can get things wrong too, because they can be bullied and manipulated by a narcissist. Judges are lawyers, not psychologists, and they have no training in personality disorders or PTSD. They don't recognise the difficulties a victim has in the witness box and are easily swayed by the smooth talking narcissist. They have no comprehension that someone who sends 50 messages an hour is likely to be dangerous. As a result, they get things wrong in children cases over and over again. And even if they were to realise they'd been manipulated and got it wrong, few judges are likely to want to admit this. Some would rather continue to accept the narcissist's narrative. But others are good:

A judge warned the perp and his mother with a non-mol over their behaviour and asked me whether I really wanted him in my child's life. Three years later, another judge questioned the social worker on whether she'd even bothered reading the court order or bundle as she'd totally ignored the fact find which found 7/10 findings against the perpetrator - who made concessions but then went on to deny any abuse for S7. The judge ordered the social worker to go away and do an addendum. He also had a go at the perp's solicitor about her client. He wasn't happy at all. But I'm still in proceedings ...

Judges say they don't want to make decisions about the minutiae of family life and parents should decide between themselves things like the time and place for handovers. They don't seem to understand that if parents could make those decisions they wouldn't be in court in the first place. The narcissist has no interest in agreeing any such detail – where's the fun (i.e. drama, chaos and control) in that?

Judges are tasked with applying the law, not punishing someone because they cheated or abused the other person. It's not their job to say who was right and who was wrong, but to work out the best way forward. But they have difficulty in seeing what's before their eyes, particularly that some people use the court system to continue their abuse of their ex.

The first step in improving the family courts is a lot more education and training for magistrates and judges. Although no amount of training is going to change the most dreadful of the judges who simply aren't fit to sit in the family court at all. Such judges are protected by the outdated privacy law, which makes it a contempt of court to publish (that includes on Facebook!) information about what happened in court. This is meant primarily to protect children from publicity about their cases, but it also works in the favour of bad judges.

The following case demonstrates the huge value that good judges can bring to difficult children proceedings.

> *My ex-husband was all smiles one minute and ranting the next; he cancelled contact on one occasion due to his concern at not being able to stop himself 'kicking off' in front of Jamie.*
>
> *But when he told me he was 'in a dark place with me, wanted bad things to happen to me, had terrible depression, was going through an emotional breakdown, was seeing a counsellor, could understand why these men kill their wives and kids, had a lot of anger welling up inside him for a long time, it was a f.....g game and I wasn't going to win, and that he needed to use Jamie as a bargaining tool' I contacted my solicitor and an emergency hearing was made.*
>
> *The judge that day happened to be a Crown Court judge on loan to the family court. That judge showed great concern for my son's safety and ordered contact to be supervised. I felt extremely happy with the court's decision and the whole approach by that particular judge as he seemed to be only concerned with the safety of the child. His comment to my ex-husband at the time was, and I will never forget it, 'I am sure you are a reasonable man, however, in these circumstances, reasonable people can do unreasonable things'. My barrister commented to me afterwards that the judge would have experienced cases of child abduction and filicide and that is the reason she felt he took it so seriously. I truly believe that if I was not fortunate enough to have had a judge with such experience as he that day, that the outcome would have been very different.*
>
> *Jamie has direct contact with his father every other year (his father's choice), and once a month on Skype. I feel lucky that my ex lives the other side of the world and I don't have to deal with the usual 'every other weekend' scenario.*

Despite the contact being supervised, my ex told his son that he is disgusting, a liar, rude, mean, not nice, ignorant and despicable (explaining to his four-year-old child that it meant horrible). When Jamie responded that he wasn't, his father just kept repeating it and failed to recognise that Jamie was getting increasingly upset by this. He told Jamie that he owns him, his mother is a liar, and not to make him angry (by not cleaning his teeth quickly enough). On another occasion he told Jamie during a Skype contact that he would take away all of his Christmas presents if he refused to speak to him the following week. Jamie was understandably distraught and needed lots of reassurance from me that would not happen. Jamie asked me after one contact if he was 'going to live with Daddy in Australia' and said that he didn't want to and pleaded with me not to leave him. He became very clingy, upset and needed lots of reassurance that this would not happen. My ex appears to have no capacity to recognise the damage he is doing to his son. I do not believe he deliberately sets out to harm him but when I highlighted the distress this caused to Jamie, as he had failed to recognise it for himself, he just shrugged.

He continued to have emotional outbursts, accusing me of poisoning Jamie against him, shouting, and being angry and aggressive towards me, causing Jamie anxiety, upset and distress and leading to me ending contact on one occasion. When he was just four, Jamie asked his father 'Why are you being mean to my mummy?'

Jamie continued to display distress during Skype contact, asking me to take it away, hiding behind my legs, a table, boxes or leaving the room. When asked if he would like to talk to Daddy he mainly replied 'I don't want to' or 'No thank you Mummy' and tried to turn the webcam around or close the lid. As he got older he simply refused to enter the room where Skype was set up and got frustrated and angry with me for continuously asking him if he would like to speak to Daddy. On the few occasions that he did speak, it was for just a few minutes before he either requested me to end the call or simply removed himself. I tried telephone contact as an alternative, which unfortunately was also unsuccessful, with Jamie displaying the same distress. His father witnessed all of the above and simply told me that I should force Jamie to do it, which I refused and advised that this would only give Jamie a negative association to his father. Jamie did not want to use Skype or telephone as a method of contact with any other family members either and I felt that he was not alone in that as a young child.

The next year his father came over, contact took place at the contact centre (supervised). After a couple of days Jamie became upset, crying and pleading that he did not want to go. He clung to my husband's legs and became angry with me when I told him he had to go. He was only persuaded after lots of reassurance from myself and my husband. While he does have fun with his father during his visits, he also suffered a lot of distress, became withdrawn, unsettled and lost confidence until the visits were over.

Despite his limited time here, my ex was late for contact, rearranged agreed contact at short notice, reduced the agreed contact time, ended contact early stating that he had had enough, and missed contact completely stating that he had either forgotten, was asleep or was too busy.

My ex continued to show that he is untrustworthy, unreliable, unpredictable, unstable, has displayed an inability to empathise with Jamie, and has questionable motives for contact. I feel that his motives towards contact with Jamie are about 'winning a game' rather than what is in Jamie's best interests and above all I fear for Jamie's emotional, psychological and physical welfare.

Five years after the first order, my ex applied to court for unsupervised contact. I was advised by my solicitor and barrister that I had very little chance of the judge agreeing to continue the contact as supervised. The barrister told me that judges systematically grant unsupervised contact to fathers who have done 'far worse' than my ex-husband had, including sexual abuse! I was shocked but sadly now know this to be true. I was advised that the best way to stay in control of the situation was to agree to unsupervised contact but request conditions.

For example:

- *The father shall not make or display any threatening behaviour, written, verbal or physical to Jamie, the mother or mother's husband.*
- *All locations for contact are to be agreed prior to any contact.*
- *The father is to be reliable and punctual.*
- *If during contact Jamie wishes to talk to his mother or requests to return home, the father will facilitate the same.*
- *The father is not to say or write anything derogatory to Jamie about the mother or her husband.*
- *The father shall not include his partner at contacts and if he seeks to introduce a new partner he shall notify the mother in advance.*

All 12 of my requested conditions were agreed by the judge. He also made two specific issue orders: one to continue the direction to the UK and Australian Passport Agencies not to issue a new passport for Jamie without leave of the court and the other to change Jamie's surname to double-barrelled. Jamie had become very upset because I had remarried and had another child, leaving him with a different surname. He said even the dog was made by someone else but had the same name as the rest of the family and he didn't want to be different. The Judge agreed to the name change stating that children did not like to feel different, which completely contradicted the recommendation of the Cafcass officer who had stated that we should 'celebrate differences'.

The contact between Jamie and his dad has improved with Jamie getting older (he is now 13). My relationship with my ex has continued to be strained and I recently passed over all communication regarding arrangements for Skype contact, etc. to be direct with Jamie, which seems to be working okay and is a huge relief for me.

In all I attended 13 court hearings with my ex-husband relating to contact, financial remedy and divorce.

I had to apply to the court myself last year for permission to apply to the passport agency to obtain a new passport for Jamie, which shows that the order made in 2010 worked. When I spoke to the judge at the family court she stated that she had never heard of such a condition being placed in an order. This again confirmed to me just how lucky I was back in 2010 to have had the judge I did.

CHAPTER 10:
LITIGANTS IN PERSON
– SPECIAL CONSIDERATIONS
FOR REPRESENTING YOURSELF
(SOME OR ALL OF THE TIME)

It should be clear by now that this book is all about strategies – how to get through your separation, cope with court proceedings and deal with your ex, all without losing your sanity. I therefore take a more strategic look at being a litigant in person. For a detailed how-to, step-by-step guide to navigating the family court without representation, I recommend *The Family Court Without a Lawyer* by Lucy Reed.

Having read about what it's like to work with a solicitor, it should be clear that there are advantages and disadvantages to *not* having a solicitor acting for you. Obviously you save yourself a huge amount of money. You also stay in control of your case; whilst a solicitor should check with you before they send anything out, they don't always and they might do or write things you're unhappy with. What's more, if you're the applicant in the case, and if your ex has a solicitor and you don't, then his solicitor will have to do some of the work that would ordinarily fall to your solicitor, if you had one. In essence, some of the paperwork for court is always the job of the applicant – but if the applicant doesn't have a solicitor and the respondent does, the respondent gets the job. This means your ex's solicitor would have to prepare the court bundle, draft letters to experts and draft court orders. All at your ex's expense! (The flip side of this, of course, is if your ex is the applicant in a court case and he doesn't have a solicitor but you do, this work will fall to your solicitor, at your expense…)

A solicitor, especially if they're following the Resolution code of conduct, will always write a 'letter before action' to your ex before issuing any court proceedings. A narcissist doesn't usually deserve this courtesy and it may give him an advantage knowing what you're planning. As a litigant in person you can just go ahead and issue the court proceedings with no warning, which may fit better with your strategy.

You may be happy handling the paperwork yourself but feel unable to represent yourself in court, in which case you can instruct a barrister to represent you. If you can't afford to be represented at every hearing you may have to choose the hearings you most need help with. As I said in Chapter 9, the three hearings I would always recommend having a barrister for, if you possibly can, are the final hearing in financial remedy proceedings, a fact finding hearing in children proceedings and any appeal.

Whether you're working with a barrister some of the time, or none of the time, this chapter will help you represent yourself with confidence.

Don't be scared by letters from your ex's solicitor

Solicitors' letters can be a source of huge anxiety but it's important not to be intimidated by them. They're just words on some headed notepaper, which means your ex has paid a lot of money for them.

Your ex's solicitor may try and tell you what to do, and issue all sorts of threats about what will happen if you don't, but remember that only a court can order you to do something you don't want to do, not a solicitor. Ask yourself what will happen if you don't do what they say, or don't do it within their time limit. And whether that would really be so bad – sometimes they might actually be doing you a favour, such as issuing court proceedings when you can't afford the fee yourself.

Solicitors often threaten litigants in person with costs orders. In which case, read the letter carefully; what it should say is that their client will apply for an order for costs against you. Well he can apply for anything he wants, but getting it is another matter entirely. Costs are very rarely ordered in children proceedings so you can take those threats with a big pinch of salt. Costs are ordered in financial proceedings, but not nearly as often as applications for them are threatened.

Don't be afraid to fight back. Look at their website and see if it says the solicitor is a member of Resolution. If so, you can tell them when you write back that their threats, rudeness, disrespect, etc. towards you are against the Resolution code of conduct and if they write to you like that again you'll report them to Resolution.

If a letter from your ex's solicitor has made you anxious, get a friend or relative to help you pick it apart. Make sure you really understand what they are saying between all the threats, accusations and legalese. Rewrite it with just the questions that really have to be answered, and if there aren't any, don't reply. Don't be drawn into all the allegations against you – again, you can just say 'all your allegations are denied'. In fact, the shorter your reply the better – treat your ex's nonsense with the contempt it deserves and don't give them anything they can use against you later.

18 months after the final hearing, his solicitor sent me a seven-day demand to disclose our address – he was suggested to be within his rights to know where his daughter was and that she was safe. I duly wrote back reminding him I had filed a Form C8 with the court to keep our address confidential, and that our residence had not only been signed off by Cafcass and social services as suitable, the social worker had then spent over 12 months visiting us fortnightly so that should have presented him with enough evidence to know that she was safe and living in appropriate conditions.

Fourteen days later I received a second seven-day demand for the address with a 'do it or else' threat. I sent this to the police domestic violence unit and spoke to the highest manager I could in the Looked After Children Team at social services. She advised me that as far as social services were concerned, he would need to apply to the court to have address disclosure and they would not support his claim.

The police also suggested I quote them and timestamp the conversation, allowing his solicitor to contact them if needed. They agreed with social services and said they would support a non-disclosure in court too. They again for the umpteenth time suggested a restraining order too may be appropriate.

I sent my response back to his solicitor and also pointed out that an email address that we set up for our daughter to be in contact with him the month we split up was still active and open and he had never contacted her on it since she asked him not to in 2015. My parents also live at the same address they have for 24 years and have the same phone number and I have the same email address and phone number so he could contact us all at any time without the need for my actual home address. I also advised him that whilst no court case was live I would no longer be responding to any further email from them (his solicitor liked to email me on a Friday at 5pm with outrageous demands/questions/statements) unless it was a court order.

I've heard nothing since.

Before you appear in court, prepare your paperwork well

I've heard barristers say that litigants in person often do a better job than lawyers in children cases, so prepare well and you have every reason to be confident in your abilities.

But it's really important that your paperwork is in order, and the best it can be. If you can go to court with a good position statement and maybe a chronology, you won't have to say as much to the judge in court – always a good idea when you're nervous. I talk more about writing a good position statement later in this chapter, and chronologies in Chapter 14.

Please make sure that you give a copy to your ex of absolutely everything you send to the court, or hand in to the judge. This is a very basic rule and not obeying it is likely to cause you problems further down the line. If you don't want your ex to see it, don't use it.

Be kind to yourself – you will make mistakes

Solicitors and barristers spend years learning the law and gaining experience in court. In contrast, you're coming to it afresh, with no knowledge of the law, and usually at one of the worst times in your life when your confidence is likely to be at a low ebb. This means you're going to get things wrong, misunderstand things, and miss things. Try to see it as an occupational hazard. Although I've had clients get upset when things have gone a bit wonky or they've made a mistake, so far not one has said, 'I wish I'd spent £2,000 on a barrister for that hearing as this wouldn't have happened'.

It's important to keep things in perspective and to ask yourself how far off course (from your goal for the end of your proceedings) this error has taken you (probably not very). Then turn your attention to how you can get back on track.

When you're writing to your ex's solicitor – and when you're in court for that matter – don't be afraid to ask for what you want. You're not a lawyer so you may not know whether you're entitled to ask for it or not, but don't worry – you'll soon be told if you're not entitled! So if you think, for example, that police records, GP records or even a psychological assessment would be helpful to you, go ahead and ask for it. As long as you remain calm, polite and respectful – and just apologise if you do make a mistake – you won't go far wrong. (Court staff aren't allowed to give you legal advice, so they can't tell you whether it's a good idea for you to ask for something. But if you need to make an application for it they should be able to tell you which form you need to use.)

My advice is to read and learn as much as you can about family court proceedings – the Resources section at the end of this book will help.

Give yourself credit where credit's due

There's no doubt that it's a tough job being a litigant in person and it takes courage to go to court unrepresented. Legalese isn't anyone's first language and for quite a few of my clients English isn't either and I'm full of admiration for what they all achieve in court. As well as saving yourself a lot of money, you'll discover skills you didn't know you had by self-representing. It will give you a big confidence boost and it's something you can always feel very proud of. And hopefully some of the skills will be transferable to whatever you go on to do next. Several survivors have gone on to be McKenzie Friends (more on these coming up) as, having learned so much about the court process themselves, they're in a good position to help others.

Dealing with your ex's barrister

When you first meet your ex's barrister at court, don't immediately adopt an attitude of hostility. It's hard to believe, but sometimes they may be as much on your side as their client's. In any event, they are supposed, as officers of the court, to help litigants in person with court procedure, so if you can get along with them it will make the proceedings a lot easier for you. And don't be alarmed if they then adopt a very different attitude towards you in the courtroom – their client is paying a lot of money and feels entitled to a good performance!

That said, I'm afraid some barristers are just downright rude and nasty, so if that proves to be the case you need to toughen up quickly and not take any **** from them. Whenever there's a lawyer for one side, the judge expects the parties to have spoken before going into court, but if you get nothing but rudeness and bullying you can refuse to speak to them, and if necessary tell the judge why.

Stand your ground in court

Judges aren't keen on litigants in person but they've had to get used to them, and better at dealing with them. Since legal aid was cut in 2012 there are now over 85% more unrepresented people in court. Judge's responses to litigants in person vary enormously – some will bend over backwards to help you and to be seen to be fair, while others can be dictatorial bullies.

This means you need to be prepared to work hard to get the judge to listen to you. For example, if your ex's barrister is trying to persuade the judge to do something that you don't want and can't afford, or if they're arguing against something that you do need, stand your ground. If necessary, keep repeating yourself like a stuck record until the judge acknowledges that s/he has heard what you've said – s/he may not agree with you, but at least you will have been heard.

Sometimes it may feel as if the judge and your ex's barrister are having a private conversation in a foreign language. Don't hesitate to ask for anything you don't understand to be explained to you and/or to ask the judge to slow down so that you can understand and take a note.

Don't go alone when you're going it alone

If you can't afford a barrister or prefer to represent yourself, do take a professional McKenzie Friend to court, if you can afford one. There's more on McKenzie Friends coming up next.

I'd also suggest you take a friend, or your new partner if you have one, too. They won't be allowed into the courtroom, but they can walk from the car park into the building with you if you're worried about bumping into your ex, go and get a coffee for you if the wait to go into court is interminable, and make sure the coast is clear, or go with you, if you need to go to the loo. They can help you with any decisions that need to be made, help you check the order over, or just be there to hold your hand. Remember, you need all the support you can get.

McKenzie Friends

I'd always recommend having a McKenzie Friend to help you in court. (In case you're wondering where the name came from, the right to a McKenzie Friend was established in the case of McKenzie v McKenzie in 1970.) A McKenzie Friend can't speak for you, but they will sit next to you and take notes, and they can quietly prompt you with what to say. Judges and barristers can talk pretty fast, and in legalese, and it can be hard to follow everything when you're not familiar with the procedure, and even more so when the hearing is by phone. So it's important to have someone with you to take notes as you can't hope to note everything yourself while you're trying to put forward your own case.

If you're terribly nervous, tongue-tied or distressed, some judges will allow a McKenzie Friend to speak for you, at least in a limited way to assist the court. It's always worth asking. As a victim of abuse, you may also – whether you are represented or not – ask the judge to allow you to have a friend or supporter in court with you. This could be an IDVA, support worker or an Intermediary (someone who supports vulnerable people in court proceedings). It needs to be someone who hasn't been involved with your ex and who understands that the proceedings are confidential.

There are professional McKenzie Friends who are not lawyers but have experience in the family court and of course charge very much less than lawyers. You can search online for a McKenzie Friend (but be careful who you choose – some of them are on a crusade of their own and not child-focused). Failing that, drop me an email (diana@dealingwithdivorce.co.uk) letting me know which court you're in and I'll tell you if I have a recommendation.

Alternatively you can take a friend, relative or work colleague who won't charge you. While there are professional McKenzie Friends, anyone can act as a McKenzie Friend in court. You'll need to either inform the court and your ex/their solicitor in advance of the hearing, telling them who your proposed McKenzie Friend is, or you can just turn up at court with them and ask the judge if you can have a McKenzie Friend with you. If possible, find someone your ex doesn't know as the other party does have a right to object to a McKenzie Friend. And given how objectionable narcissists are, you can assume your ex will object. However, they'll have to have a good reason for their objection to be upheld, as the normal procedure is to allow a McKenzie Friend. That said, if it's someone who's been very involved in your relationship, their involvement may be refused.

If you've not followed everything properly during the hearing it'll be hard for you to check the draft order. This is another reason to take a McKenzie Friend with you – if they've got a good note of all that was said you're on much stronger ground to object to things that shouldn't be in the order, and to ask for other things to be included or for something to be changed.

Another advantage of having a McKenzie Friend with you at court is to stand up for you outside court if your ex's barrister is trying to bully you into agreeing to something before you go in to see the judge.

How to write a statement for the court

Statements are, as the name suggests, written statements given to the court before (or occasionally on the day of) a hearing. If you have a solicitor they will write your statements for you (and your barrister will write a position statement), based on the information you give them. If not, you'll have to write your own statements and send them to the court and your ex's solicitor (or directly to your ex if they are also a litigant in person).

There are two types of statement you may need to write:

- A **position statement** is a short statement that sets out what you want to happen and what you are asking the court to order, i.e. it is your position in relation to what other people are saying they want or should happen. This may be sent in advance of the hearing (certainly if it's a remote hearing) or can be handed in on the day. You can write a position statement before any hearing in the family court – financial, children, etc. – and you don't need permission from the court.

- A **witness statement**, usually just referred to as a 'statement', is your evidence for the court and is usually longer than a position statement. You can only write a witness statement when the court gives you permission, and you would write it before a contested hearing instead of taking the oath and telling the court what you say has happened. It should be sent to the court by the specified date, which will always be in advance of the next hearing.

- However, in an urgent case such as to suspend contact or to prevent an abduction or school move, you can write a statement and take it to court with you. You can ask the judge for permission to file it with the court, which is more likely to be granted if you've sent the statement to your ex in advance.

Before you write anything for the court, ask yourself what you want the court to do. If you're not clear about what you want from the court, or fail to state it clearly, the court will assume you don't have a strong opinion and is likely to do what the narcissist wants. He'll always have an opinion!

Let's look at each type of statement in more detail.

Position statements

It's helpful to the court if you write a position statement before every hearing because it tells the court what you want to happen. And if you're a litigant in person who is nervous about speaking in court, a position statement is especially helpful because you'll need to say a lot less on the day.

Basic rules for formatting your position statement are:

- At the top of the first page you must include your case number as well as your name and the other party's name.
- Next, centre and underline the heading: 'Position statement of the [Applicant] [Respondent] for hearing on [date] at [time].'
- Then you can type your statement.

A position statement should be short – three pages at the most. The shorter it is, the more likely the judge is to have time to read it so keep it concise and clear. It should not contain your evidence – see witness statements below – just what you want the court to order at this hearing. If you know what you want as a final outcome of the proceedings you can state that too – for example, 'I would like an order that the children live with me and have supervised contact with their father'.

For a financial case you'll set out the issues still in dispute and what you want the court to do about it. For example, your ex may be saying he wants a professional valuation of your home and you might say you oppose it as being an unnecessary expense when estate agents will value it for free.

Your position statement may also need to respond to what other people are suggesting the court do at the hearing. For instance, before your first children hearing you should receive a safeguarding letter from Cafcass (see Chapter 14), in which they will usually suggest how they think the court should proceed. In your position statement you can say whether you agree with their suggestions. And if you don't, you can either suggest some other way forward and/or ask for any extra directions that work for you.

If you are raising allegations of abuse towards you and/or your child, you should already have sent a Form C1A to the court (see child arrangement orders in Chapter 14). In your position statement, you then need to ask the court to consider Practice Direction 12J (also covered in Chapter 14) and ask for a fact finding hearing if your ex is denying the abuse.

It's really important to be clear in your mind what you want the court to order *before* you start your statement, although in practice you'll write this at the end of your position statement.

So how do you start your position statement? At the beginning you need to give a few brief details of what has happened to bring you to this point, and to explain why you want a particular court order.

When writing position statements for hearings involving an abusive ex, you need to consider carefully what to put in and what's better left out. If you're trying to get a fact finding hearing then you probably need to throw the book at them and describe the abuse (in general terms, not in the detail you'll put in a witness statement). But if you're further down the line and the abuse has been dealt with in a previous hearing, it may not be wise to antagonise the judge or your ex by going over old ground again, especially if you're on the back foot at that point. Basically, think carefully about what you want to achieve and the best way of getting that – and if the abuse isn't relevant to what you want to achieve, it is perhaps best left out. Unlike you, the judge is not usually interested in the truth, just the outcome. This is why you need a clear strategy for court.

Your case will shift and morph as the months go on and it's really important to take the time to work out what your current position is both for the final outcome and the next hearing before you start writing your position statement. It's a harsh fact that the court is not interested in how you feel about what's happened to you and your children and somehow you need to get out of your heart and into your head before you start writing. And if at all possible, get someone else to read your statement through before you submit it, to check that it's clear what you're asking for and why, and that there's no emotion in the statement, just hard facts.

To close out your position statement, just write a clear description of what you want the court to order and add your name at the end.

When you're done, email your position statement to the court (google the correct email address for your court) and to your ex or to their solicitor if they have one. If you've not managed to send your position statement in advance, give it to the usher as soon as you arrive and ask them to give it to the judge. Give a copy to your ex or their barrister as soon as you can. And if it's a remote hearing – i.e. by phone or video – be sure to check right at the start that the judge has received your position statement.

Rights of Women have an example of a position statement on their website (see Resources) and Google will offer more help if you need it.

Witness statements

You can only write a witness statement (again, often referred to just as 'a statement') if the court gives you permission to do so. The exception to this is if you're applying for a non-molestation and/or occupation order (Chapter 13), in which case you will need to send a statement with your application. Otherwise, your court order will give you a date by when you have to send your statement to the court and to your ex (or their solicitor if they have one). Your court order may also set out conditions for your statement, such as how many pages you're allowed to write, so be sure to check your order before you start.

Exhibits are not included in the number of pages allowed so you can usually attach as many pages as you want at the end of your statement (number each exhibit with your initials first – for example, VG/1, VG/2, etc. and mark the initials and number on each document). Exhibits could be emails, or a report or letter from a third party, such as the police or your GP.

Basic rules for formatting your witness statement are:

- Your statement should have your case number at the top, and be set out the same as for a position statement.
- The heading will be 'Statement of [your name]'.
- The introduction will read: 'I, [name], of [address], make this statement following the order of [date of order].' If you have an order to keep your address confidential, you can say 'of an address I wish to keep confidential'.
- After that your paragraphs need to be numbered.

Witness statements are the most important statements in family proceedings as they are where you give your evidence. In other words, instead of you telling the court verbally what has happened, you describe it in your statement. So, if you have a contested hearing your statement is instead of you giving evidence, and you will just be cross-examined on the contents of your statement by your ex or their barrister. If your ex is saying something very different to you, the judge has to decide which of you they believe. It's therefore important that you spend as much time as you can (at least a week or two) to make your statement the best it can be, so don't leave it until the last minute. You also need a night or two to sleep on it and come back to it to make sure it's all correct, you haven't forgotten anything, and that it reads as well and succinctly as possible.

Always bear in mind how little time the judge has, and the shorter your statement is, the more likely it is to be read. If you start rambling on about things which may be important to you, or have angered or upset you, but which don't help the judge to decide the issues before the court, you weaken your case.

Your statement is just that – yours – so it should be written in your own words, in the first person, as if you were speaking it in court.

In children proceedings a lot of your statement will be about what has happened in the past – the behaviour of your ex, the effect on the children, etc. – as well as what is happening now and (usually) what you want to happen next. Be as specific as you can with dates, exact words used and what was said or done as a result of what happened.

Keep in mind that, in children proceedings, the judge will rarely have concern or sympathy for what you've been through or the abuse you've suffered, so keep the focus of your statement on the children instead. For example, after writing 'The children were in the kitchen when he pushed me so hard I fell over and caught my head on the edge of the table', instead of saying 'I had a huge cut just above my eye which bled so much it made me feel sick.' you could say 'As I lay on the floor I could see the horror on the children's faces as the cut to my eye was bleeding so much, before they both burst into tears. They were inconsolable and I couldn't get them to bed that night. They were subdued and clingy for 10 days afterwards and seemed frightened and frozen in the presence of their father.'

It's important not to get bogged down in defending yourself against his bogus allegations when your case is about his behaviour and the effect of it on your child. He'll try to deflect everyone's attention from that and put it on to you. Don't fall for it. Just put 'I deny [his] version of events' and carry on with yours. And when it comes to countering what your ex wants, deal briefly with your ex's position in your statement; this is what he says, and this is what I think about that. For example, you could say something like 'The 50/50 shared care that he wants won't work because it needs parents to communicate and co-operate well together.' Keep this free of your emotion.

If your ex is a narcissist another reason for keeping your emotion out of your statement is not to give him any further 'supply' so reread it to make sure it passes the 'grey rock' test (Chapter 5). Your emotional reaction keeps him feeling powerful and in control so when you leave that out you take back your power and help to derail him.

Just as with a position statement, in the witness statement, after setting out your evidence, you simply state the order you want, and why you want that order. For example, 'I want the court to order that the children live with me and for the time they spend with their father to be supervised in a contact centre.'

At the end of a witness statement (but not a position statement) you need to add a statement of truth, as follows:

'I believe that the facts stated in this witness statement are true. I understand that proceedings for contempt of court may be brought against anyone who makes, or causes to be made, a false statement in a document verified by a statement of truth without an honest belief in its truth.'

Finally, you need to sign and date the statement, which again is not necessary for a position statement.

Always check your order

The draft order – i.e. the written document recording the decisions made by the court – is another area where things can go wrong. It's not impossible, but it's very hard to get an order changed once it's been made, so you need to check it very carefully.

If both parties are litigants in person the judge will write up the order, and it will then be typed up by court staff and posted to you for your records. This may take two or three weeks to reach you, so do make sure that you've made a note of any dates in the following few weeks when anything has to be done by.

If one party is represented, their lawyer will be expected to do the judge's job for them and draft the order (which may be done then and there or later). They should allow the unrepresented party (i.e. you) to check the order before it's submitted to the judge. But not all of them do, and they sometimes try to sneak things into the order that haven't been agreed, or ordered by the judge. And because the judge is busy, and (mis)places a lot of trust in lawyers, these things slip through the net.

So never leave court without either checking the draft order first, or, if it's going to be drafted later, having the barrister say, preferably in court in front of the judge, that it will be sent to you for approval before being sent to the court. And make sure you have the barrister's email address, so you can chase them up if the draft order isn't sent to you.

When you get the draft order, check it very carefully. If there's anything in it you're not 100% clear about, ask the barrister to explain it. Don't be afraid to query anything, or ask them to add anything that was said in your favour but has now been omitted, or to take out anything that wasn't said and has now been included.

But preferably don't leave court without having agreed the order because otherwise by the time it's drafted the narcissist will have decided it doesn't suit him and will haggle over every last detail – in which case, it'll take days or weeks to get it finally agreed. Also note that there will often be 'recitals' at the beginning of the order. These record the position prior to the order being made, so any agreements you reached before going into court, or maybe things the judge said at the hearing. Make sure these really do reflect the whole situation and are not just slanted towards your ex to give him the advantage going forward. Sometimes barristers will try to slip things in that weren't agreed or ordered at all. Check very carefully both what is there, and what isn't.

CHAPTER 11:

DIVORCE PROCEEDINGS (AND HOW THEY FIT IN WITH CHILDREN AND FINANCIAL PROCEEDINGS)

The Divorce, Dissolution and Separation Act 2020 is due to come into force on 6 April 2022, bringing in the long-awaited 'no fault' divorce. After that there will be no more divorce petitions based on 'unreasonable behaviour', adultery, or two years' separation, and the process will be much easier for litigants in person. The language will also be updated so that a decree nisi will become a 'conditional order' and a decree absolute will become a 'final order'.

It will, however, take longer to get a divorce as there will be at least 20 weeks between the petition (application for divorce) and the conditional order, and then another six weeks before you can get the final order.

Overall, though, the introduction of 'no fault' divorce is a huge improvement for people divorcing narcissists. Although it really doesn't matter at all what's said about someone's behaviour in a divorce petition, survivors were regularly outraged to read the lies told about them in petitions and find their ex had projected many of their own narcissistic traits onto them. But under the new law, people get divorced without having to describe the behaviour of their ex. In other words, you can get the divorce part of your separation – i.e. the legal dissolution of your marriage – completed with much less mess. Which is good, because the children and financial arrangements are messy enough, so you'll want to save your strength for those.

In what order would you apply for divorce? Well, if you need a financial order from the court, you have to issue divorce proceedings before you can make a financial application. In which case, the divorce needs to be applied for early on. But if you're just going through children proceedings and/or injunctions – so no financial proceedings – then it doesn't really matter when the divorce is started.

You can apply for your divorce online on the government website and the form is pretty straightforward. You don't need a solicitor to do this for you – save your money for when you really do need legal advice or representation.

CHAPTER 12:
FINANCIAL REMEDY PROCEEDINGS

Children proceedings would ideally come before financial proceedings – if there isn't enough money for both parents to have adequate accommodation for the children, deciding where the children are going to live is usually a priority. But there's nothing to stop either party issuing either financial or children proceedings whenever they want. Indeed, you may want to get in first and issue a financial application to distract him from using the children as a weapon (assuming he only wants to fight you on one issue at a time).

In other words, you may or may not have been through children proceedings before you get to the financial stuff. But since the children proceedings can rumble on for many years, let's cover the financial proceedings first.

The majority of people getting divorced don't ask the court to decide their financial settlement. They want to be fair and they sort it out over the kitchen table, go to mediation or get solicitors to negotiate an agreement for them (circle back to Chapter 8). Then a solicitor puts their agreement into a draft order and sends it to the court for a judge to approve. And that's it, their financial settlement is sorted.

Usually, none of that is possible with a narcissist and you will end up in court sooner or later. I normally advise sooner; why waste another year of your life (and maybe thousands of pounds in costs too) just to give your ex more narcissistic supply while he strings you along? Just issue your divorce petition and then your Form A (the application form which starts the process of requesting a financial order from the court) as soon as you can. Although you are starting the process of asking the court to decide the financial settlement for you, this doesn't stop you mediating or coming to an agreement between yourselves before then – but it does keep the narcissist within a timeframe and stop them from threatening you with court and/or stringing you along.

Don't be afraid of financial proceedings

If you're a mother who's had a bad experience in children proceedings in the family court, you may be dreading having to go to court again in financial proceedings, but they're rarely as bad. The judge might still be rude and disrespectful to you, and take the side of your narcissistic ex, but they won't go as far wrong as they do in children proceedings. There's a limit to what your ex can lie about when the figures are all there in black and white. (Well, some of them at least!)

There's also a limit to how unfair the judge can be to you without being appealed, and they'll want to avoid that. Plus there's a limit to how long your ex can prolong the financial proceedings – he may be able to get an extra hearing or two by delaying and failing to disclose his documents, or by making other applications to hold things up, but once you get your final order that's the end of it. In other words, he won't be taking you back to court again and again for extra decisions. (Although, if he doesn't comply with the financial order, you may have to go back to court to enforce it.) Whereas in children proceedings he can keep taking you back to court until the children are 16.

Deciding what you want as a starting point

Some survivors just want to walk away and not fight for what they're entitled to financially. And just occasionally that's the right thing to do; there's plenty more money in the world and it may be more important to run for your life or save your health and sanity, which are at high risk when divorcing a narcissist. I would recommend taking legal advice first so that you know how much you're entitled to under English law and what you're giving up. Remember too that even if you walk away and give him everything it's still not usually enough; he wants blood too. He wants to continue to control and upset you and, if you have children with him, he'll simply find another way to do so. Consider too that if you're trying to protect your children, financial proceedings may serve to distract him from using them as weapons against you (especially if he's more interested in money than his kids). These are all reasons to consider fighting for a financial settlement.

But you'll need to hold on tight because it's a bit of a roller coaster ride and the amount of paperwork can be overwhelming. Take it one step at a time and you will get through it.

Where the children are going to live usually needs to be resolved first unless there's enough money for both parents to have a property big enough to accommodate them after the divorce. This means the narcissist will often fight for at least 50/50 time with the children, if not actual custody of them, so that he'll get an equal or bigger share of the property (in order to house the children). And of course he doesn't want to have to pay you child maintenance, which he'll have to if the children spend more time with you. You can put his earnings into the calculator on the CMS (Child Maintenance Service) website to check how much he should pay, and apply to them if he doesn't pay. The courts don't deal with child maintenance, only spousal maintenance.

Recognise from the start that you won't get all you're entitled to financially; the narcissist has to win, and he's a master manipulator who will probably hide and obfuscate his assets and income. Decide what the minimum settlement is that you could live with, or live on, and aim for that rather than spending years and thousands of pounds in fees trying to unearth what he's hidden. But, having decided what you'll settle for, don't tell him. You'll need to be strategic and use reverse psychology. You can make him think he's won by asking from the start for much, much more than you want or need – so that when you 'give in' he'll think he's beaten you down and won. Or you can ask for things you know he really wants and might be fooled into thinking you want too, such as his pension. Then you can magnanimously give them up in exchange for something you really want, such as the house, and make him think he's won.

To start this process:

- Make a list of all the financial things that have to be decided in your financial proceedings: properties, savings, pensions, maintenance, house contents, etc.
- Highlight the things you really want in one colour.
- In a different colour, highlight the things you definitely don't want.
- And in a third colour, highlight the things you would quite like to have but are willing to give up.
- Whatever you do, don't let your ex know what's on your list.
- Keep referring back to this list and keep your focus on what's really important to you.

Who's really entitled to what? Dividing the assets, the former matrimonial home and rehousing

The narcissist may or may not take legal advice (because he always knows best so why would he, although in my experience they usually do). And if he's been the one earning most of the money or who has most of the assets, he won't like the advice he's given; it won't suit his sense of entitlement to be told you'll be entitled to a bigger share than him and he'll try all sorts of tricks to get you to agree to more than he's entitled to. Again, you should take legal advice to clarify what exactly you're entitled to under English law.

A 50/50 split of all of the assets is the starting point but it's very rarely the end result. If you don't have children, or have independent adult children, and earn about the same then there'll usually be an equal division. Otherwise other factors will tip the balance one way or the other. If the children are going to be spending most of their time with one parent, that person is likely to get a bigger share of the house because a settled home for the children is always the court's priority.

The mortgage on the former matrimonial home is often the big problem. The property can't be transferred from joint names into your sole name unless your lender agrees. And if you don't have enough income to meet their affordability criteria, they won't agree.

It's possible to have a Mesher Order, which means the property and mortgage remain in your joint names until a defined event triggers the sale, often the youngest child reaching the age of 18. This is never a popular order because the person who's paying the mortgage but not living in the house can't get another mortgage elsewhere, and the courts prefer to make a clean break order (to sever financial ties) if at all possible. Plus, from your point of view, a Mesher Order can be a dreadful solution because not only do you remain financially tied to your narcissist, if you're relying on him to pay some or all of the mortgage, or maintenance to enable you to pay it, it means he still has enormous control over you; step a toe out of line and he'll be threatening not to pay, or he'll stop paying and you won't sleep at night. You'll be back to begging him to do the right thing, which never worked before and won't work now.

A better solution, if you can make it work, is to sell the property and buy a smaller one. The court may agree that you should have all the equity in the first house to buy a new one in your sole name to make sure the children have a home until they're 18 or leave university. The house would then be sold (or you would buy him out) and your ex would get his share of the money then. In the meantime he would have a charge over your property (which means you can't sell the house without him getting his money), but you remain very much in control as he'd have to take you back to court if you refused to sell or buy him out at the time ordered.

Applying to the court for a financial settlement

If the narcissist has had unpalatable advice it may be down to you to issue the court proceedings to resolve your financial situation as he'll want to keep out of court, and keep control of you.

The divorce petition (Chapter 11) is your first step as you'll need the court number from the divorce case to put on your Form A, which is the form used to apply for a financial settlement.

Before you can make an application to court, you are required to attend a Mediation Information Assessment Meeting (MIAM) to see if mediation could be used to reach an agreement with your ex rather than going to court. However, you can just tell the mediator that you are a victim of abuse and say you don't wish to try mediation. Instead, you can just ask them to sign a Form A and send it to you (find the cheapest mediator you can to do this). Then you complete the rest of the form, put your postcode into the government website (google Divorce form A) and it will tell you where to send your form.

Form A is also used if you're not married, to make an application under Schedule 1 of the Children Act, for example to secure a home for yourself and your children until they are 18.

The court will then send you a notice setting out the dates of the next steps: when you have to exchange your Form Es (more on that coming up), when you have to send your other documents for the first court hearing, and the date of your FDA (first directions appointment, more on this coming up too). Usually the court will send this notice to your ex or his solicitor too, but sometimes they tell you to serve it – i.e. send it to him, or his solicitor if he has one. Be sure to read the letter carefully and if it's down to you to serve, make sure you can prove you've done so, for example, by sending it recorded delivery, or by email.

Interim maintenance and legal services orders

If your narcissist is earning good money and not paying you any, or not enough, you can make an immediate application for interim maintenance for yourself.

(You have to apply to the CMS for maintenance for your children.) Indeed, that may be why you had to issue your Form A in the first place. It's usually best to write to him or his solicitors before you do this – asking for the amount you need, and including a list of your income and expenses. If that doesn't get you anywhere, you can then apply to the court on Form D11 for interim maintenance, sometimes called maintenance pending suit (MPS).

If you can't afford legal representation and your ex can or is controlling all the assets, you can make an application for him to pay for your legal representation too – this is known as a legal services order. You will have to show that you can't obtain a loan and have no other means of paying legal fees. You can apply for this on the same Form D11 as your maintenance application, so you'll only have to pay one court fee.

You can attach the form to an email to the court and ask them to ring you to take the fee over the phone. Then you'll know they've received it and are dealing with it.

Form E: Financial statement

This is different to the other court forms you'll encounter and there's a clue in the name – although it's called a form (all 29 pages of it), it is essentially a financial witness statement. Such statements are evidence and far more important in court proceedings than forms, which just get the process going and aren't usually looked at again. So don't be confused by the word 'form' – the Form E is, in fact, a crucial statement. It is therefore very important to get this one right or it can come back to bite you.

If you have a solicitor they will usually complete this form for you, but will charge you for doing so, as well as for asking for any bank statements or pension information on your behalf. So it's much better to prepare it all yourself and just ask your solicitor to check it when you've finished. If you're a litigant in person, it falls to you to complete though you may be able to get some help from an accountant if you need it. Your ex (or his solicitor) will also have to complete his own Form E.

You'll have about three months from when the Form A is submitted until your first court hearing. Your Form E will be due before this hearing (the court will confirm all the dates after you issue the application). Given that the form is so long, it may well take you three months to finish it all. Don't ever leave your Form E until the last minute – if you have a pension, it could take your pension provider the best part of three months to supply the necessary valuation needed for the form, so make that the first thing you ask for. In addition to a pension valuation, there may be lots of other documents you might need to hunt for or apply for copies of, which is another reason to start the form as soon as possible. It's a good idea to make a list at the start of all the documents and information you'll need to gather to complete your form, then methodically work your way through gathering or requesting this information.

The information and documents required by Form E are intrusive and most people are aghast at all the information they have to give to their ex. Not only do you have to send your bank statements for the last year, but you have to keep updating them before each court hearing. So if there are things you don't want your ex to see, find another way of paying that doesn't involve your bank account! Of course your narcissistic ex may be even more reluctant to produce his documents than you are, depending on what he's hiding, and you may receive an offer to settle. Please take legal advice before you agree to anything.

Be sure also to make full disclosure of all your assets, liabilities and income on your Form E. Don't be tempted to hide anything. The income needs (i.e. your expenses) section of the form is also very important, particularly if you're not the main earner, and it could take you two or three months to remember everything you pay out for over the course of a year, so start a 'regular expenses' list and keep adding to it. I have a comprehensive list of typical expenses and you're welcome to email me (diana@dealingwithdivorce.co.uk) for a free copy. This should ensure you don't forget anything.

Section 4.4 of Form E asks about bad behaviour and says it'll only be taken into account in exceptional circumstances. So if your ex had injured you and reduced your capacity to work, or drunk or gambled away the family money you'd want to put that down. But just because it won't affect the outcome isn't necessarily a reason not to mention his behaviour. If a solicitor is doing your Form E they will probably advise you to leave this section blank, but if you're a litigant in person you can always plead ignorance and write what you want! And it may well be worth you mentioning if he's been financially controlling as this may alert the judge to look more carefully into what he's been up to.

Section 5 asks you what you want the court to order. You don't have to complete this section, so don't rush to give the game away on what it is you really want; be strategic and think very carefully about the best things to write here, if anything. If possible, use reverse psychology and put the opposite of what you really want as well as asking for the moon. However, don't say the house should be sold if there's any possibility you might want or be able to stay. Say you want a pension sharing order even if you'd rather have a bigger share of the house instead. Honesty is not the best policy when it comes to stating what you want!

If you're not in court proceedings – i.e. if neither you nor your ex has sent a Form A to the court, and you are attempting to reach a financial settlement without the court – you don't have to do a Form E. If you or your ex has a solicitor they'll no doubt ask you for one, but you're entitled to refuse as you can make full financial disclosure without putting it all on this form or producing quite so many documents. If you can reach agreement between yourselves, or in mediation, you need only complete a Form D81, which is just six pages long and requires no documents to be sent with it.

Even if you are a litigant in person, you may want to get the advice of a solicitor or accountant before you finalise your Form E. If your case settles before the final hearing this will be your only statement in court, so it's best to maximise this opportunity. You can find more information on the Advice Now and No Family Lawyer websites.

You are ordered to exchange Form Es with your ex and send them to the court by the date given, but on no account should you send yours to the narcissist without being sure to receive his at the same time. Part of his tactics will be to send things late to raise your anxiety levels. That's fine. Let him play his little games and just send your Form E to the court on the due date and start a list of all the dates he misses and how late he is. And if you still don't get it, you can ask for a penal notice to be attached to the court order, which would enable you to apply for his committal to prison if he still failed to produce it.

Questionnaires

Having exchanged your Form Es, you then have to exchange questionnaires. The questionnaire is where you set out any questions you have regarding your ex's Form E, and ask for any further documents that you think are needed.

The problem with him being late with his Form E is that you'll have less time to prepare your questions on his Form E, but if your questionnaire is late you can just explain it was because his Form E wasn't on time. Generally speaking, it doesn't matter as long as the judge has everything on the day of the FDA (more on the FDA coming up next). Besides, it's usually better to do it right than on time.

Key tips for completing your questionnaire are:

- Check carefully through his bank statements and ask for any that are missing.
- Check whether there are payments to or from other accounts that haven't been disclosed; you can also ask for credit card or PayPal statements if relevant.
- You can ask for explanations of any large sums on the statements that you don't understand. Actually you can ask for anything you want; it'll be up to the judge at the FDA to decide which questions will stay in your questionnaires and have to be answered, and which questions will be struck out. (You'll be given a date at the FDA when these questions have to be answered by, questionnaires don't have to be answered before.)
- If you suspect he's got stuff hidden, make a guess at what it might be and ask for it! If the judge tells you you're not allowed to go on a 'fishing expedition' and strikes it out so be it, but you might just strike gold.
- If you don't want to answer questions you've been asked by him, be ready to tell the judge why not, or put it in your position statement.
- Prepare your questionnaire on a Word document (not a pdf, so that the answers can be typed underneath), with the usual court heading and 'Applicant's questionnaire of the Respondent' (or vice versa) as the heading. Then refer to the paragraph numbers on the Form E as you list your questions.

First directions appointment (FDA)

This is a directions (or case management) hearing where the judge will decide what needs to be done for the case to be ready for the next hearing, the FDR.

So, there may be directions given for valuations of properties and/or businesses, or a pension on divorce expert (PODE) report or for disclosure of further financial documents. You may be ordered to supply a letter showing how much you could borrow on a mortgage, and to send estate agents' particulars of properties you say would be suitable for both you and your ex. You will be given a date – usually a couple of weeks before the FDR (see next section) – by when you and your ex must make offers to each other to settle your financial claims. These should be marked 'without prejudice', which means that if you don't settle they cannot be put before the court at the final hearing.

Your application for interim maintenance or a legal services order may also be decided at this hearing if you've applied in time and there is court time – if not, a date will be set for another hearing. Sometimes both parties can agree on all the directions that are needed and send an agreed order to the court so no one has to attend the hearing. Obviously it's rare for a narcissist to agree but it's always worth a try!

Before the FDA hearing, you'll also need to prepare a 'statement of issues'. This sets out the things you and your ex don't agree on that the judge will eventually have to decide – for instance, the value of your property, or how much one of you is earning from a business. If you have a lawyer, they will prepare this for you.

Financial dispute resolution hearing (FDR)

This is where a judge will look at all the papers – including the without prejudice offers of both parties – hear what both parties say about the issues in dispute, and then indicate the orders they would make if it were a final hearing. Basically, the judge indicates how they would decide the case but without making an order. You're then asked to go outside – with your representatives, if you have them – and negotiate to try and reach an agreement.

This hearing will be listed for at least two hours but you should be prepared to be at court all day and make sure you have someone to pick the children up if necessary. If you reach an agreement, this will be your final hearing and the financial settlement is sorted. If neither parties are represented, the judge will draw up the order to be typed up in the court office and sent out to both parties. If one of you is represented, the lawyer will draw up the agreement. Be sure to check this very carefully – ideally you wouldn't sign it without taking legal advice. Most likely, you'll be asked to sign your agreement to the general principles and then the draft order will be sent to you a day or two later, at which point you can get a solicitor to check it for you.

The majority of cases settle at this hearing, or very soon after. Lots of people just want to hear 'what a judge would order' and, once they know that, they're very often willing to reach an agreement, even if they don't much like it. This doesn't necessarily work with a narcissist, though, as their main aim isn't to settle the matter and move on, it's to destroy you or to continue to control you. So no matter how creative the judge and lawyers may be in trying to find a way forward that would be acceptable to both of you, the narcissist will keep objecting to parts of it and you're likely to leave court after a very long day of arguing the toss feeling utterly defeated.

That's assuming you don't cave in and agree to take something less than the judge has indicated you're entitled to. This is why it can be so helpful to have a friend or relative with you at this hearing – as well as your barrister (if you have one) or McKenzie Friend – so you can talk it through with them, and they can encourage you to stay the course and not let your ex have a win they're not entitled to. Of course if you are represented, your solicitor or barrister should be telling you this too, but they may see it as a professional failing if they don't get an agreement and try and persuade you that it's not such a bad deal.

Some people worry more about how they may be seen during the proceedings than getting the right outcome for themselves. The judge or your solicitor, or both, may try to pressurise you into an agreement, which might make you feel you should do what they want. But it's you who has to live with this order for the rest of your life so be very sure you can. Don't be afraid to ask for a few days to sleep on it – you don't have to sign on the dotted line on the day (though if you've been offered a good deal the narcissist may go back on it if you don't both sign on the day). And if you're not represented, you can always ask for a week or two so you can take legal advice on the offer. Whether or not you then do that is up to you, but at least it gives you a chance to think it through and be sure it's right for you. If you do ask for more time to consider the offer, the case will be listed for a final hearing.

Likewise, if you don't reach an agreement at all, the case will be listed for a final hearing. The court will give directions for the final hearing, meaning you will be directed to file a witness statement (called a section 25 or narrative statement – Wikivorce has a template) and anything else that's still missing.

Form H: Estimate of costs for financial remedy cases only

Form H records all the fees that have been paid to solicitors and barristers to date so that the judge can keep an eye on the costs, as they can get very out of hand – especially when a narcissist is involved. Each party has to complete a Form H before every financial hearing, unless you're a litigant in person and have not paid any fees to a solicitor or barrister for advice or representation for financial proceedings.

If you have a solicitor they will complete this for you before every hearing. If you have a direct access barrister, you'll need to fill in the total of all your barrister's fees. If you had a solicitor previously you need to add those costs in the appropriate places. You must include all fees paid or owing to a solicitor or barrister for the financial proceedings only; do not include legal fees paid for the divorce itself, or any children or injunction or other proceedings. And you don't include any fees paid to a McKenzie Friend, financial advisor or any other professional who you may have paid for help with your case. This form is just for the fees of solicitors and barristers.

If you're a litigant in person and have never had a solicitor or barrister you don't complete this form – you just have to be prepared for the eye-watering figure your ex discloses if they're represented!

The final hearing

If you haven't managed to reach a financial agreement with your ex by this point, the final hearing is where you and your ex will both give evidence and the judge will make a final decision on who gets what.

You really do need to be represented for this if you possibly can be, even if it's by a very junior barrister. Unless maybe you're an accountant, or figures come so easily to you that you can deal with all that as well as addressing the judge and cross-examining your ex and coping with your own cross-examination.

The final hearing may last one or several days and at the end of it the order has to be drawn up – the judge should look out for you if you're a litigant in person and make sure your ex's barrister doesn't slip things in or take things out, but there's no guarantee so having a lawyer to oversee this important legal document is always recommended. See Chapter 10 for more tips on checking a court order.

Final tips for financial proceedings

I'll leave you with some final pointers to help you navigate financial proceedings:

- Depending on your financial circumstances, it may be advisable for you to take financial advice from an independent financial adviser and obtain a cash flow forecast to ascertain how much you really need for your future.

- If you're getting divorced later in life, be sure to get a state pension forecast and compare it to that of your ex so that you can be compensated if there's a big discrepancy.
- If there's an order for the sale or transfer of your house, ask for a clause in the order to say that the solicitor who does the conveyancing can sign the contract and transfer document if your narcissist fails to do so. It's not uncommon for them to refuse to sign and it can leave you in an awful mess, or having to make an urgent application to the court.
- If the order is for the sale of your house, try and get it to say that you have sole conduct of the sale (meaning you are the one dealing with the estate agent and the conveyancing solicitor). Failing that, agree the agent in the order and the minimum price the property can be sold for. This prevents the narcissist from messing you around over the sale.
- If you have an order for spousal maintenance make sure the dates of the payments are specified and exactly when the payments are to stop.
- Never agree to cancel or adjourn (delay) a court hearing just because the narcissist has promised that he'll reach an agreement with you. He'll never agree anything which is why there were court proceedings in the first place so don't be taken in and always say you're going ahead with the hearing.

CHAPTER 13:
INJUNCTIONS (NON-MOLESTATION AND OCCUPATION ORDERS)

Separate from children and financial proceedings, these two orders are basically injunctions designed to help protect you and your children from abuse.

Non-molestation orders (non-mol)

Many narcissists are very subtle in their abuse and gaslighting of you and it's hard enough trying to explain to a friend, let alone a court, what he's doing. But if he's more overt with his abuse a 'non-mol' can protect you and your children, not just from violence from your ex but also from harassment, stalking, threatening or intimidating you, being abusive, his smear campaign, controlling you, coming near you or your home, or contacting you at all.

You can apply to the court at any time by completing form FL401 and writing a short witness statement about the abuse. Make a list at the end of your statement of exactly what you want the court to order him not to do. If you need help with your application, you can ask your local domestic abuse agency, such as Women's Aid. A non-mol won't stop him from seeing his children, but you may have to make different arrangements for handovers so you don't come into contact with him.

If you're worried about how he'll react and that he may be violent when he receives the application from the court, you can apply 'ex parte' – i.e. without the court telling him, so that you can have a non-molestation order first to protect you. You then both go back to court a short while later so he can oppose your application and tell the court his side of the story if he wishes to, which of course he will as such an order would cause a big narcissistic injury.

Survivors can be reluctant to apply for a non-mol and you do need to think it through. You know your own narcissist – how likely are you to win? If it's just your word against his, and knowing that his lies are more convincing than your truth, what are your chances? If, however, you have loads of emails or messages in a very short time, or abuse in writing, or other evidence, you've got a much stronger case. How is he likely to react to a non-mol order against him? He won't be able to do any of the things he's been ordered not to, at least not without risking a fine, or a prison sentence of up to five years – none of which looks good for an image-polishing narcissist! But if he's having unsupervised time with his children is he likely to complain to them about what you've done, or try to alienate them from you? If so, be sure to include in your order that he's not to involve the children in any way.

In short, you'll need to think this through carefully and consider how it fits with your overall strategy. Will a non-mol enable you to take back some control, to fire a shot across his bow and let him know you mean business now and won't be messed around anymore, or even give the judge in your children proceedings a message about how frightened you are of him? (Although injunctions are completely separate from children proceedings, they will usually go on the court file for children proceedings so the judge will see it all.)

Sometimes there is ample evidence for a non-molestation order (e.g. photos of bruising or other injuries) and in some cases the police should be taking criminal action. Instead they advise victims to apply for a non-mol – an example of the institutional buck-passing that is rife in abuse cases. Try again to get the police to take action, or ask someone to try and persuade them on your behalf.

Having applied for a non-mol, the case will usually be listed for a short (directions) hearing first to see if it can be agreed by the perpetrator giving undertakings (i.e. promising not to do something), or agreeing to move out of the house. If agreement can't be reached directions will be given, usually for your ex to file a witness statement in response to your statement. If either party wants to call witnesses, the judge can make orders for them to file statements too. Then the court will give a date for a contested hearing.

Occupation orders

If you're not safe in your home you can apply for an occupation order, which will force your ex to leave. It's better to do this than to leave yourself and then try to return to live in the house later without him, which is very difficult to do (the courts are always reluctant to deprive a man of his castle). Unless he's got somewhere else fairly locally he can go, such as his mum's, or he's got enough disposable income to be able to afford to rent somewhere else, it may not be worth applying if he's not a huge danger.

An occupation order just defines who can live in the property and it only lasts for six or 12 months (but you can apply to extend this). Importantly, the order doesn't change ownership – so in that six- or 12-month period, you'll want to sort out who is going to own the property going forward, or whether it needs to be sold. This will be agreed or ordered as part of your financial proceedings (Chapter 12).

Having applied for an occupation order, the case will usually be listed for a directions hearing to see if your ex will give an undertaking to move out. If he won't, directions will be given for the filing of witness statements and a date fixed for a contested hearing.

Undertakings

Instead of having a contested hearing for a non-mol or occupation order these applications are often resolved by one or both parties giving undertakings to the court. This is a promise to the court (verbally and in writing) not to do any of the things that you asked for in an order.

An undertaking is not an admission of anything that's happened in the past, it's simply a promise not to do any of those things in the future. Breaching an undertaking isn't a criminal offence but it is contempt of court so can still be punished by the family court if the other party applies. But unlike an official court order, the police will not get involved if your ex breaks an undertaking.

It's up to the perpetrator whether he's willing to give an undertaking – and up to you whether you're willing to accept his undertaking. If not, it'll go to a contested hearing.

A narcissist may insist that you also give an undertaking (called cross-undertakings) as a condition for him giving one, especially if he's making false allegations against you. There's usually no harm in this as you wouldn't dream of doing the things he's doing and it will save you having to give evidence in a contested hearing. Just be aware that he may try to trick you into breaking one of your promises to the court and you can be sure he'll then apply to have you punished for it. But don't panic if that does happen; applying for an order does not mean he'll actually be able to persuade the court to make that order.

CHAPTER 14:
CHILDREN PROCEEDINGS
(CHILD ARRANGEMENTS ORDERS)

I don't think I will ever fully recover from the trauma of the process, how it was able to go on for so many years, and why no one was able to step in and say 'stop this man' rather than just trying to appease him so he could continue to try to destroy my family with no consequence. It was like being forced into a boxing ring over and over again with my hands being tied behind my back. I really do feel like I went the full 10 rounds that's for sure. It's frightening to think how terrified I was about just showing up for the hearings, and I am generally a really strong minded person.

The first thing to understand is that, while it's usual to have a financial order in divorce proceedings, the opposite is true of children proceedings. The Children Act specifically states that the court shall only make an order if it's better for the child than making no order. In other words, parents are expected to work out their arrangements for their children between themselves. They can of course get help from a mediator to do this, but at the end of the process there's no official record of it, no court order, no need to go to a solicitor. Though I'd always recommend having a parenting plan (see Chapter 6) signed by both parents if at all possible.

Of course if you're divorcing a narcissist you're very likely to end up in court.

People would be shocked if they knew, and probably won't believe you when you tell them what happens in children proceedings, but as they're held in secret no one can know what a dangerous place the family court is for children.

It's appalling that even when a child discloses abuse, which has been backed up by police, social worker or a doctor, the court still often orders that they have to continue seeing that parent despite their fear and cries for protection. It's not just the court that's the problem, the other agencies such as social services and the police also lack understanding of abuse and personality disorders and fail to protect victims.

A man's biology seems to have more sway in the family court than what he does, and women and children are expected to bear the brunt of his abuse without complaint. The very language used in court bears this out; mothers may be referred to as being 'implacably hostile' whereas a father's abuse is rarely labelled. A barrister may refer to his client as 'Mr Smith' but the other party as 'the mother' which is also divisive.

There are some good judges, and good social workers and Cafcass officers but it is a lottery. If you don't win the lottery this week, you buy another ticket next week i.e. you may need to keep going back to court (by appealing or making new applications) until you do get the right judge or Cafcass worker and 'win' safety for your child.

Remember, the courts rarely recognise a narcissist

It's very hard to get a diagnosis of narcissistic personality disorder as the narcissist can manipulate and gaslight the professional assessing them. And without a formal diagnosis, you should never call your ex a narcissist in court. It will only work against you.

In fact, I'm only aware of one family court case in which the narcissism was diagnosed (Re P (A child) in 2015) and another one in which it was mentioned (Re F (Children; contact, name, parental responsibility; HHJ Duggan) in 2014). All direct contact was stopped in both cases.

In Re F the Judge gave five examples of where the father had 'let himself down' and one of those was where, 'The mother has insulted him by quoting his psychological assessment of narcissism, so, if she is insulting him, he is going to insult her.' And he certainly did, calling her 'a drug-addicted alcoholic surrogate who has suffered from sexually transmitted diseases'.

Not just to one or two people; he told this to the providers of nursery education in the mother's home county – all 723 of them! This was because he didn't approve of her choice of nursery and was trying to stop her acting contrary to his wishes.

Though I'm actually more surprised about the fact he didn't try to deny his diagnosis of narcissism. The father had a very public online blog about his children's case, which he updated almost daily, and even included the names of his children (it's against the law to name children in court proceedings but he's a narcissist and got away with it). He included in his blog a medical report relating to a deformity of the penis of one of his sons. And said he hoped his children would see his postings when they got older. There was more, and worse, but I won't go on. The case reference is in the Resources section at the back if you wish to read it.

The father played the victim a lot of the time and kept threatening to walk right away from his children. Maybe if the judge had had some understanding of the personality disorder he wouldn't have been so desperate to keep the door open for him 'if he is able to take a different approach'. Judges are in desperate need of education in personality disorders.

As well as an order for no contact, and to be able to change the children's name, the mother succeeded in obtaining a barring order for five years, which is also very unusual.

In Re P, the father was diagnosed with both histrionic and narcissistic personality disorders, and he also suffered from bipolar disorder. His behaviour during the relationship was so bad that it took the mother four years to recover enough from the abuse to be able to resume the care of her child. It appears that the little girl had a bruise on her forehead when she was three and the father coached her to say the mother had done it. The original judge found that the little girl had lied to please her father, but maybe she was frightened of him. The judge said, 'As a result of his personality disorder, the father was unable to identify P's needs as distinct from his own; that factor, together with his inability to have his opinion challenged and his need to control those around him, rendered P vulnerable to harm.'

This father didn't like his personality disorder diagnosis so got a report from another psychiatrist who said he could find no evidence of a personality disorder. The Court of Appeal wasn't impressed by this as the psychiatrist didn't have the father's medical records, but did know about the court proceedings and the father's restricted contact with his daughter and was happy to base his report on the father's own account of things.

The father didn't follow the correct procedure for obtaining this report, which is to apply to the court for permission to obtain a second opinion. If the court agrees, the second expert is given all the medical and legal information in the case so they are on an equal footing with the first expert.

The father originally had contact with his daughter but it was badly supervised by the local authority and her behaviour started to deteriorate after seeing her father. He was oblivious to her upset and intent only on continuing his obsession with his 'campaign'. The Court of Appeal refused to change the five-year barring order made by the lower court.

The key takeaway here is that the diagnosis itself isn't necessarily important, especially as judges don't really understand narcissists or the consequences of narcissism or the fact that narcissists are untreatable.

So, rather than try to bandy the word 'narcissist' around in court, just focus on the behaviour of your ex and the effect of this behaviour on your child and yourself. Make a list of their traits – such as sudden irrational rage, punishing the children harshly, an inability to empathise, pathological lying, stonewalling, etc. – and back it up with any evidence, such as abusive texts. If you can show their behaviour in court, you'll inflict a narcissistic injury and they may eventually crack and show their true colours. You have to know which are the right buttons to push to make him flip. Be calm, tell the truth and don't be intimidated or let him rile you. If you give him enough rope he'll go on and on and show himself up, all while thinking how marvellous and impressive he is.

And if your case is similar to either of the cases mentioned above, you can use them to try and persuade the court to make an order for no contact, or a barring order.

How to deal with the narcissist's tactics in court proceedings

A narcissist needs to win – because winning is a huge dose of narcissistic supply and losing or losing face is more shame than they can bear – so try not to be thrown by their dirty tricks.

If the narcissist needs to win, what do you need? What is your goal for the court proceedings? (Refer back to your strategy, Chapter 5.) Keeping your goal firmly in mind is the first step in dealing with his antics in court.

Prepare yourself for his lies

What will happen to you when he lies in court? Will you smile to yourself saying, 'That's the first one. I wonder what the next will be?' or will you be stunned by it and unable to focus or hear what comes next?

Your narcissist knows you, and exactly how to trigger and destabilise you. You may have to work hard, perhaps with a therapist, to be able to put a stop to him having this power over you. It's more a battle with yourself than with him. You know he's going to lie so instead of being shocked, angry or upset, make a game of it in your head – wonder how many times he's going to lie today, and what about. Then count them off and see how many you got right instead of jumping to defend yourself. If you're not actually in the courtroom, consider deflecting it with something totally random. For example, if he's just accused you of taking the children to school late every day for a week, you could say something like 'Oh look, I've just noticed that really pretty book cover'. That will throw him, and you can start to turn the tables.

Survivors are often concerned about 'looking good', particularly to the court. But what good does that do? The narcissist also wants to look good so he'll agree with things professionals and the judge say, and will agree to do as they recommend, but he won't actually do it. He knows how to play the game, and he gets away with it. He also knows you, and that you'll do exactly as you say you will. Take him by surprise and do something different!

Let's say the Cafcass report (covered later in the chapter) didn't go his way and just before the hearing he sent 100 pages of lies to the court to try and rewrite history. You've barely had time to read it, let alone think up any response and you arrive at court upset and flustered. Bingo, he's won again. The first thing to do is stay calm. Yes, he's within his rights to file a position statement before a hearing but he'd be lucky if the hard-pressed judge reads 10 pages, let alone 100. (That's why I recommend keeping your position statements to three pages at the most if you possibly can, see Chapter 10.) In other words, the judge won't read his 100 pages before the hearing, so why get upset about it? It won't be a healthy thing for you to read just before a hearing, so ignore it.

Next, ask yourself whether he had permission to send his document to the court – look at your last court order and see if the judge has asked for witness statements. A 100-page document is clearly not a normal position statement and likely contains his 'evidence' … which makes it a witness statement. In which case, you can object on the grounds he didn't have permission to submit a witness statement. You can also object to reports going into evidence if they're not correct – just tell the judge why you don't want them included.

When he tells a lie about you, instead of going into a long explanation as to why it's not true, you can just say 'There's no proof of that' and ask him to file his evidence. Remember, it's up to him to prove what he says, not for you to prove a negative. Keep telling the truth yourself, and hopefully he'll trip himself up eventually.

As well as lying about you, he'll lie about himself and when he's telling the court what a brilliant dad he is you'll be wanting to scream that he's never been a parent to his children. But that doesn't work, so don't do it. Poker is the game to play here; don't let even a flicker of emotion cross your face. He will remain calm throughout and the more emotional you get, the more likely you are to be considered 'unstable' and cause the focus to be put on to you, when it's not you who's the problem. The calmer you are, the more he will fall apart. So let him lie as much as he likes which will give him every possible opportunity to trip himself up later.

You too can play the long game (narcissists are very good at this) and give him enough rope to hang himself. Sadly this may take more than one lot of court proceedings – sometimes the long game can be long indeed. You won't get far trying to prove his untruths yourself, so it's far better to get him to expose his own lies by showing that what he says and what he does are two different things. A narcissist is manipulative and flies under the radar, which means you have to keep scrupulous records of events:

- Keep a list of his lies, and his actions which are the opposite.
- Use chronologies to record factual events (more on this coming up).
- Keep lots and lots of evidence on his time with the children – everything that happens and everything the children say. Make sure it's all dated, as that's your best hope of eventually being believed by the court. I talk more about gathering evidence later in the chapter.

Avoid being labelled a 'high conflict case'

'Parental conflict' are the words I dread hearing in children proceedings because once a case is labelled like this, it can be very hard to turn it around. The question is: is it conflict, or is it abuse?

There's often conflict between parents immediately after they separate, until they can find their feet again as individuals, settle down, and co-parent successfully. That can take a year or more, and they can find themselves in the family court in that time. That's on a 'normal' divorce.

And then there's narcissistic abuse, which doesn't stop. The abused parent can't settle down and can't co-parent with a narcissist. These are the parents who find themselves in the family court time and time again. And when it's labelled as 'a high conflict case' it derails the children proceedings and the abuse continues unrecognised and often facilitated by the family court.

Of course there is conflict because the narcissist is out to destroy the other parent who fights to protect their children. But it's the abuse and intent to control that's the underlying problem – the conflict is the result of that problem, and it won't go away as it does with 'normal' couples for whom the mutual distrust and disagreement is the result of their separation. The professionals and judges don't understand personality disorders and they view you as equals: equally unreasonable and equally to blame. Sometimes they'll even tell you they want to bang your heads together to stop you fighting and they remain totally ignorant about the huge power imbalance.

The narcissist has a high-conflict personality and he thrives on drama. His aim is to draw you in by upsetting or angering you so that you continue his 'supply'. But if you take the bait and engage with his drama – and enter into a bitter 'he said, she said' – the court can't tell the difference between the two of you and just labels you a 'high conflict case', which basically means they see you as two halves of a toxic whole. Judges have no idea which parent is telling the truth and they don't have the time or resources to find out so tend to come to the conclusion that both parents are as bad as each other and equally to blame. This is why it's so important to have therapy or coaching, which will help you to become strong enough to resist being taken in like this.

It's also important to politely contradict anyone who tells you your case is 'high conflict' or 'parental conflict'. Explain that it's abuse, not conflict.

The narcissist may perpetuate the 'conflict' myth by saying that the relationship was mutually destructive. He may even admit that he did get angry at times and did some 'pushing and shoving' but says your claims are grossly exaggerated.

Once this 'high conflict' label is applied, it's very difficult to turn it around. So don't play the narcissist's game, ignore their allegations against you and don't get drawn in. The problem is that the truth is important to you, and you want everyone to know he's lying, but this emotional response is your weakness. And your ex knows your vulnerability because you've argued with him about his 'truths' in the past.

If you absolutely have to respond to a lie, all you need say is 'That's not true' or 'I disagree with your version of events'. The more you get pulled in to where he wants to put you, the further you get from where you need to be and your own case. So keep your eye on the ball and don't get distracted. It's key to winning a game on any court!

> CAFCASS, the same officer who had previously seen our case as high conflict recognised the control this time round. She used the words 'the mother and the children deserve to live their own lives'.
>
> Judge second time around immediately said it was wrong we were forced to have a contact schedule that fitted to his shift pattern and that his constant changes clearly made my life and work difficult. She told him 'you need to work around your children, they are not designed to fit your excel sheets. It's not the mother's job to work around your needs'. The MOJ harm

report came out between our two lots of proceedings and I think that had an impact. I also learnt not to talk about the abuse, I let his words do the work. The best decision I made was not having a solicitor, I think they drive up hostilities as hostile cases earns them more, but damages DV victims cases.

Keep the court focused on your children

In order to help keep the focus on your children when the narcissist wants it all on himself, you can give the judge a photo of the children. This will serve as a reminder of who they're dealing with, and that your children are real people – not just another case. Just tell the judge or magistrates at the beginning of the hearing that you'd like them to have a picture of your children; you'll have to show it to your ex first as you can never put anything into court without the other party seeing it, but otherwise there shouldn't be a problem. Alternatively, you could include a picture at the end of your position or witness statement.

Using chronologies to your advantage

Abuse cases tend to get muddled and messy, so it's helpful for the judge and other professionals to have all the events set out in chronological order. Drafting a chronology – a timeline of events – can clarify things and sometimes make it obvious how one thing led to another.

In fact, it's helpful to write two chronologies. The first one, which you can give to the court or attach to your position statement, should contain only hard facts that can be proved by written evidence – i.e. these are things your ex can't possibly argue with.

To write this first chronology, put the usual court details at the top, followed by 'Applicant's/Respondent's Chronology' as the heading. Then you'll want to put dates on the left-hand side of the page, then the relevant events that happened on those dates to the right. You would include the dates of birth of all of you, date of your marriage and separation, date of the application to court, dates of all court hearings and brief details of what was ordered, and dates of any incidents that social services, the police, GP or your children's school will have a written record of. You can also add anything else that is relevant and can be proved (for example, in emails); a good example might be the date when the other parent's contact with the children started and stopped.

Your second chronology has the same dates and events as the first chronology (you can copy and paste the details into this new document), but also includes things that your ex may argue with. This version can be used with a social worker or Cafcass, or as an attachment to your witness statement. You can add in all your allegations of abuse that your ex denies, and anything else he will dispute.

These chronologies are most effective when they tell a story very concisely. So try to keep each entry to just one or two lines – remember, the shorter a document is the more likely the judge or professional is to read it.

Double binds and what to do about 'contact at all costs'

The family court forces protective parents into some impossible dilemmas – hence the phrase 'double binds'.

One such situation is the culture of 'contact at all costs', in which the court presumes that having both parents in a child's life – even when one of those parents is abusive – is more important than anything else (including the abuse). With this in mind, ideally you will go into court proceedings with the abusive parent currently having as little contact as possible with their children – because the court is very likely to give the perpetrator more time with them than they're having now. This also (generally) means you must be seen to be promoting contact – even when your child is telling everyone she doesn't want to go. If you aren't seen to be promoting contact, rather than focusing on his abuse the court will blame everything on 'parental conflict' (for which of course you are responsible for at least half), or you will be accused of parental alienation.

If social services have been involved with your family, you may well have been told that unless you protect your children from your partner's abuse – i.e. by leaving him and stopping his contact with the children – they will have to intervene and take you to court, i.e. in care proceedings. So you manage to extricate yourself and protect your children, only to find yourself in the family court anyway when the father applies for contact. At which point you will probably be told that the children must see their abusive parent. And the social worker who was previously doing a good job then abdicates all her responsibility to the court, who she views as a higher authority – and anyway her huge workload means she's only too happy to pass the buck.

Of course you want to protect your children, as every mother should, but it's likely that you won't get any help from the court to do so. This means you have to say you promote contact while actually trying to do the opposite – another impossible double bind.

Every case is different and only you can decide how much contact you think is safe for your child. You can always say that you want your child to know her father and have a relationship with him but you need it to be safe. Cards, letters and video calls are generally safe. The main thing is that you're seen to be encouraging contact, so it's harder for you to be accused of alienating your child from her father.

If contact is safe (or as safe as it ever can be with a narcissist) you can try reverse psychology – as in, make out that you want him to have more contact if he's already having the children for considerable time. It's a high-risk strategy but it's one that can work, because whatever you want, the narcissist is going to try and do the opposite. His natural reaction is to fight you, especially if he thinks you're using him as a babysitter, which is way below his dignity. To see whether this strategy might work for you, you could tell him you want him to have the children while you go away on a hen weekend. Chances are he'll say no!

The bottom line is divorcing a narcissist can put you, the protective parent, into some awful situations and decisions that no parent should have to face. You may need some therapy to help you reconcile the choices you make.

I was able to remove him from the home following an incident with drink (and later I found out drugs too) where he had put our nine-year-old at risk in her own home.

We had argued earlier as he insisted on taking Evie for Friday 5pm pub drinks, even though she never wanted to go. He insisted he could 'care' for her although she was scared of his volatile nature and they didn't have a good relationship. I went to my pal's for coffee and Evie knew I was on stand-by. She knew he had drunk three pints of beer in the pub and driven home with her. He then started drinking whiskey from the bottle and she excused herself to her room to ring me after she had seen half a bottle gone. He wanted her to go in his car again after he had drunk a further quarter of a bottle and she knew he was so drunk he could barely stand.

By the time I got home he had passed out on the staircase. We left him there and locked ourselves in the bedroom. Evie begged me that enough was enough and he had to go. She divulged that she had secretly witnessed violence in our bedroom a few weeks earlier but had been too scared to say or do anything. I woke him at 5am and asked him to leave before he realised what was happening.

Evie thrived at school literally weeks after her dad left the home and her school reports since then continued to be amazing. This was an actual fact backed up by the school but was completely disregarded in court.

My ex is an inside devil outside angel. He can put a smart suit on, turn on his phone voice and charm and convince people he is all that and more.

My daughter and I faced a barrage of lies against us both, and the authorities became complicit with him because who calls their nine-year-old a liar? Well he did and he got away with it, with full authority support for a full four years.

He presented me as a woman scorned and a bitter ex-wife and sadly Cafcass and the legal guardian fell for it hook and line. The guardian met Evie's dad twice before meeting Evie! When she finally met Evie she said, 'I don't know what your problem is, your dad is a lovely man'. It was a turning point for Evie. She was 10 and had just told this lady how much her dad had frightened her with his verbal and physical abuse in her bed (grabbing and dragging her) and what she had witnessed him do to me that made her not want to see him, and that was the reply from a person in a trusted responsible role. After that she withdrew trust for any person in power presented to her.

I was treated like a scorned ex-wife. I was never privy to pre-court information sharing or meetings that a representing solicitor would have been, and there were gaps in processes because I simply didn't have all the legal tools to challenge along the way. The Cafcass representative knew his solicitor and worked with her, not with Evie. She made recommendations in court about contact without ever having met or spoken to Evie.

Cafcass also interviewed Evie twice without allowing a trusted adult to be present. They interviewed his family members (who saw us only at Christmas each year) yet didn't meet my parents who have provided care for Evie weekly since she was 10 weeks old. It's like they didn't want to seek the truth.

I'm a believer in fate and that lies eventually unravel, so Evie and I hung off the truth as we knew it would be his downfall. The fright in her bedroom tipped the scales for her; he really did scare her and to this day he calls her a liar.

I self-represented and asked for a consistent district judge over magistrates (who barely ever read the paperwork and just agreed with the ex's solicitor) and I think that helped. The judge was a father of two girls and he showed me grace and acknowledgement in every hearing, making sure I had a voice and understood what was happening. My ex had a Rottweiler of a barrister.

I employed a barrister (financed via a family member) for the last two hearings as I was simply wrung out. My barrister had been a family law solicitor for many years. She re-wrote the whole case from the paperwork before I met with her. The first day in court she listed all the failings to the district judge and his response was that he was glad I had managed to get representation and he accepted what my barrister brought to the hearing.

The aim of all the time in court had been to restore Evie and her dad's relationship – despite the police being 100% insistent that he shouldn't have any contact at all and it was inappropriate to be trying to manifest a relationship. It was proven in our last hearing that Cafcass had acted with bias towards her dad and ignored the facts presented to them.

My barrister tore shreds in how this had been allowed to happen. In court she pointed out the many failings that had happened in the process that meant the dad had been favoured and the child had remained unheard despite her age. My barrister secured zero contact for my ex, who was allowed one letter per month to be given to Evie via social services, if Evie wanted to accept it. She also got us a Family Assistance Order to give us support and protection as the house repossession was in full swing, and there was vandalism happening at my folks' home that the ex was suspected of, amongst many other things. The final order meant that Evie's wishes were to be seen as hers and not as parental alienation by me.

We now have full support from social services and the police. Cafcass and the legal guardian solicitor sloped away in shame.

Deed Poll agreed to allow Evie to change her surname last year without his permission based on the court paperwork we presented. She also moved to a school where none of my ex's friends' children go and where the school were fully versed in her rights to withhold certain personal information (as a 13+ year-old) from a non-resident parent. They have been amazing.

I am not divorced. He went bankrupt behind my back and caused ALL manner of financial distress, which he used as leverage to keep control by refusing a divorce. We couldn't get him to agree to a financial closure so I'm still tied to him eight years later but legally changed my name some years ago. My divorce lawyer is useless, to be honest.

Evie and I won't ever be completely free from him but we are safe and repairing.

Child arrangements orders

Typically, a child arrangements order sets out who a child lives with, and how often they see the other parent. But child arrangements orders can also include 'prohibited steps orders', which stop a parent doing something (such as taking a child abroad, or moving to a different part of the country), and 'specific issue orders', where the court decides something the parents can't agree on (such as which school a child should attend, or whether a child should have medical treatment).

You're more likely to be on the receiving end of an application for a child arrangement order if your ex is abusive and wants more time with the children. Think very carefully before making an application for such an order yourself as you may just pave the way for your ex to get what he wants. Obviously if the narcissist has manipulated the children into living with him and you're not seeing enough of them – i.e. he is alienating them from you – you'll need to apply quickly.

But if the children are mostly with you and you're thinking that you either need a 'lives with' (custody) order, or the court to decide on how much time the children should spend with their father, think twice. You may be shooting yourself in the foot if you make an application, as it's not wise to enter the dreadful family court system if you can possibly avoid it. After all, the abusive parent usually comes out of it much better than the protective parent.

Instead, remember that 'possession is nine tenths of the law' and be bolder than you've ever been before with your ex. What will happen if you say 'no' to him having additional contact? Use reverse psychology – tell him you think it better that the court decides how much contact he has and ask him to apply. If he thinks it's what you want it's the last thing he'll do and he certainly won't want to do your 'dirty work' of form filling and paying a fee to the court.

If you do need to apply yourself for a child arrangements order, you'll use the C100 form. It's a long form (20 pages) but most of it is quite straightforward. The form asks you whether there has been any harm, or if there's a risk of any harm to your child, and you do need to consider this carefully. It won't help your case at all if you make false allegations but equally it could harm your case if you don't say at the outset what concerns you have. There's a question about domestic abuse on the form – and my advice is to mention the domestic abuse, whether or not it's physical abuse. After all, the form is asking you whether your children have been harmed – if children witness abuse, they're harmed by it. Likewise, when you come to the question asking about child abuse, remember this doesn't have to be physical – constantly criticising or shouting at a child is abusive too.

The question asking what you want can be answered briefly; for example, 'I only see my children once a month and I want the court to order that they can see me every week.' Keep it short and factual with no emotion or statement about the other parent's possible motives. You are not writing a statement here – although, that may come later – you are just telling the court, Cafcass and the other parent why you're making the application and what you want to change.

If you want to say that the other parent has harmed you or your child, or if you fear there is a risk of harm or abduction in the future, you must also complete a form C1A detailing the allegations of harm or domestic abuse. If you are the person applying, you send this form with your C100. (If you apply online the two forms are consolidated into one.) If you receive a C100 from the other parent, you need to send a form C1A to the court and other parent as soon as possible. But don't worry or agonise about this form – the purpose of it is to flag up that there are allegations the court will need to look into. You will give a lot more information later to Cafcass or a social worker, and probably in a statement too, and you'll be able to alter or add to what you've said then; so it doesn't matter too much what you say on this form now, as long as you say something. It will be harder to make, or be believed about, an allegation of abuse later if you've said nothing at the start.

If you are frightened to make your allegations now, maybe because you haven't felt able to tell anyone what's been happening before, just put something vague. For example, you could say something like 'The Respondent has been abusive and controlling throughout our relationship' or even 'I need help with this but cannot afford a solicitor' or 'I wish to make allegations but am frightened of repercussions'. And in section 4 you could just tick 'yes' to say you do have other concerns about your children and then write 'I will make a statement later'.

Just as with a financial application, before you can make an application to the court for a child arrangement order, you are required to attend a Mediation Information Assessment Meeting (MIAM) to see if you can reach an agreement through mediation. Again, just find the cheapest mediator you can, tell them you're a victim of abuse and that you don't wish to try mediation, and get them to sign your form.

Once you've made your application, the court will send a Notice of Hearing with the date of the first hearing (the FHDRA), and Cafcass will get in touch during their safeguarding checks (more on Cafcass later).

What to expect from the FHDRA: First hearing and dispute resolution appointment

This directions hearing is the first court hearing in child arrangement proceedings. As well as the judge and your legal representatives (if either of you have one), a Cafcass officer will also be present to talk to you and your ex and may try to broker an agreement.

You should have had a call from Cafcass and received their safeguarding letter before this hearing. And hopefully you'll have received that letter in time to comment on its recommendations in your position statement.

If you're frightened of your ex you will hopefully have arranged a separate waiting room in advance (see special measures, Chapter 9). If not, get to court as early as you can and try to secure one of the little interview rooms that most courts have, so that you can hide away and feel a bit safer. Give your name to the usher as soon as you can so they know you've arrived and where to find you.

And remember, even if you're represented by a solicitor or barrister, it's good to have a friend or family member with you on the day, although they won't be able to go into court with you.

If your ex is represented, his barrister will come and talk to you or your barrister to see if any agreement can be reached. If you're both represented, your barrister may spend a lot of time talking to his barrister (yet another reason to have a friend with you, so you're not sat alone). If you're not represented, don't let a barrister bully you. They may say they want to talk to you without your friend or family member there but you're entitled to refuse; they're not the judge and there's no reason that your friend can't be present in your discussion. They may also tell you what the judge will or won't do in an attempt to coerce you to agree to what your ex wants. But unless they're married to the judge and know which side of the bed they got out of that morning they can't know this! So you can just say you don't think what they're suggesting is what's best for your child and you'll wait to hear what the judge says.

There will usually be someone from Cafcass at court, though not the person who wrote the safeguarding letter (or the person who will prepare the Section 7 report, if one is ordered) – more on Cafcass and their involvement later in the chapter. The Cafcass representative will also try and negotiate an agreement between you and your ex – again, don't be bullied. The judge may also try to bully you into an agreement. Basically, all the professionals present want you and your ex to sort this out and take up as little court time as possible. This may include your own barrister – who's supposed to be on your side but sometimes they really aren't. If that's the case, be sure to get someone different for the next hearing.

It's so important to prepare well for this hearing, and to be able to remain calm and withstand the pressure you're likely to be under. Be crystal clear as to what you will and won't agree to. If you cave in under pressure and agree to an overnight stay, for instance, there will be no going back on that, he'll only get more next time. Ideally your position statement (Chapter 10) will have said you'll agree to less than you actually will so that you have room to negotiate at the hearing and look as if you're being reasonable. (Not that it really matters what you look like. The most important thing is to get the right outcome for your children, not to score brownie points for yourself.)

When you go into court, the Cafcass officer may start by telling the judge the results of their efforts to get the two of you to reach an agreement and whether they have any different advice to the court from that set out in the safeguarding letter. The applicant (or their barrister if they have one) will normally speak first and then the respondent. Both parties ask for what they want – such as a fact finding hearing, to file statements, a Section 7 report, etc. And the narcissist will no doubt want more contact with his children in the meantime.

In theory, at this hearing (or any other directions hearing) the court can't order you to do anything different to what you're doing now, unless you agree. This is because the court should hear evidence from both of you before making a decision. But because there's a culture in the courts of 'contact at all costs' and because the court is so short of time, orders are sometimes made that really shouldn't be. It's so important that you stick to your guns at this hearing and don't consent to anything you don't truly agree with – if you do, an order will be made 'by consent' and you won't be able to appeal it or go back on it. You simply can't afford to be agreeable or worry about what people think of you if your aim is to protect your children.

If your ex is having no contact and you believe that any contact will harm your child you cannot afford to make any concessions. If you accept that there should be some contact then there's usually room for compromise though you may have other 'red lines' e.g. that the contact should be supervised, or only daytime and not overnight. Be very clear in your own mind before you go to court where your 'red lines' are and don't be pressured into crossing them. Once contact is accepted in principle it's very hard indeed to resist 'progress' from supervised to unsupervised, or visiting to overnights. Having a friend with you, even if you're represented, can help you to withstand the pressure and do the right thing for your children.

The judge will decide what's going to happen next and this will be recorded in the court order. Sometimes the order will be drafted before you leave court, and sometimes it will be sent to you at a later date. Either way be sure to check it carefully (see Chapter 10 for more on checking orders).

Practice Direction 12J (PD12J) and what it means for your case

This is a direction to courts, made by the President of the Family Division, which may be relevant to your FHDRA hearing. It's not the law, which is made by Parliament; rather, it's the rules and procedure the court should follow. The law (i.e. the Children Act) says there is a presumption that it's best for the child if both parents continue to be involved in the child's life. The bit that seems to have been forgotten since 2014 when the law changed is, 'unless the contrary is shown'. Instead we have a culture of 'contact at all costs' and the cost to children can be huge.

In 2017 PD12J was amended to try and redress the balance. PD12J applies in any application relating to children where there are allegations that an adult or child has experienced domestic abuse by the other party. According to PD12J, the court should ensure that any order for contact will not expose the child to an unmanageable risk of harm and that it will be in the child's best interests.

How to use PD12J

You can find a link to PD12J in the Resources section. Do read it in full and use it where you can – as in, be prepared to ask the judge to follow it if you think they're not. If it's used properly, PD12J can disarm the narcissist and their quest for more contact.

If the other person denies the allegations of abuse, and if the allegations will make a difference to the court's final decision, the court should hold a fact finding hearing. Therefore, the court has to decide at the FHDRA whether a fact finding hearing is necessary. These fact finding hearings usually take two or three days, if not more, and there's likely to be a long delay before the court has that amount of time free. During that time, contact with the alleged perpetrator won't usually be increased, which doesn't fit well with the 'contact at all costs' culture of the family courts. So the courts do all they can to avoid fact finding hearings. One of the things the judge has to consider at the FHDRA is whether their final decision about the children seeing their father would be different if they did find the allegations of abuse to be true. Very often the court decides that even though someone has been abusive to their partner, they won't abuse their children, so the fact finding hearing would be a waste of time anyway.

Bottom line, referring to PD12J may help you argue for a fact finding hearing, but getting the courts to use PD12J isn't always easy. Be prepared to say what it is about your case that makes a fact finding hearing necessary.

Sometimes a hearing is ordered which is a combined fact finding hearing and a welfare hearing, so that Cafcass will prepare their report before the hearing (not afterwards, as is usually the case). This isn't ideal as Cafcass don't have the benefit of knowing whether there was abuse or not before making their recommendations as to the way forward.

Consider carefully whether or not you need to fight for a fact finding hearing. What are you hoping to achieve as the final outcome of the proceedings? Will your argument for supervised or limited contact stand up without findings of abuse being made? If there has been abuse or neglect, there are safeguarding issues – how do you want your children to be protected in the future? Is the court likely to order that if no findings of abuse have been made?

If you're still not sure whether to fight for a fact finding hearing, do take some advice if you can afford it, as cases can go horribly wrong if this decision isn't made properly.

If the judge does decide to order a fact finding hearing they will give directions about witness statements. If you have any witnesses who can give evidence about your abuse, be ready to tell the judge how many witnesses you'd like to call, and to give their names. Because court time is short you're likely to be limited in how many you can call, but a third party can make a big difference to your case so do have at least one if you can. Your mum or dad, or best friend, can be a witness for you – anyone who has seen or heard your ex abuse you or your child, or has seen your bruises or other injuries. As well as anyone else your ex has abused before or after his relationship with you.

Scott schedules

If a fact finding hearing is ordered, you may be asked to prepare a 'Scott schedule' (basically, a table-style template where you detail your allegations). Unfortunately the survivor is often limited to making just five or six separate allegations of abuse. This is fine if it's allegations of physical violence, for instance, but it's almost impossible to describe a pattern of behaviour where each incident could appear trivial on its own. And as a result, coercive control is still just as hard to prove in the family courts as it is in criminal proceedings.

However, the 2021 Court of Appeal decision in Re H-N (see Chapter 16) makes it clear that Scott schedules are not fit for purpose in cases of coercive control and hopefully they will soon cease to be ordered. So if you're asked to provide a Scott schedule when making allegations of coercive control, you should be able to argue against giving one. However, if the allegations are about physical abuse, the Scott schedule can still be used.

Pre-trial review (PTR)

The court may list this hearing before your fact finding hearing (or any other contested hearing). This will be a short directions hearing for the court to check that all the statements and other evidence is in, whether all the witnesses really need to be called to give evidence and if the time estimate for the fact finding hearing is still correct.

Interim contact order

If there is going to be a fact finding hearing, the court should only make an interim order for contact before then if it's safe for both child and parent. In other words, if your ex pushes for an interim contact order while waiting for a fact finding hearing, you can potentially argue that it is not safe for either you or your child for him to have any or more or unsupervised contact before a decision has been made about his alleged abuse.

Fact finding hearings (FFHs)

If the court does order a fact finding hearing – a contested hearing, where you'll give evidence – what can you expect?

When it comes to abuse, the 'truth' is rarely obvious

When Caroline Flack died I read a lot of posts on social media. Some were saying how abusive she'd been to her partner, while others were saying she was the one who was abused.

As I was reading all this I was struck by how similar it was to what the family courts regularly have to decide: which of the two is the abuser. In fact, I had never heard of Caroline Flack before she died so knew nothing about her, which meant I read the social media posts a bit like a judge in a family court comes new to the evidence presented to them. And I had absolutely no idea which of them might have been the perpetrator and which the victim. As one poster on social media put it, 'Nobody knows what goes on behind closed doors and I guess nobody will ever know.'

So it's clear that the family courts are faced with an almost impossible task when they have to decide cases involving abuse. This is why fact finding hearings are so important.

What to expect from a fact finding hearing

Fact finding hearings are more like criminal trials than normal family court hearings as both parties and any witnesses have to give evidence on oath about the allegations and be cross-examined. The person making the allegations will often go first (rather than the applicant) and then be cross-examined. At the end of the hearing, the judge says which allegations they find to be true, and which they don't. But unlike in a criminal court, if an allegation is found to be true that doesn't make the perpetrator 'guilty' or mean that they will have a criminal record. In legal terms, 'findings of fact' are made if the court finds something is 'more likely than not' to have happened, whereas a criminal court has to be sure that it did.

Even though it isn't a criminal trial, the court still has to make black and white decisions about situations that are usually messy and very far from clear. Because of this, how the parties present themselves when they give their evidence, and how they behave in court, will have a big influence on the final decisions.

This is a big problem because:

- The judge has little, if any, training in domestic abuse and none in personality disorders but probably has stereotypical assumptions about how both abusers and victims should perform.

- The narcissist is a brilliant actor, and remains cool, calm and collected while being charming and persuasive in his lies.

- The victim may be traumatised by the abuse, triggered while reliving it in evidence and barely able to string two words together, let alone relate the events in a coherent and chronological order.

The judge doesn't have a crystal ball or any other way of knowing whether someone is telling the truth or not. Coercive or controlling behaviour in particular can be difficult to prove and there's no guarantee that the court will come to the right conclusion as to who is the abuser and who the abused. If the abuser is projecting – i.e. accusing the other parent of what they are actually doing themselves – how is the judge supposed to know who is telling the truth?

This means it's really important that you conduct yourself properly in court and prepare for the ordeal of giving evidence. There's more on giving evidence coming up late in the chapter.

The wrong findings made at a fact finding hearing can be devastating and make things much worse rather than better for the abused party. But if you do get findings against your abuser, it's a huge step forward in your case. Cafcass then have to prepare their report on the basis that your allegations are true, and the more your ex protests they're not, the more it'll go against him.

Dispute resolution appointment (DRA)

After the fact finding hearing, Cafcass will prepare their Section 7 report (more on this coming up), and then there will be a directions hearing – a dispute resolution appointment (DRA). If both parents agree with the recommendations made by Cafcass it will be the last hearing and a final order will be made. But if one party does not agree with the recommendations, directions will be given for a final hearing – i.e. for more witness statements to be filed setting out what each party says the final arrangements should be and why they do or don't agree with the Cafcass report.

Final hearings

> Yes it was a final hearing (even though it was only listed for a few hours). Yes it was brutal, game playing, collusion and lies, but I am becoming an expert in this (it wasn't all terrible, it could have been worse, but my god the system is screwed). Anyway, the music to my ears this evening is 'The Guardian has been discharged'. She was one useless, incompetent person.

If you don't reach an agreement after the Cafcass Section 7 report the judge will list your case for a final hearing – a contested hearing, which is likely to last for at least one day depending on how many people there are to give evidence. Usually there will be at least three: both parents and the Cafcass officer.

Don't be tempted to agree to something you're not happy with just to avoid this contested hearing. You have to live with the result for a long time, so it's worth a few uncomfortable hours to try all you can to get the best outcome for your children.

If your ex made the application, he will give his evidence first. He'll stop at nothing to win and when he's giving his evidence it's easy to be distracted by his lies and character assassination of you. Refer back to the tips earlier in this chapter on dealing with his lies in court. If you've made the application, you will give your evidence first. After giving your evidence-in-chief as it's called, you will be cross-examined by your ex's barrister on what you've said and written in your statement. And after both parents have given their evidence, any witnesses or experts will give theirs. That's the theory, but in practice the Cafcass officer may well go first so they can leave court and get on with their work. And experts may be fitted in to suit their timetables rather than the court's.

There's more on giving evidence and being cross-examined coming up later in the chapter.

Your final order – and why you must stick to it

The last court order in the process, this decides the application that was made in the first place and ends the court proceedings. It can happen at any time during the process if the parents reach an agreement – if not, the judge decides at the final hearing. In the context of children proceedings, the final order sets out all the arrangements for the children, such as who they live with, how much time they spend with the other parent and all the other details as set out in this section.

It's really important to have every last detail recorded in your final order so that there's nothing left for the narcissist to argue over in the future. The lawyers and the judge may lose patience as you try to get the order right, and you'll probably want to give up and go home too. But you'll regret it in the months to come if you don't finish the job properly.

For example, you'll want to check things like:

- Does the order provide for who does the handovers and where and how they take place, both in term time and holidays? (So, if it's 'Wednesday after school' is it still 3.30pm on Wednesdays in the holidays?)

- Does it say where the children will be on birthdays, Christmas Day, Mother's Day, etc? And does it have the exact hours on those days?

- What about school holidays? Is there a formula set out so you don't have to negotiate with your ex over which weeks they have them every year?

- How about school uniforms – do they need to be washed/returned at the end of a weekend?

- If your order is for 50/50 shared residence, what happens if one parent signs their child up for a weekly activity – does the other parent have to agree to take them on their weeks?

Make sure there's nothing in your order that says it's 'to be agreed' between you in the future. A narcissist doesn't agree, not now, not ever, so don't agree to that being in your order. Also make sure that any provisions (that suit you!) from previous interim orders are included in the final order so the narcissist can't argue later they don't apply now.

When the order has been typed up and sent to you, you'll obviously need to check carefully that it covers everything agreed.

Having got your very detailed court order, unfortunately you have to stick to it through thick and thin. There's no give and take with a narcissist (only take) and unfortunately neither you nor your children will be able to deviate from the court order. They will have to go on exactly the times and dates set out in the order and you should only change it in cases of emergency.

The narcissist will keep trying to get you to do something different to what's in the order, with a sob story here, a bribe or two there and plenty of manipulation and gaslighting in between. If you agree to the slightest variation, you're sunk. He'll keep pushing for more and bigger variations, and you won't be able to say he's got to stick to the order when you've previously given in on other changes (however small) to the agreed arrangements. And you can be sure he won't agree to any variations of the order that you might want. As always, it's the children who suffer because they probably won't be able to attend parties or sporting events during his time. But this is the nature of parallel parenting (see Chapter 6). Ultimately, sticking rigidly to the order will make your life much easier in the long run.

Barring orders

Having got your final order, the narcissist will probably keep taking you back to court until he gets bored (because you've managed to disengage), or he's run out of money (and for some reason doesn't want to be a litigant in person), or your child is 16. The only way to stop him continuing to control you in this way is by getting a 'barring order' under S.91(14) of the Children Act (which restricts his rights to make another application to the court). Barring orders aren't easy to get as people are only barred from accessing court in exceptional circumstances. And even if you do get one, you'll need to keep in mind that:

- It's not a complete bar as he can still apply for permission to make a further application, so it's effectively just another hoop he has to jump through.

- It may only last for a year or two.
- You will probably be barred from making another application too.

You're unlikely to succeed in an application for a barring order the first time you ask, so if you've been taken back to court for the second time without good reason that could be a good time to start asking the judge for a barring order (verbally or in a position statement).

In the 2019 Court of Appeal case of Re G (Children: intractable dispute), the father lost his appeal against a three-year barring order. He had made 56 applications to the court over three years. During that time, there had been about 30 hearings, 50 orders and there were 13 files of documents. And this was only since the previous appeal – the judgement doesn't say how many hearings there were in the two years before that! What's more, in the eight months between the barring order and this appeal, the father had made six applications asking for permission to make another application. The Court of Appeal agreed with the judge that the mother and children were entitled to protection from incessant litigation.

This was an extreme case and it's unfortunate that the courts won't make these orders more often. Don't let that stop you applying, though, and hopefully this reluctance to issue barring orders will change as the courts (gradually) begin to understand that this is yet another tactic of coercive control. And when the Domestic Abuse Act (see Chapter 16) comes into force, hopefully before the end of 2021, section 67 will make things a lot easier; the courts will then be able to make a barring order if they are satisfied that another application would put you or your child at risk of harm, and that's without the need for lots of previous applications having been made.

You can tell Cafcass at your interview for the Section 7 report that you'd like a barring order and ask if they would support your application.

Evidence, evidence, evidence

If you were a detective in a criminal investigation you'd have to keep meticulous notes. Many of those notes wouldn't be needed or relevant in the end but you don't know where the case is going at the start, and sometimes putting all those clues together can lead to gold. You need to do the same. Gathering evidence is a critical part of navigating the family court and getting what you want from children proceedings.

Shutty shutty, write it down – creating a log of what he says and does

Keep notes on every last detail – for example, was he late, did he ask to change the arrangements (even if court ordered), did he bring a girlfriend, are his parents always there, did he over-react? Over time, mundane details can show patterns and so your logs can make good exhibits to witness statements. You may even be able to give your log to Cafcass at the Section 7 interview, if they'll accept it (they won't always). But if nothing else, having a log will help you describe specific examples of his behaviour when talking to Cafcass or when writing your statement for the court.

The narcissist is very persuasive. People listen to him and believe what he says. Your word against his rarely works so you want to show that his words don't match his actions. By keeping a daily log on a spreadsheet, you can eventually (hopefully) expose his behaviour.

In general, you're looking for patterns of behaviour, rather than one-off incidents. While one-offs can be helpful, and certainly need to be noted down too, it's easier for the narcissist to explain away single events; patterns, on the other hand, are much harder for him to get away from. Disordered personalities don't change their behaviour so if you look back over the years you'll be sure to find a pattern.

> *He treated her the way he treated me. All her confidence had gone and he had drilled into her that she was fat, stupid and ugly 'just like her mum'.*

For instance, how does your ex react if someone says something he doesn't like or doesn't agree with? Does he shout, argue, change the subject, shut the other person down, or walk off if they try to discuss things with him? Does this include his children? What is the effect on them? Or does he have a pattern of responding with unwarranted or excessive anger? Or an inability to control his anger? Or does he often display impulsive or self-destructive behaviour? Think of three or four of his patterns of behaviour and then find three or four examples of each.

Analyse his parenting carefully. You've got used to it, but what would another parent who didn't know your family think of it?

- Does he expect his children to be perfect (like him)?
- How does he deal with any disabilities or difficulties they may have? Does he show a level of denial about them, or a failure to accept their imperfections?

- How does he react when his children have different wishes or views to him? Will he support a son who wants to play cricket when he only loves football himself?
- Is he helping his children to become independent or does he limit, inappropriately for their age, where they can go and who they can see?
- Does he micromanage their lives now, like he used to yours?
- Does he violate their boundaries, for example, by walking into their room without knocking, reading their diaries or telling them how they feel, rather than asking them and validating their feelings?
- What messages, overt or implied, does he give his children about how women should be treated?
- Does he drive fast or dangerously with the children in the car?
- Does he prepare them well for big events, such as meeting a new partner, or does he ambush them?
- Does he treat one child better than the other? Are there messages on their phones that evidence this?
- How does he discipline the children? Is it proportionate and age appropriate?

And look at his behaviour in general. Narcissists can only behave the way they behave; they're not usually capable of reflecting on their behaviour and adapting it when it doesn't work as most of us do. So if you can identify his patterns of behaviour, you can probably predict what he'll do next. For example:

- Does he see some people as all bad and others as all good or have other black or white thinking?
- Does he have a habit of blaming others (even his children) or finding fault with people or complaining, rather than taking responsibility?
- Does he say he's trying to resolve a dispute while actually increasing it, maybe by shouting, drawing other people into it or running away?
- What happens when you try to discuss a current issue? Does he stay focused on it or distract you with past grievances or his victimhood? Does he stay calm but drive you to anger or exhaustion?
- Are his emotional reactions more intense than other people's or out of proportion with what's happened?
- Can he control himself when something untoward happens, or does he throw his toys out of the pram like a two-year-old?

- What does he do when he doesn't get his own way? Does he shout or threaten or stonewall you for a week?

I recommend you create a spreadsheet log of events, reactions and behaviour. Your spreadsheet can have several columns:

- The date of the incident
- The incident itself
- His behaviour or reaction
- The effect on the children
- Whether you reported the incident to anyone else (such as the police or a social worker)
- Any action taken by that third party
- You may also want to record things he says and things he does so you can show how they differ

When listing the effect on the children, describe how each incident harmed your child's health, wellbeing, education, or self-confidence (physically or emotionally). It doesn't matter if each incident is only tiny, it all builds up and you're slowly but surely building evidence of patterns of behaviour. This might not come easily to you (you could be so used to his behaviour that it's become totally normal for you), so if you're not sure whether something is 'normal', talk it through with a friend or your coach or therapist.

You can also consider what you would have done in each situation. Most of us modify our behaviour when something doesn't work, and try something different the next time; parents in particular have to do this. But a narcissist can't or won't change their behaviour and will keep doing the same thing. So keep writing it all down, and be sure to look back over your log before talking to Cafcass, writing your statement or giving evidence.

Importantly, when you know he's lied, don't tell him. Shutty shutty, write it down! Work out the best time to use it (which may be when you've got even more ammunition further down the line) and produce it then. If you tell him straight away that you've caught him out, he'll just figure out a way to make you wrong, not him, and he won't make such a mistake again. So hold your fire, however tempting it might be to shout about your little victory now. The narcissist will be inconsistent in his lies or 'facts' so it's important to note them all down and show how he said one thing one week and the opposite the next week. With a more comprehensive record of his lies, it'll be harder for him to get away with it.

Gathering other evidence that may help you in court

Social media messages and updates can be very helpful in court, especially if you get into a 'he said/she said' situation, so screenshot them before they disappear. If it's triggering for you to read his social media pages, ask a friend to keep an eye on them for you and just give you anything that may be relevant. A good example is him showing off his lavish lifestyle while pleading poverty to you and refusing to pay child maintenance. Or maybe he's foolish enough to post about a wild weekend away when he was supposed to be with the children, or does he first announce a new relationship on Facebook?

When it comes to your children, make sure you scrupulously keep every bit of evidence that may help at a later stage – and make sure all that evidence is dated. If your children come home upset or injured, awful though it is, photograph it all (ideally without them seeing you do it) as well as writing it down. If they have meltdowns, video them (again, preferably without them knowing). If you're doing handovers yourself, video them if there's any possibility of abuse or untoward comments. If he gives or sends them anything inappropriate, be sure to photograph it before you bin it.

It's also a good idea to keep diary entries every day, whether that's in a notebook you keep by your bed, in a notes app on your phone, or on another page of your evidence spreadsheet. Use these entries to note any activities your children did that day, followed by how they behaved, if they were unwell, how they were emotionally, any relevant comments they may have made. (Again, always make sure every entry is dated.) Record the good as well as the bad, the happy and the sad – it all helps to identify patterns. How are your children different before or after going to their father? Can you see a build-up of behaviour in the days leading up to contact? Or are they subdued or do they have bad attitudes in the days afterwards?

Get evidence from your child's school if possible. (Cafcass should do this, but rarely do.) Teachers often don't want to get involved and, if they have to deal with the narcissist themselves, you can hardly blame them. However, you can ask the court to request a factual report from the school about your child's behaviour, performance and attendance; and to give dates which may then relate it to time spent with the abusive parent, or your child's reaction afterwards.

What about audio recordings? Both the abuser and victim are likely to make recordings of each other, though for different reasons; victims do it because they no longer trust their own memory, while narcissists do it because they want to use it against their victim. And both may record meetings with Cafcass and other professionals because they don't trust them.

Recordings are difficult as the court will often refuse to let you use them as evidence. (Voice recordings and video can't be attached to a witness statement – unlike photos, which can easily be attached.) They may even accuse you of escalating the 'parental conflict' by recording things. Don't let any of this stop you, although it's best if you can avoid letting your children see that you're recording difficult handovers with their father. You can always transcribe your recording for court, and attach it to your witness statement as an exhibit. Outside of court, you may be able to play it back to Cafcass or a social worker or psychologist in your case, after the narcissist's convinced them how reasonable and charming he is. If nothing else, you'll be able to quote word for word any abusive interchange.

Keeping your evidence safe and orderly

I'm afraid gathering all this evidence is a tedious job which you're likely to have to continue for years to come. This means it's best to create a workable system from the outset. Otherwise you'll have an overwhelming amount of evidence all in different places and formats.

That's why I recommend keeping your written evidence in a spreadsheet – but do make sure it's backed up to cloud storage (obviously to a cloud account that your ex doesn't have access to). Photos, videos and audio should also be stored digitally and backed up safely. Alternatively, you could send a daily email to a friend, or to another email account you set up for yourself (with an address your ex doesn't know), but this may not be so easy to trawl through when you need to find a specific piece of information.

You may also want to blind copy (bcc) your solicitor or a friend, as well as yourself, into every email you send to your ex, and/or to professionals. You've then got this evidence in chronological order if you need it against false allegations later.

The truth, the whole truth ... or economical with the truth?

As I've said throughout this book, the truth doesn't always prevail. In fact, the more you try to expose a narcissist, the less people believe you. So whenever you're at a court hearing or talking to Cafcass/social services, don't launch into a huge defence of yourself (if you need to refute an allegation, a simple 'That didn't happen' or 'I deny his allegation' will suffice). And don't blame your ex.

The more you try to point the finger negatively at the other parent the worse the court will view you. Far better to use your evidence to demonstrate a pattern of behaviour, or how he says one thing and does another.

Although it may sound counterintuitive, it's often best if you limit the information you give. Remember, the court is a cold and emotionless place, and the judge wants evidence (i.e. facts and figures), not your feelings. So it's best to calculate your words and keep them largely devoid of emotion.

An abuser will often try to convince the court, Cafcass and social services that you are the abuser and he is the victim, and will paint the picture of you as being the unreasonable and unfair one. If a professional person doesn't ask you for specific information don't volunteer it. And always talk about how the abuse affects the children rather than how it affects you, because if they become aware of how you are upset or traumatised by the abuse, they can use that against you to support the abuser's narrative that you are unstable. This is especially true if you don't have hard evidence of the things you know they did (all the more reason to gather as much evidence as you can). In some cases, the abuser even frames the victim's allegations of abuse as evidence of parental alienation, resulting in some mothers losing residence of their children.

It was after the birth of our second daughter that things really got bad. Up until this point I thought that I was able to protect the children from the worst of his moods, his anger, his aggression. But my oldest daughter was petrified of her father. When she had done something that aggrieved my ex and he picked her up by the scruff of her t-shirt, dragged her up the stairs and threw her onto her bed – she was four at the time – I realised that actually I wasn't able to protect them and I needed to leave. I told him that we couldn't continue like this, it wasn't fair on the children and I would not allow them to grow up thinking this behaviour was okay.

The children and I remained in the house. Over the course of the next week or two, my ex repeatedly came into the house in the early hours of the morning and climbed into bed with me. I kicked him out each time. I was told by the school that my daughter had been making comments about how she was so scared of her father and that I needed to contact social services. So I contacted social services, and was advised that I needed to get a solicitor and go to court to apply for a residency order and a prohibited steps order to stop my ex taking the children. I was also advised by children's services not to let my ex have contact for the time being.

My ex would repeatedly call if I didn't answer. He would do this up to 60 times. It was incessant, and on the few occasions I did answer I let him know that I had been in contact with children's services and been advised not to let him see the children for now. I put in an application for a residence order and a prohibited steps order and my ex put in a counter application for contact. We went through two years of hearings at the family court. The judge denied him contact each time. He admitted in court to much of his behaviour, although denied that it was domestic abuse – he said it was just conflict between a couple. Eventually he was allowed supervised contact at a contact centre every two weeks. He went to the contact centre for six months and then he was allowed to take the children out for a couple of hours unsupervised and return them to me. After this the judge ordered that overnight contact could take place and this should be on an alternate weekend and half the holiday basis. That very first weekend of overnight contact, my daughters came back very distressed. My youngest daughter, who by this stage was four-and-a-half, came back with a red raw genital area – a repeat of how she had returned from seeing him two-and-a-half years prior to that. I was quite concerned about this fact and alerted the GP, who arranged for my daughter to be seen by a forensic paediatrician. When she was examined it was found that she was very red and sore inside as well as outside but they could not definitively say whether any penetration had taken place. This report was then sent to children's services who said that contact should continue because they could not definitively say that penetration had taken place. I was forced to continue sending both my daughters for contact.

My youngest daughter's personality completely changed. She became withdrawn. She was petrified of her father. She would hide as soon as she knew that he was coming to collect her. A lot of the time, she completely refused to go, but he would pull her screaming from my arms. My eldest daughter went for each and every single contact and at this point there were no signs that anything was going on with her.

Five months later, after my youngest had been for contact, as I was putting her to bed she said to me that she was red and sore again. She had continued to be red and sore each and every single time she had gone for contact. I asked her what was going on and said that we needed to get to the bottom of why she was continuously coming back sore. She said to me, 'Mummy, it's sore when they poke me.' I asked her what she meant and she said 'It's sore when they poke inside my fanny.' I asked her who poked inside her fanny and she didn't seem to know. She said that it was too dark to see who it was but it was big fingers not little ones and it really hurt. She was trying to go through the list of all the other children in the house, naming them one by one, ruling them out saying it couldn't be this one because he was in a cot, or it couldn't be that one because he was asleep. It genuinely seemed to me that she didn't know who it was. She eventually settled on the fact that it must have been the puppies because my ex and his wife had puppies in the house at that stage.

I immediately called the NSPCC to report what she had told me. The NSPCC alerted children's services again and also the police. I was told I had to take her to the GP first thing the next morning for an examination, which

I did. My daughter jumped up onto the examination table, pulled down her pants and splayed her legs immediately without any prompting. This was really concerning to the GP. The GP again arranged for my daughter to be seen at the hospital by a different forensic paediatrician. This paediatrician said the same thing, that he could not definitively say whether full penetration had happened but he definitely could not rule out digital penetration. He said unfortunately in these situations they often see kids six or seven times before they actually have enough evidence to definitively say something has happened. This was reported to children's services who decided that once again contact should continue.

I was very concerned by this stage because, not only was my daughter physically coming back displaying signs of sexual abuse, her whole personality had changed. She was showing sexualized behaviour. She was petrified of her father, and refusing to go to contact. I was now being forced to send my daughter, plus my other daughter, despite what my youngest had disclosed. I was told by the social worker that I must not believe anything a child says because children make things up and it's a very complicated situation so she will tell me what she thinks I want to hear. There is no way that a five-year-old would be able to make that sort of stuff up unless it actually had happened to them or they had witnessed or heard about it, all of which are abusive situations.

Six days after she first disclosed to me she started speaking about it again, saying that she didn't want the puppies to be locked up. She very quickly changed from the puppies being locked up to the person being locked up. In the space of a 10-minute conversation she must have mentioned about 20 times that she didn't want the person to get locked up. Once again, what five-year-old equates what has happened to her with getting locked up? It was at this moment that I realised she knew exactly who it was that had done this and that she'd been threatened to keep quiet. That night she went into a lot more detail of what had happened, although she still didn't say who it was.

As a result of this, both my children were put on a child protection plan, but unfortunately they were not put on the child protection plan under the category of sexual abuse – they were put on under emotional harm due to the animosity between my ex and myself. I was devastated! Children's services were ignoring my daughter's disclosures and her worrying behaviour, and they were minimising the whole thing. Children's services told the police that they did not need to investigate, and my daughter was never given an interview by the police.

My ex's knee-jerk reaction to this was to accuse me of parental alienation and state that I was coaching my daughter to say these things in order to stop contact. He then applied to the courts for a residency change, claiming that I would always obstruct his contact and I would never allow him to have a relationship with his daughters. Not once did he ever ask or seem to want to try and find out why his daughter had said the things she did.

Surely as a parent, if your child has stated what she said about sexual abuse, you would do your damndest to get to the bottom of it. Not once did he do that. His only reaction was to say it wasn't him. No one had ever said it was him. There are two adults in his house – him and his now wife – and her six children. According to my daughter, this had happened on numerous occasions so it ruled out someone visiting the house. It had to have been one of the adults, either my ex or his wife. We still to this day do not know, and we may never know.

We went through another year or so of hearings with this case, and initially social services were completely wrapped up by my ex, who had them eating out of his hands. Social services initially supported his application for residency change. But over the course of the year, through the work that social services had done with my children, they changed their tune. Three days before our final hearing, they put in an addendum report saying that they no longer supported his application for a residency change.

For our final hearing, unfortunately we got a different judge to whom we had had all the way through. I freaked when we heard who we had because this judge had himself been in court on charges of sexual abuse against a minor. He was cleared, which is why he was still practising but nevertheless he should not be overseeing cases like this. This judge had also been named as being very pro-father in all cases, regardless of the situation. I knew from the first few minutes of the first day of the three-day final hearing that I'd lost my children. The judge ignored the fact that my ex was proven to have lied throughout his statement and under oath on the stand. The judge ignored the fact that the social worker had put in an addendum report – he said the initial Section 7 report would have been much more carefully considered and this addendum was a later change. It was too late in the day so he would not listen to the addendum. This was despite the fact that the social worker was cross-examined and once again stated that she did not support a residence change. The judge also ignored the wishes of both children, who did not want to move to their father's house at all. The judge ordered that the children were to move in with their father and that I was to have alternate weekend contact and holidays, as well as Mother's Day.

I was granted permission to appeal. The order was stayed and the children remained with me until the appeal was heard a few months later. Sadly I lost the appeal and was told that the children would still move in with their father. Two days later the children were picked up from school by the father and his wife. I was not allowed to be there to say goodbye. Bearing in mind that this wasn't a simple residency change – it was a move from everything the girls had ever known, to a new house three hours away, away from their school, their friends, their extended family, basically everything they had ever known their whole life. This was in December 2016.

Since this time the children have been living with their father. For the best part of a year after the move, I would have them in tears every time they were with me, begging me not to send them back to their father. They would hide when he was due to come and collect them and beg me to keep them with me. The father has repeatedly taken it back to court since this time, trying to stop me having any contact with the children at all. He hasn't got his way in that respect, but each time he's got that little bit more control and an extra order on me. I now have a prohibited steps order against me preventing me from taking the children for any medical appointments or medical care whatsoever. This is a result of the father claiming that I was over-medicalising the children and taking them for repeated medical appointments and obtaining prescriptions that they didn't need. I submitted all the children's medical records to prove that actually this was not the case. I had letters from the GP to say they did not see the children too regularly. All the records showed that in the period of three years, my eldest had been to the doctor once and my youngest had been seen three times. This is not excessive. However the judge decided to grant the prohibited steps order on me.

My ex then applied for a barring order stating that the children should not be coming backwards and forwards to court (not that they have ever actually been to court themselves). He applied for the barring order on me, even though from 2012 to the present day I have only made two applications to the court: first for the residence order and prohibited steps order and then the appeal hearing for the residency change. Every single other application was my ex (we have had well over 20 applications), yet he was asking for a barring order on me. The judge granted the barring order for three years. She granted it on both of us, though, and said that the case was not to return to court for three years. This expires in April 2022.

This means that during the three-year period, my ex has been able to do whatever he wants with no repercussions. He's withheld contact, he stops telephone calls, he's prevented the children coming to me on numerous occasions and he knows that I'm powerless to do anything about it. I cannot take it back to court. The children are very heavily manipulated not only by my ex but his wife too. In fact, I would say his wife is 80% responsible for all the issues that we have now. She is intent on turning my children against me and will do everything in her power to do that. She tells them that if they don't come to me that she will take them for horse riding lessons, or take them shopping and buy them lots of new clothes. Initially this didn't work with my children, but unfortunately it's starting to work now.

When my girls are with me they're full of love and cuddles and we have an amazing time. Unfortunately, whenever we're in a situation where it's myself and the children and the stepmother, or the children's father, the girls are petrified to be okay with me. They get rewarded for treating me badly in front of them. My children are now 13 and 11. They are at a very difficult stage of their lives. I find myself playing damage control all the time, trying to limit the effects of the manipulation they're going through. This is a very, very hard thing to do as I refuse to denigrate them, but at the same time I need to let my children know that this behaviour is not okay.

I don't know where we're going to end up. I don't know whether my children will ever come back to me. I feel like I'm losing them. I feel like I'm losing them really quickly now. My children are now being turned against me. My youngest tells me that what Daddy says to her is right, that I lie all the time. This isn't the life I wanted for my children!

While you may well be suffering from PTSD, anxiety or depression due to the trauma of the abuse by your ex, you may need to downplay these effects during proceedings, especially if your ex is trying to prove that you are mentally unstable. No matter that it's been caused by him, it won't stop him trying to use it against you to prove you're an 'unfit mother'. If this is the case, it may be wise to tell the court, your social worker, GP, Cafcass, etc. that you've taken steps to deal with the stress and anxiety and that you're coping well under the circumstances. Tell them you have the support of your family and friends. In other words, you're admitting that his abuse has caused you stress, anxiety, or worse, but making it clear that you have all this under control.

Otherwise you risk professionals saying they're worried about your children and bring residence into dispute. There's no confidentiality for mothers in this situation; your GP records can be requested (if you refuse they'll say you have something to hide) and a social worker may tell the court you have mental health problems to protect their own back if they're worried about your children.

Try not to be so concerned about the truth – that's not what the family court is about. Focus on your strategy and goals (see Chapter 5) rather than exposing your ex as an abuser. And rather than asking yourself 'Is this right?' or 'Is this true?' ask, 'Will this work?'

Giving your evidence in court, and being cross-examined

Giving evidence and being cross-examined is scary. For anyone. Even professional witnesses such as social workers, Cafcass and doctors can feel nervous and anxious about being in the witness box. The one person who isn't worried is the narcissist (the overt narcissist, the sociopath and the psychopath that is. The coverts and borderlines may be adversely affected).

Your ex is going to love his day in court, hearing the sound of his own voice, playing to the room, and lying and manipulating all concerned. It's a hard act to follow, but you may live to regret it if you back down now and reach an agreement (that doesn't work for you) before you have a chance to give evidence in court. Here I go through the main considerations for giving evidence in children proceedings (although much of the advice applies to financial proceedings and injunctions, too).

Preparing to give evidence

If you know you're going to have to give evidence at a contested hearing, prepare well. Failing to prepare is preparing to fail.

- Keep thinking about what you might be asked and how you will answer it. Write down your possible answers and learn them.

- Do some role play with a friend, asking them to fire questions at you (including lies that will shock you), until you can remain calm and answer well. Get used to listening carefully to questions and answering succinctly without getting upset or angry.

- Attend the Court Confidence course or a witness familiarisation course (listed in the Resources section) to help you give your evidence and prepare for court.

- Prepare yourself emotionally with a therapist or coach so that you're not triggered by the lies or aggressive questioning.

- Read through the all documents filed in your case (statements, reports, etc.) until you're familiar with them all, but especially your own, which you'll be questioned on. You won't receive the court bundle – a PDF or hard copy of all the important court documents in your case – until a few days before the hearing and it will help you to feel less flustered when giving your evidence if you can find your way around it quickly and easily. You'll usually have had court bundles in previous hearings, so you can at least be familiar with the sections they're divided into and the documents already in there before you receive the updated one.

- Finally, prepare yourself practically for what may be a long day. Contested hearings can last several hours, so make sure you take something to drink and eat to sustain you through the day.

Giving your evidence

If you're the applicant in the proceedings, you'll give your evidence first. You'll have written one or more statements (see witness statements), and these will be your main evidence. Your barrister will ask you a few questions first, just to confirm what's in your statement and add anything that's happened since. If you don't have a barrister, you simply confirm what's in your statement is true and give any other updating evidence.

The first thing to remember when you're in court is not to look at the narcissist, or his barrister, and to give all your answers directly to the judge. If you have a screen in court this will help you (and infuriate your ex). On the other hand, if you don't have a screen and can manage not to look at your ex, this may infuriate and unravel him even more, especially if you have a new calmness about you and he sees he's unable to affect you as he used to.

If you know you're going to find it difficult to answer the questions when you're later cross-examined, it's a good idea to have your barrister ask you about this at the start. For example, your barrister could ask you if you suffer from PTSD and what effect that has on you, and you could reply that if you're triggered your brain freezes and you just end up staring and unable to speak. This means that you will need a few moments to think things through before you can answer.

It's important that the judge knows this because, when witnesses pause before answering questions, they're sometimes perceived as making it up. You may want to say that so much has happened it's all muddled up in your head and you're worried about not making sense when you give your evidence. Or that it's been so traumatic that you've tried to put things out of your mind and now you're having trouble recalling them all. This may be worth doing if you're worried you can't give a good account of yourself.

When giving evidence, you must always tell the truth – but how much you say, and how you say it, makes all the difference. Ultimately, these proceedings are about your children, although of course the narcissist will try to make them all about him (but definitely not about his abuse) or about how dreadful you are. So always bring your answers back to the children if you possibly can – talk about what they witnessed and the effect it had on them. For instance, instead of saying 'I was really scared when he threw the plate that just missed my head and smashed into the wall and it upset me to see the children looking so frightened,' you could say something like 'The children were whimpering under the kitchen table after the plate smashed into smithereens; it took me ages to coax them out even after their father had left the house. After that they clung to me constantly and wouldn't go near him for over three weeks.'

When you're cross-examined

Don't rush to answer his barrister's questions. Breathe and think before you answer. Be very clear about what you're being asked – never answer a question by rambling on in the hope that you're giving them the 'right' answer somewhere along the way. Don't hesitate to ask for the question to be repeated if you're not crystal clear on exactly what they're asking. Remember, the only time you speak to the barrister is if you need to ask them to repeat the question. Otherwise, all your answers should be aimed at the judge.

Once again, don't say too much: 'yes', 'no' and 'I don't know' are often the best answers as they can't be twisted to mean anything else. Don't try to tell your story – it should already be there in your statement(s) anyway. Just answer the question being asked and shutty shutty. A common barristers' trick is to keep looking at you without saying anything when you've finished talking, so that you feel obliged to fill the silence and carry on speaking (hopefully, in the process, admitting what they're trying to get you to say). If you keep looking firmly at the judge when you give your answers you won't fall into this trap. Another barristers' trick is to not look directly at you when they're asking you their questions in order to unnerve you. Again, just do this right back at them and reply directly to the judge, not them!

You'll probably already know most of the allegations he's going to make against you. Just answer with a simple denial, like 'No, that's not true' or 'No, that didn't happen' or 'That's not correct, no.' It will be your natural instinct to try to defend yourself against his lies and accusations but don't be tempted to explain why it's not true – it's his allegation and it's for him to prove it, not for you to disprove it. Though you could say something like 'No that's not true but x did happen and that harmed our child by....'.

You'll no doubt be accused of lying, or told 'but that didn't happen did it?' so have your answers to these ready-formed. You could say something like 'I'm not lying. I was brought up to tell the truth and that's what I do' or 'Yes it did happen, I don't make things up'. And however many times you're told you're lying, just keep looking the judge in the eye and calmly repeating your prepared phrases.

You may feel embarrassed to answer some questions truthfully but don't let that stop you; dying of embarrassment is just a figure of speech and you will survive even if your face goes very red and you want the floor to open and swallow you up. You could be asked why you didn't leave before if things were as bad as you say; don't be afraid to give your real reasons, such as you were too ashamed or embarrassed and didn't want to tell anyone what was really going on, or you thought things would get better and you wanted to keep your family together.

If your ex's barrister is being really aggressive, or asking questions you shouldn't be asked – such as things that you've done in the past that aren't relevant to the children, or new allegations that weren't in the Scott schedule or statements – you could say to the judge that you're feeling intimidated and ask them to ask the barrister to stop rolling his eyes, making disparaging remarks, asking these questions, or whatever else he's doing to antagonise you. Whether they'll stop it will depend on the judge. If you're really desperate not to answer a certain question, you could ask the judge (not the barrister) if you really have to answer it – but it's best if you can leave that line to the narcissist. If your ex doesn't like the questions your barrister asks him, he might ask them if he has to answer, or how long they're going to keep asking questions for. As it is the job of the barristers to ask questions and not answer them he shouldn't get away with this, but as we know, narcissists get away with an awful lot they shouldn't do. From your perspective, don't be tempted to ask his barrister a question back (except to clarify their questions of you). You certainly won't get away with it!

Think about agreeing with certain questions that his barrister asks, as it's a good way of shutting down their line of argument. Though be careful not to answer with just a 'yes' if you've more to say as there's a risk his barrister will jump in and stop you, moving quickly on to their next question. So, for instance, if you were asked 'But you screamed hysterically at Zac on Mother's Day last year, didn't you?' it would be better to say 'Zac's football rolled into the road just as I saw a bus coming round the corner and I did scream loudly at him, yes.'

Or if you were asked 'Do you agree that you're over-anxious?' it wouldn't be a good idea just to say 'No' if they then go on to point out all the things that they think show you are anxious. After all, they may ultimately be trying to show that you're unstable and unreliable. Instead, you could say something like 'I'm very anxious standing here right now' or 'I'm anxious about my child being abused by her father' or 'I can't imagine any mother who knows her child is being abused, not being extremely anxious. I think my anxiety is proportionate to the abuse my child is suffering and my feelings of total helplessness at being unable to protect her' or 'I'm anxious about whether the court will believe my daughter' or 'I'm anxious about the effect of my ex's behaviour on my children and how it will impact their relationships as adults.'

If you're asked whether you think your anxiety impacts badly on your children you could say, 'I don't believe it harms them as much as their father shouting at them/telling them what a terrible mother I am/threatening them.'

If you're asked about parental acrimony you could say, 'You call it parental acrimony but I call it child abuse. You are right to the extent that I will always fight as hard as I can to stop my child from being abused and so long as his father keeps abusing him we will never agree. So yes there is and will always be parental acrimony but it's the child abuse that's damaging our child, not the parental acrimony.'

By agreeing with certain parts of their questioning, they have less chance of starting an argument with you. They have nowhere else to go.

But beware the short, quickfire questions designed to trip you up. A barrister may ask you several questions in a row to which the only answer is 'yes' or 'no' and they may speak more quickly as if to hurry you to answer quickly. Don't fall for it because at the end of these inconsequential questions will be the one they want you to give the same 'yes' or 'no' to and you will have fallen down a big hole when you do. So don't give in to the pressure – pause, breathe and take your time.

A lot of people worry about breaking down in tears when questioned. As I've said, it's best if you can remain calm in court (if only to avoid giving your ex narcissistic supply). But don't beat yourself up if you break down during your cross-examination. Narcissists often 'break down' in court – all fake of course, but they've been to the best drama school and are utterly convincing that they're the victim and are distraught about their children. Unfortunately you can't win either way – if you cry in court you may be considered 'unstable' and if you don't, the conclusion could be that you're cold and uncaring. So don't put undue pressure on yourself either way. You've got to get through the day whichever way you can. And if you do end up in tears, the court will give you a break so you can pull yourself together again before you carry on.

Finally, what if your ex doesn't have a barrister – can he cross-examine you himself? Under the Domestic Abuse Act 2021 (see Chapter 16), no, he cannot. But that Act isn't in force at the time of writing and they haven't yet drafted the rules on what will happen instead. So it's not clear whether another lawyer will be appointed for him, who will pay or how it will work. At the time of writing, the judge will often put the perpetrator's questions to you, so you don't have to be questioned by your abuser. Or you may be able to find a barrister to do this for you free of charge – google 'pro bono schemes', such as Advocate.

When your ex is cross-examined

Survivors are shocked when narcissists lie in court. Don't be; lying is what narcissists do and no oath or judge is going to stop them. It's particularly difficult for you when your ex lies under cross-examination because your barrister often doesn't know the truth and you can't tell them quickly enough for them to be able to correct it. You can always try passing your barrister a note, so have Post-it notes or small pieces of paper ready to do this.

The same rules apply here as when you're giving evidence: don't react in court no matter how monstrous his lies or allegations are. Shutty shutty. That means no pulling faces, shaking your head, sighing loudly or drawing attention to yourself in any other way. The judge is there to decide who they believe and they won't thank you for trying to influence them by indicating your view of when the other parent is lying. It'll do more harm than good. Learn to play poker if you're going to have trouble containing your emotions!

Know your narcissist – think about what pushes his buttons so you can get your counsel to ask the right questions to make him angry. Shame is probably what he fears most so think about what he's most ashamed of and what questions can be asked around that. It could be a simple question about a mundane thing that no one else would think twice about that will cause an outburst in court. Then the judge will see for themself how your children would be affected by his behaviour.

Another way to bring out his anger is to get your barrister to inflate his ego and then burst his bubble. If he's presented with a challenge he's not expecting, his arrogant composure (which hides his fear of exposure) may crack and he'll respond angrily. When narcissists say something negative about their ex they say it as though they care – 'She's a good mum, and I want my family to be together but she has a mental health problem' or 'Unfortunately she's not willing to allow me to take my responsibility as a parent'. He may build you up with praise and then knock you down, and you can ask your barrister to do the same to him in cross-examination.

As an example, your counsel can build him up by saying how he's a great dad, who takes his children on fun outings or holidays, and then take the wind out of his sails by asking how he could leave his child with no food, or frighten his child by shouting so angrily. Or if he talked about how important both mother and father are to the children and how much he wanted to be in their lives, and how it should be 50/50, your barrister can start by asking questions he'll agree with, such as 'Is it right that it's the responsibility of both parents to care for the children?' and 'Is it true that you want to be with the children 50/50?' Then your barrister can catch him off guard by asking things like 'Isn't it true that you've done little or nothing with your children to date?' and 'Is it true you've not paid any child maintenance?' Hopefully this building up and knocking down will bring his anger out – which is what you want the court to see – as well as show that his actions are not in line with his words.

In an appropriate case, a good question to ask is whether he would prefer to see his children go into care than remain with you. For most parents, the last thing they'd want is their children going into care, but a narcissist has no such qualms as he knows it will destroy you, and his answer may show him up.

You can also note the parts of his evidence that are all about him rather than his children, and then ask your barrister to point this out – both in their cross-examination of him, and in their closing speech. They could, for example, ask why he's more focused on himself than his children. Hopefully the judge will take notice of this and start to view the narcissist differently.

Another advantage of starting with questions he'll be happy to answer is that you may be able to compare how he reacts when telling the truth to when he's lying a bit later. If you were to lie in the witness box (not that you would) you'd probably look uncomfortable, get fidgety and look down rather than looking the judge in the eye. The narcissist is very comfortable with lying, but he may have 'tells' of his own. While you would be fidgeting, he may become more still than before, or he may pause and hesitate. The narcissist usually talks about himself (I, me, mine) but may shift responsibility when lying, so you'll hear more 'her' and 'him' instead. Make sure your barrister knows to keep pressing him to answer the question properly if he becomes evasive.

And, of course, if you're a litigant in person representing yourself in court – although I really do recommend you have a barrister by this point – these are all strategies that you can employ yourself when cross-examining your ex. (If you want to, and indeed if it is allowed under the new Domestic Abuse Act. Survivors rarely want to cross-examine their abusers.) At the time of writing, when an abuse victim doesn't have a barrister, the judge will usually put their questions to the perpetrator, in which case you can use the above strategies when preparing your questions for the judge to put to your ex.

Dealing with Cafcass and social services

I told Craig about the court order and when I said he had to go and stay with his dad every other weekend he burst into tears. I said that he must have told Cafcass that was what he wanted and Craig said she kept interrupting him and putting words in his mouth.

Cafcass, or the social worker, are the 'eyes and ears of the court', the people tasked with finding out how the children feel and what they want, the 'experts' the court will rely on when making their decisions – because judges are lawyers and social workers/Cafcass are the people supposed to know what's best for children. It's therefore hard, though not impossible, to get a court to go against the recommendations made by Cafcass and they have to give their reasons if they do so. All this means that your interactions with Cafcass and social services are vitally important.

How and when Cafcass get involved

Whenever it receives a C100 application for a child arrangement order, the court will ask Cafcass to prepare a 'safeguarding letter' with recommendations to the court as to how to proceed with the case. To prepare this letter, a Cafcass officer will contact the police and local authority to see if your family is known to either, and speak to both you and your ex on the phone (they will usually speak to the applicant first). All this will happen before the first hearing, the FHDRA.

Then someone else from Cafcass (i.e. not the person who wrote the safeguarding letter) will attend the FHDRA and try to get the parents to reach an agreement. If the parents don't reach an agreement at the FHDRA, the court has to decide whether Cafcass should prepare a Section 7 (of the Children Act) report – essentially a report about the children's welfare. This is used to help the court determine who the children should live with and how much contact the other parent should have. To prepare that report, Cafcass will interview both parents, the children, and any other relevant people. (If a fact finding hearing has been ordered, the Section 7 report won't be ordered until the end of that hearing.) The Section 7 report will be prepared by a third Cafcass officer, not either of the ones previously involved.

Occasionally the court will order the local authority to prepare a Section 37 report if they feel things are more serious and that social services may need to be involved, or more involved, with your family. There's no need to panic if this happens – it doesn't mean the court is thinking of taking your child into care. And even if a care order were to be made, it doesn't mean your child would be removed from you into foster care. It usually means that you might get a little more help from social services and protection for your children.

If a social worker is already involved with your family, the court may say they should prepare the Section 7 report rather than Cafcass. Both of these services are underfunded and overworked so they are each likely to say the other should prepare the report. You can make your view clear to the court – if you like the social worker you can argue that the children already know her and shouldn't have to meet someone else. If you don't like her you can say you feel she's biased or whatever your complaint is, and say you feel Cafcass will be more independent.

Unfortunately Cafcass is a big part of the 'contact at all costs' problem and there's no guarantee at all that they will be any better than the social worker. And they may just ring the social worker and put her opinion in their report. Or they may be equally taken in by the narcissist and come to the same opinion anyway. Like judges and lawyers, most professionals working for social services and Cafcass have no knowledge or understanding of personality disorders. They expect both parents to 'get along', often blame the protective parent for the 'parental conflict' and try to bulldoze them into giving the abusive parent the contact they want.

The safeguarding letter and phone call

You can expect this call to take place after you've received the C100 application and date of the FHDRA. The time of your call will be arranged with you beforehand, and if you've submitted a Form C1A (detailing allegations of harm or abuse) it's a good idea to check Cafcass have received it before they speak to either you or your ex.

Your call will only be around 20–40 minutes so you'll need to prepare well and decide on the three or four main points that you want to get across in your call – depending on what's most important and relevant to your case, this could be things like his abuse and how it affects the children, his poor parenting, his relationship with the children before you separated, any disabilities or special needs a child has, and whether the children want to see him or not. Have these points written out in front of you so you're not distracted by all the questions you're asked.

After the call, you should receive the safeguarding letter before the FHDRA hearing. Once you've received it, you can comment on anything you disagree with, or clarify other directions you want the court to make, in your position statement.

The Cafcass Section 7 interview

If the court has ordered a Section 7 report, you'll have an interview with a Cafcass Family Court Advisor (often known as a Cafcass officer or FCA – this person is a social worker, qualified for at least three years). This interview, which normally takes place in person, but not at the time of writing due to COVID-19, will take place after the FHDRA hearing (and after the fact finding hearing, if there is one).

How should you handle this meeting?

When first meeting a Cafcass officer, the narcissist aims to charm, flatter and impress them with the widest smile and impeccable manners, mentioning how well qualified they are and 'what a great job you're doing'. The protective parent, on the other hand, is more likely to stumble into the meeting a bag of nerves intent on defending themselves or explaining how dreadful their ex is. Nine times out of 10, the professional is persuaded to take the side of the narcissist and, as they have no training in personality disorders, they get it wrong time and time again. So when you're meeting these professionals remember the Spanish proverb: flattery makes friends and truth makes enemies.

Be prepared, and have a strategy. You too can be charming. Social workers aren't always popular but they are human too, despite what you've heard or the dreadful experience you may already have had with them. They have a difficult job to do, and too little time to do it in. So start by asking about them – for example, are they rushed off their feet? – and say you appreciate their call to you. If you're meeting in person, compliment something they're wearing. Do whatever feels right to you and be yourself – you don't want to come over as insincere!

One form of flattery is to ask for their expert opinion. Just as in the courtroom, when talking to Cafcass or social services, you must never say you think your ex is a narcissist, or what you think is the aim of his behaviour (for example, to destroy you). They don't understand personality disorders and will just dismiss you as the crazy one being over-dramatic. Instead, you'll want to lead them to conclude for themself that his behaviour isn't normal and has a detrimental effect on the children; it really doesn't matter whether they slap a label on his behaviour – all that matters is they recognise it. You can help them along the way by asking questions and asking them for their expert advice; for example, you could use questions such as, 'Why do they think a father would behave like that with his child?' 'Have you come across this before?' 'How can we find out what the problem is?' 'What should I say to the children when they come home from their father's house upset?' Pretend that you think they know best and can come up with the answers!

If your ex has made the application to the court, he will usually be seen first by the Cafcass officer. You know your ex will have lied to her and made all sorts of false allegations about you. You know how intensely emotional and how convincing he can be. So she'll come to you thinking at best you don't care about your own children, or at worst that you abuse them. Either way, you're on the backfoot when Cafcass has seen your ex first. How are you going to deal with this problem? Don't ignore it. Be prepared. Think it all through.

You've got two options. If you've got some good evidence – such as a voice recording, an email or photo of damage he's done – you can blow him out of the water straight away. You can say that you've no doubt she found him utterly charming and the perfect gentleman/father but before you go any further you'd like her to listen to him shouting at you or the children, or to read how he writes to you. Show, don't tell. Getting into 'he said, she said' is only going to get you labelled as a 'high conflict case'. You need the evidence to speak for you.

If you've no hard evidence to give of his abuse, your best option is to talk about your children. Give detailed descriptions of them, what they're like, what they like and what you do with them. Show a couple of photos of them, including one with you in it that demonstrates how close you are. The narcissist probably doesn't know much about his children and will have talked about himself and how wonderful he is with them, as well as his grievances and his criticisms of you. The FCA probably won't realise till afterwards she's got no information about the children! Smile when you talk about your children. Make it clear how much you love them and how proud of them you are.

Your ex will have made allegations against you, possibly including some you've not heard before, so keep one step ahead and don't be taken by surprise. He may have said you suffer from mental health problems. At best he'll have said that you're unreasonable and unfair, and at worst that you're the abusive one and he's the victim. Try your best not to get upset or angry, as you risk confirming his allegation that you're unstable.

If you're asked about a specific incident, tell them what happened, but just give them the bare facts. If they want to know why you did what you did, or how you felt about it, they'll ask; but if you go into a long spiel justifying yourself it can look defensive and suspicious. Be careful how much information you give as it can end up being used against you. Tell the truth, and then shutty shutty! If you know you tend to give long-winded explanations for things, do some role play with a friend or a coach to prepare for this important interview.

When preparing, make a list of all the things you want to get across. Then, during the interview, keep your eye firmly on those things you want to say – don't allow your interview to be derailed by his allegations. When responding to his allegations, you can just say calmly 'That's not true' or 'That didn't happen' without wasting precious time giving a long explanation of why it's not true, or what he might have meant. If they want to know more, they'll ask.

If your ex is likely to have said you're trying to alienate the children from him, you can say you'd never stop them seeing him (if that's the case), you just want it to be safe. If it's the case that they clearly love him, or enjoy spending time with him, say so. If you believe it's important for them to have a relationship with him, say so. If you can't honestly say that, say you believe it's important for them to know him. (Which it is, otherwise they can come to idealise him and believe he's their hero, but you don't need to mention that bit!) If you have concerns about his drinking, or the fact he's hit one of the children in the past, or the harsh way he disciplines them, you can say that and that you want to ensure it's safe for them.

Be ready with a list of what you've done to promote contact, and what contact he's actually had (which he's probably not been truthful about), whether that's been face to face, supervised, video or messaging, letters, etc. You may already have all this in your chronology, which you can hand over. Say if he's not always taken up the contact that's been offered and how that made the children feel – for example, rejected or confused – rather than mentioning how put out you were by it.

You'll want to spend the time getting across how his abuse has affected your children. Not you, always the children. Sadly, how affected you are is way down the court's list of priorities and it's more likely to go against you and be seen as you trying to alienate the children from their father if you dwell on it.

Whatever he's done to you, it does affect the children, and they are finally recognised as victims in their own right in the new Domestic Abuse Act (see Chapter 16). It affects them if they've experienced the physical abuse, the shouting at you, the way you're controlled, or the stonewalling. And it affects them if you're distracted and forget something important to them, if you're distressed and have to leave them alone or with someone else while you pull yourself together, or if you're worried or frightened and not able to be fully present for them. And it affects them if they're worried or frightened for you. So think it all through in advance and make notes of how the abuse of you affects your children. This is what you should focus on in your interview.

If it's your child who doesn't want to see their other parent, give concrete examples of the behaviour that's upset them. You can explain if your child is fearful of her father and wouldn't have the courage to challenge him in any way or tell him she wanted something to happen differently. Describe specific events that have brought her to that position. The more detail you can give about the bad behaviour or parenting, the more convincing it will be.

Does your child feel safe or settled with your ex? Can you give examples of why they don't, and why they feel more settled with you, or how they're thriving with less contact with the abusive parent?

Don't be afraid to challenge Cafcass or a social worker on what they say, though be sure to do it politely and respectfully, however angry you may feel. You can ask them to repeat something to make sure you've understood correctly and you can ask them to explain their reasons; and you can say you respect their opinion, but you don't agree. If you have phone calls with Cafcass outside your main interview, or any phone calls with your social worker, it's worth emailing them afterwards to confirm what they said, as all too often they will deny it later. If they don't reply to contradict you, it's good evidence for you to use in future if they do go back on it.

Remember, this is about abuse, not conflict

If 'parental conflict' or 'acrimony' has already been raised as an issue, maybe in the Cafcass safeguarding letter or in the court order made at the FHDRA, it's important to dispute this during your interview. Tell them it's not conflict, it's abuse, and that any acrimony is the result of the abuse, not the cause of the problem. You can say that if there's conflict it's because you're trying to protect your children and yourself from further abuse, not because you bear him any animosity or want a fight with him. Give examples of the abuse, again focusing on how it's affected the children.

Cafcass have a screening tool to help them differentiate between domestic abuse and harmful conflict. It says:

'Domestic abuse and harmful conflict are distinct from one another and require different assessment/intervention techniques. This tool is designed to be used early in the life of a case to assist Family Court Advisers (FCAs) in deciding which will be of most assistance in their assessment: the purple domestic abuse tools and guidance or the orange harmful conflict tools and guidance. It is not designed to be a diagnostic tool in and of itself and does not replace professional judgement.

Where cases contain characteristics of both, it is strongly advised to proceed with an assessment using the domestic abuse tools and guidance first as this will ensure you are able to explore the pattern of behaviours in the safest context.'

Despite this advice, they still get it wrong, which is probably because their 'indicators of harmful conflict' are more like indicators of a personality disorder. And why they list 'Incidents of verbal abuse' under the conflict section (when it is clearly abuse) is a mystery! That said, the very fact that this tool exists can help you. It may be worth you asking if they've used this 'tool' and which indicators they have found that led them to the conclusion it's conflict rather than abuse. You can either ask towards the end of your Cafcass interview if you feel they're still focused on conflict rather than abuse, or in cross-examination at a final hearing. You can also ask what they think is behind the conflict, and how much they think you are each contributing to it. Tell them the last thing you want is conflict and ask them what they think you can do to reduce it, given that he's not going to stop his abusive or controlling behaviour.

Be sure to explain what your ex's relationship with the children was like before you separated. One of the factors on the 'harmful conflict' list is 'loss of focus on the child'. But often the abusive parent never had their focus on the child, so it can't be lost now and it's crucial to state this at an early stage.

Be sure too to praise something your ex does well, such as that he has a good imagination and does fun things with the children, or he works hard and provides well for his family. No one is all bad, despite the fact that the narcissist's black and white thinking makes him say that you are. You will come over as more balanced and objective if you can point to a thing or two in his favour, and you're more likely to be believed.

You'll probably be pressured to 'get on', to co-parent, maybe even to go to mediation or family therapy. If so, you can say none of this is possible as there's no effective communication between you and there's no co-parenting – you do all the parenting and you try not to let him disrupt it. You can say you don't want to sound obstructive but you're not willing to be further controlled or abused by your ex and none of those things will be possible, which is why you've ended up in court.

Who else will Cafcass talk to for the Section 7 report?

Schools are usually reluctant to get involved in court proceedings, although they will speak to Cafcass if asked. So if you think a teacher has some important evidence, do ask Cafcass to speak to them, although there's no guarantee they will. If there's someone else who knows you both, maybe a childminder or someone from your church or your child's sports team, you could also ask Cafcass to speak to them. They rarely do, though, as they don't have enough time, but if you've asked they can at least be cross-examined in the final hearing on why they didn't do it.

Cafcass will usually only speak to your child once, typically after speaking to both parents. Ask for Cafcass to meet your child at school and ask the school to make sure someone stays with them throughout the whole interview. As with the narcissist, Cafcass can bully and pressure children, and they sometimes ask the teacher to leave before the end of the interview. So find out who will be there with your child and ask them not to leave even if they're asked to do so.

Social workers and Cafcass are supposed to listen to 'the voice of the child'. But if he has the opportunity, the narcissist will manipulate or intimidate the children into saying that they want to live with him. Even if they don't, children often try to please the disordered parent to keep them calm whilst knowing that the stable parent won't overreact if they say something that upsets them. And children will lie to social workers if they think that's the best way of keeping themselves safe. The professionals don't usually have the time or training to get to know a child and build enough trust for them to be honest. So Section 7 reports can cause a lot of heartache to protective parents. Expect the worst, even if you feel your interview has gone well, and then you can only be pleasantly surprised.

Guardians and psychologists/psychiatrists

Sometimes in more serious or complex cases the court appoints a guardian for the child (sometimes referred to as a 'Rule 16.4 guardian'). The guardian will usually be from Cafcass, and may be the officer originally appointed if they are senior enough to act as guardian. Sometimes the National Youth Advocacy Service (NYAS) are asked to provide a guardian, so if you're not happy with Cafcass you can ask for this. The guardian will appoint a solicitor for the child as they are now a party to the proceedings and will be represented at every hearing.

The advantages of this are that your child will have legal aid and a good guardian and solicitor will take a more investigative role and seek information from other people who know the child. The guardian will be more involved in the case than Cafcass normally are (who will typically just see each person once, make their recommendations in their report and not do any more). The guardian should see the child more often, and the solicitor should present your child's wishes and feelings properly to the court. If the child is old enough they should have the opportunity to write or even meet and speak with the judge. But be wary of pushing for this, as it can be seen as manipulative.

The guardian tells the court what they think is best for the child (and, if the child is old enough, what the child wants to happen). An older child may disagree with the guardian's recommendations, in which case the child's solicitor can put forward what they want to happen, leaving the guardian to tell the court what they think is best for the child.

A guardian may recommend that an expert (i.e. a child psychologist or psychiatrist) be instructed to make an assessment of the family. You may be asked to contribute to the cost of this if you can afford it; if not, your child's legal aid will cover the cost.

Personally, experts concern me as there seem to be few good ones about and they're very busy so there are long delays in getting their reports. And of course the guardian and the expert are two more people for the narcissist to charm and manipulate into siding with him – which means getting them to see that you're suffering with anxiety or PTSD as a result of his abuse will be an uphill struggle.

You may be worried about a psychological report because you are anxious. If that's the case, get in first and say you're anxious about protecting your child, and going through court. Don't give them the chance to say you're an over-anxious mother. You could even say something like, 'I expect you're going to label me as an over-anxious mother but I'm not anxious about Jack when he's with me or at school. I'm only worried about the abuse he's at risk of suffering when with his father.'

Child power

Emily, a family law solicitor, told me her story of divorcing a narcissist – a story that's sadly typical of many I hear and confirms my view that 'child power' – i.e. children taking matters into their own hands – is about the only thing that works in family courts at the moment. Parents are powerless to protect their children from a narcissist in the family court culture of 'contact at all costs', and only the children bold enough to find a way out for themselves succeed in escaping further abuse.

As a solicitor, you may think Emily would have had an advantage in the family court, but that wasn't the case at all. Here is her story.

He was controlling and manipulative; he was bullying and threatening and he was totally self-centred. I never thought it at the time but the reality was that, over the years, I was abused. I coped with it on a daily basis as part of my 'to do' list – feed the cat, take the kids to school, placate the sociopathic husband. I never thought about it because abuse was something that happened to my clients, not to me.

By the time I worked up the courage to leave him, I was having a full-scale nervous breakdown. The family 'home' was like Fort Knox as he was in the security business and there were cameras and locks and triggers – which I didn't know how to work – all over the house. My passport was in a locked gun room in the garage; it was a room full of guns and bullet-making equipment behind a huge metal door. I lay awake at night too scared to sleep. Whenever I did, I woke in a sweat imagining him standing over me with a shotgun.

When I left, it seemed as though I had got out but I had not; it was the beginning of years of abuse by my ex using the courts against me. I thought that the legal system would help me; I assumed that as I was the victim the court would 'sort him out'. But within the court proceedings I was disbelieved, punished and found to be a monster. The court viewed me as a professional woman 'in the trade' who 'should know better'. I was accused of using my professional knowledge of what 'sometimes happens' in order to throw allegations at my ex-husband.

Initially he was awarded 40% of the time with the children. Cafcass saw him as a loving father who was not being given the opportunity to have a relationship with them by their mother. After that order, when he no longer saw any reason to put on his act, the children were refusing to go with him so I reapplied to reduce the time they spent with him. Then it was 'game on' again for him and he was back to persuading the children that he was a great father. He claimed that I was emotionally abusing the children. There was a guardian and children's solicitor involved but they did not listen to the children. They decided that I was a hostile mother and the court ordered the children to live with their father.

The adversarial system played right to my ex-husband's strengths – a great game which he could play to win. Cafcass and the professionals were quick to believe him because he was charming and believable, and he convinced them that I was bad because I was suffering from mental and emotional illness. His story seemed the 'norm' and mine did not. No one stopped to consider the risk he posed to two innocent children if what I said was true, and I was not given a chance to prove that it was.

My legal team let me down; they had no clue about what was happening or how to deal with my matter and I lost at every hearing. Initially, a London barrister gave bad advice and things went badly as a result. I lost my cool

*and was upset and angry, and the solicitor who attended court sacked me!
I had no representative and the barrister who'd given advice would not talk
to me. The next solicitor removed detailed information and evidence from
my statements and left me being accused by the judge of being 'fanciful'.*

*I felt as though I was in a net under the water and the more I struggled
the more the net tightened and dragged me down. There was no way to
struggle out.*

*Eventually I gave up the fight within the court as there was no sense or
reason to be found there – and certainly not justice. When my ex-husband
got custody, I knew he wouldn't want the children. It was his worst nightmare
having to care for anyone else, let alone two young children who needed
looking after on a daily basis.*

*I stayed still and let the water consume me. I eventually floated to the
surface and drew breath.*

*With the transfer of residence, things got worse and worse for my children
living at their father's house. He grabbed my son from behind a chair and
threw him onto the floor; my son ran away from the house. My daughter was
thrown on the bed by her father and both children called the police as they
felt threatened. But neither the police nor social services believed them as
it was assumed that I had 'put them up to it'. I was worried sick for them.*

*Then my 10-year-old son, who has Asperger's syndrome, decided that
he was not going to live with his dad anymore and sorted out residence
himself. He went mad and had an episode at school. Dad was called to
collect a small blonde whirlwind child much like a Tasmanian devil. My son
swore at his father, poking him in the face; he rampaged through the house
and made his dad miserable throughout that day. It was 4.55pm when my
ex phoned to ask me to take them back. They had been with him for less
than four months.*

Emily's story demonstrates child power at its best. Sometimes things have to get
worse before they get better, and when you hit rock bottom, the only way is up.

One mother quoted in the Harm Report (see Chapter 16) reported her
child's solution as: 'My son when he was 12 wasn't allowed a say, I had to make
him go to his dad and he hated me for it. His schooling went downhill, he was
kicking off at school. He was being hurt by his dad and I had to keep making
him go. Till one day he got naked in bed and said I had to try and dress him for
him to go.'

Another mother said, 'I received an amazing line in my court order by a
judge who understood (eventually) my ex's control over us. The line was put in
to protect the children when they didn't want to go (felt unsafe after an abusive
episode) so that the law didn't say they HAD to go to him because it was his
contact time. The line was along the lines of "whilst the mother is to support

contact, the children's wishes and feelings must be considered". Several policemen have told me what a great line this is in our court order and how they wish more court orders had this line. The judge told me to tell the boys about this line in the court order – he knew he was empowering two children with this. And he was. It has proved absolutely invaluable to us and enabled my children to create for themselves some stability over the longer term.'

Although the family court is the last place you'll want to go to again, sometimes it's necessary to apply to vary your order to get the change your children need, once they are old enough to be able to say what's happening and what they want. The difficulty is that, although they'll be listened to, whatever they say is likely to be dismissed on the basis that you coached them to say it. So the best thing you can do is to help your children practice articulating their feelings (about everything – not just your ex). With practice, they will be able to say precisely and convincingly how they feel before going to their dad, and how they feel when he does certain things, compared to how they feel with you, with their friends, at school, etc.

Breaching court orders: Enforcement proceedings

Disappointed that all the proceedings are over, the narcissist will be looking for any excuse to take you back to court and is likely to make either an application to vary the current order, or to enforce it if you've put a foot wrong.

This is why it's so important that you stick rigidly to the court order. So before you ask him if he'll swap weekends, or to allow little Liam to go to a party during 'his' time, ask yourself if it's worth it if he takes you back to court as a result. And if your ex tries to bully you into changing the order, point out to him the warning on the first page and say if he wants to do something different he needs to take it back to court.

It's hard on you, and probably even harder on your children, that you have to stick so rigidly to the court's schedule. The children are the ones who really miss out when they can't go to birthday parties or other events, especially if they're not doing anything very exciting with their dad to make up for it. But no one's life is easy if there's a narcissist in it and you just have to manage the situation as best you can.

Often the narcissist has no real interest in his children and won't keep to his part of the order and people ask if they can take him back to court to enforce the order or get the order changed when he's not complied with it. If you look at the order you'll see it says you have to make your child available to spend time with her father. That doesn't mean the father has to make himself available for the child! So if he tells you he doesn't want her or he just doesn't turn up, there's not much you can do except shutty shutty and write it down. (Technically you can apply to vary the order to reflect the amount of contact he is actually having, so you don't have to keep getting her ready only for her father to not turn up. But why bother? It's best to stay out of the courts where possible.) Just because he doesn't want her now doesn't mean he won't take you back to court in six months' time, so keep all your evidence scrupulously.

But if he has failed to return the children when he should have done (thereby keeping them for longer), or if he won't comply with the order regarding handovers, you may take him back to court for breaching the order.

If he takes you back to court because you've not kept to the order – i.e. to enforce the order – don't panic. Firstly, it's not a criminal offence, and you won't get a criminal record. You're also very unlikely indeed to go to prison unless you've breached an order several times and have already been warned by the court that if you do it again you risk prison. In fact, if it's the first hearing for a breach probably very little will happen at all; the court will always try and find another way of dealing with a breach. You could be ordered to compensate your ex if, say, he'd paid for travel or a holiday and you stopped the children from going, and ultimately you could be ordered to do unpaid work or you could be fined.

The court can also vary the existing order. This is the biggest danger if you have breached it and your ex is alleging parental alienation – the court could order that the children live with him instead of you, but again this is very unlikely on the first occasion. You would normally be warned first.

CHAPTER 15:
APPEALS, COMPLAINTS AND SUBJECT ACCESS REQUESTS

Whilst some parents do get the help they need to protect their children and themselves from further abuse, the family courts are making some dreadful, life-damaging decisions for children, and some of the judges behave appallingly, particularly towards women. Some Cafcass and social workers are little better, and family lawyers are a lottery.

So what can you do when you've been treated poorly by the court and other professionals? There are no easy answers and most people are so exhausted and ground down by the end of the proceedings, that they don't actually do anything. I would just ask you to please do something. If you do nothing, everyone assumes it's all okay. And it's not okay at all. If everyone appealed or complained the huge problems would become more obvious and change would come more quickly.

When you do have the strength to do something about it, here are your options.

Appeals

The losing party can appeal and that of course includes the narcissist. To have succeeded in front of a judge and then to have to cope with an appeal can be quite devastating and is another reason why people can feel pressure to compromise and reach an agreement. But consent orders are almost impossible to appeal and the Court of Appeal cases of Re H-N (see Chapter 16) are very much the exception.

Appeals are difficult, but then nothing in the family court is easy. You can't appeal because you don't like the decision, you can only appeal if the judge has got the law or procedure wrong. Barristers, rather than solicitors, usually advise whether you have grounds to appeal.

You only have 21 days from the date the order was made to appeal (or seven if it's a case management decision), although sometimes you can get permission to appeal out of time. And unless you're appealing a decision made by magistrates, rather than a judge, you'll need permission from the court to appeal.

Your barrister will draft your grounds of appeal and skeleton argument – which is the next step after getting the court's permission to appeal. If you can't afford a barrister, Rights of Women have a helpful pdf on their website that sets out what you need to do, and they may be able to help you if you get stuck. You will also normally have to pay for a transcript of the original hearing for an appeal, but if the cost is prohibitive you can try and proceed without it.

It's not just final orders that are a problem; cases often start going wrong when a bad interim order is made, so it's important to appeal those if they're going to derail the rest of the case. The difficulty is that your appeal may not be heard in time before the next hearing, but you could potentially ask for that hearing to be adjourned (postponed).

Complaints about judges, Cafcass, social services and solicitors

If you can't appeal, and the judge has been rude to you, bullied you or been very unfair, please do make a complaint to the court and/or the Judicial Conduct Investigations Office. Some judges really should be sacked but unless lots of people complain, no one knows. Also if you've made a complaint you have a reason to object to that judge sitting on your next hearing, should they be listed for it. But you can't complain if you just didn't like the decision the judge made and they made it professionally and fairly.

Having complained about the judge, please also complain to your MP.

If you want to complain about Cafcass, you can either write a letter or use the form on the Cafcass website. You have six months from when Cafcass was last involved with your case to appeal and you'll find a pdf on their website setting out what you need to do, and what they will do. It's much better if you can complain as soon as possible while the proceedings are ongoing otherwise they are likely just to tell you that you should have raised these issues in court.

As with any complaint, be sure to tell Cafcass what you want them to do to put things right. Don't just moan! Having complained, you may be worried about that worker continuing with your case so one of the things you ask for may be a different Cafcass officer. Unfortunately few people get any satisfaction from their complaints but please don't let that stop you making one. Like the judges, if no one tells Cafcass that things aren't right, they'll just keep getting it wrong. (Although you only have to look at the 96% 'Bad' rating on Trustpilot to see that people do register their complaints.)

And if you want to complain about a social worker, you have 12 months to complain from whenever it is they did something or decided something incorrectly. But again it's best to do it as soon as you can – especially if you want to ask for a different worker to continue with your case. Family Rights Group have a lot of helpful information on their website about making complaints to social services.

You can also complain about your own solicitor. Indeed, they will have told you what their complaints procedure is in their initial 'client care' letter to you. If they can't resolve your complaint you can go to the Legal Ombudsman. However, most survivors want to complain about their ex's solicitor, not their own! These solicitors threaten litigants in person with all sorts, as well as costs at every turn, but you can't complain to the Legal Ombudsman about a solicitor who isn't your own. You may be able to complain to the SRA (Solicitors Regulation Authority) – check on their website. The only other thing you can do is to check on the solicitor's (or Resolution's) website to see if they're a member of Resolution and complain to Resolution that they're not following the code of conduct (see Chapter 9).

You can, however, complain to the Bar Standards Board about the conduct of your ex's barrister. If it's your own barrister's conduct you want to complain about, you do this with the Legal Ombudsman.

Subject access requests (SARs)

Since 2018 you have the right to ask organisations like Cafcass and social services to see the information they have about you, and this is known as making a subject access request (SAR). The Information Commissioner's Office has clear and helpful information on their website explaining how to do this.

If you can't understand how your social worker or Cafcass have come to the recommendations they have, think they may have got their facts wrong, or that they've been colluding with your ex against you, it's worth asking to see what they have.

To make a request to Cafcass, google 'Cafcass subject access requests' to find the link for their website form and all the information about it. (At the time of writing their website gives two different addresses to post an SAR to, one in

Slough and one in Coventry, so their website form is probably best.) What you receive in response will be limited as they will only give you information about yourself, not anyone else. You can ask for the information they hold about your child – although if your child is 12 or older they will usually have to make the request themselves.

To make an SAR to social services, google SAR with your local authority's name. Each local authority has slightly different procedures.

Two social workers (one a manager) lost their jobs over my case through mismanagement identified by the head of Children's Services. The main issue was around lack of monthly DBS checks on all the adults involved in Evie's life. Her dad's monthly police checks – had they happened – would have alerted social services to an open investigation on him. There were a number of failings by our Social Worker who was a level two team manager and she no longer practices in social care. I could write a book about the whole sorry episode really.

The Children's Commissioner partly upheld a complaint that I raised about social services acting for the wishes of her dad rather than addressing why Evie didn't want to see him. The actual 'Head of' listened and acted appropriately to gather social services support for Evie.

The Information Commissioner's Office investigated Evie's high school for enabling her dad and sharing information and photos with him on a weekly basis – despite him being estranged and denied any contact.

CHAPTER 16:
FUTURE IMPROVEMENTS TO THE FAMILY COURT SYSTEM – AND WHAT TO USE IN THE MEANTIME

That the family courts are making some shocking and atrocious decisions for children is beyond dispute. You would be forgiven for assuming that things would have changed after Claire Throssell's boys were burnt to death by their father in 2014 (see Chapter 6). In terms of the family court, little has changed since then, and Claire Throssell, along with many others, is still campaigning for change.

The Harm Report

In June 2020 the Harm Report – a beacon of light in what feels like a long, dark tunnel – was published by the government. This Ministry of Justice report, which is the result of an expert panel's review of the family court (specifically, how well the family court identifies and responds to domestic abuse), sets out several recommendations to improve the family court's handling of children proceedings.

I have to admit, when the panel's review was announced two years before I was a little sceptical that they would uncover the truth or, if they did, that they would be allowed to publish it. But the report pulls no punches and lays bare the appalling practices in our family court and the damage it does to children and vulnerable parents.

The panel appear to have been shocked by the accounts of the harm children have suffered as a result of court-ordered contact with abusive parents.

There were reports of children being extremely distressed at the prospect of contact and of trying everything to avoid it. A divorce and domestic abuse professional quoted in the report said, 'I have examples of children so desperate not to go to contact they for example hide under beds, lock themselves away in rooms, run into roads whilst under supervision of an expert, hurt themselves so they don't have to go to contact, refuse to go to school, suffer severe tummy pains to the extent they have been rushed to hospital with suspected appendicitis which was proved to be emotional pains only, cry, withdraw, become more clingy to their "safe" parent, regress to a much younger age in behaviour, display mute catatonic behaviour when asked about the parent they are scared of, stop socialising with other children and have regular nightmares.'

One might have thought this report was enough to bring about immediate changes in the family courts but, once again, nothing has changed (or at least, not at the time of writing). I really hope it does change, and soon. The report certainly points to a better way forward.

There are 16 pages of excellent recommendations in the report, ranging from a complete overhaul of the system to better training for judges and magistrates. The pilot schemes proposed by the Ministry of Justice sound good: piloting an investigative approach in child arrangements cases, seeking to improve coordination between jurisdictions and agencies, enhancing the voice of the child, better training, and more generally the introduction of new design principles for private law children proceedings. But these pilot schemes are, at the time of writing, on hold due to the coronavirus pandemic.

There are four main themes in the report:

- The pro-contact culture
- The adversarial family court
- The failure to share information
- The lack of resources

Let's briefly explore each area. (Although if you are in children proceedings I do recommend you give the full report a read and pick out the relevant parts to use in court and your position statements. You can find it in the Resources section.)

The pro-contact culture

This was well summed up by a divorce and domestic abuse practitioner featured in the report, who basically said abusers cannot be good parents and it's about time the courts recognise this. I couldn't agree more.

Despite this, as the report notes, the parental rights of abusive fathers are often favoured over what the child wants.

The presumption that it's best for a child to have both parents in their lives results in allegations of domestic abuse and child sexual abuse not being believed, or being minimised. For example, domestic abuse may be treated as 'historic' to enable contact to occur, rather than considering whether the abuse is relevant. The report recognised that allegations of domestic abuse can sometimes be reframed by the court as 'high conflict' – and are increasingly being used by abusive parents as so-called 'evidence' of 'parental alienation'. In one extreme case mentioned in the report, a father physically attacked the mother's lawyer at court – as witnessed by court security guards – yet the judge simply set the incident aside.

The report says that, 'The panel is clear that the presumption of parental involvement should not remain in its present form' and recommends an urgent review on this matter.

The Ministry of Justice say they will do this, under the leadership of the Family Justice Board. Unfortunately they don't say when, just that everything is delayed by the COVID-19 pandemic.

The adversarial family court

Our adversarial legal system is unsuitable for family cases and the panel found that it puts parents in opposition to each other with little or no involvement of their child. What's more, the adversarial nature of the courts is particularly stressful, confusing and traumatic for litigants in person.

Yet, interestingly, in cases where a protective parent has legal representation and the perpetrator is a litigant in person, judges appeared to 'bend over backwards' to help them.

The report also notes how abusers and the abused appear differently in court, with the abuser coming across as calm, reasonable and, ultimately, more believable. Meanwhile, mothers report feeling seriously disadvantaged by appearing emotional and disordered. The report acknowledges that the 'disordered' appearance of the mother may be a direct result of the abuse she has endured – as well as the fact that she has to be in close proximity to her abuser in court.

That said, the report included some examples of abusers becoming verbally and physically aggressive in court. So the calm demeanour of abusers isn't universal. Unfortunately though, in some instances, judges and court staff 'made excuses' for the aggressive behaviour. In some cases, the abusive behaviour was even regarded as 'justified' – a result of the father's 'understandable' frustration at lack of contact with his children.

In other words, the report acknowledges that the abused can't win.

Lack of information sharing

The report admits that the differences between criminal justice, child protection (social services and care proceedings) and child arrangements proceedings lead to contradictory decisions and confusion. To put it another way, the lack of joined up thinking and information sharing often puts the abused and their children at a disadvantage in court.

One mother's former husband was jailed for the rape of her and child abuse offences. He was described by the criminal court as a dangerous man. Given his convictions she expected the family court process to be straightforward, but he was able to prolong the case for more than five years – indeed, the mother felt the court was bending over backwards to accommodate his attempts to gain contact – at a cost to her of more than £50,000 in legal fees. In court she was not automatically given a screen and had to ask for one each time. And because many of the family court hearings were heard in the same criminal court where she had given evidence in his rape trail, she was visibly upset and shaking, yet nobody in the family court system appeared to care. She was also concerned that there was no reference to the police or the criminal court to explain the risk her ex-husband posed – demonstrating a complete lack of joined-up thinking. She effectively had to go through her ordeal twice: once in the criminal court, and then again in the family court.

The panel went so far as to say that the lack of information sharing can be 'life threatening' and 'available evidence of domestic abuse and its impact on children is ignored by family courts'.

And we're not just talking about sharing information between the family court and police/criminal court. The time pressures of the family court system mean that Cafcass spend very little time with the child and often don't talk to other professionals who have been involved with the family and know the child much better, such as schools, domestic abuse charities, police, GPs, etc. Worse still, even when there is evidence from such professionals, the judges give greater weight to the views of Cafcass.

Lack of resources

This is obviously a political rather than a legal issue, but it's still relevant to people's experience of the family court. The result of many courts being closed and insufficient judges is that, although many people are wrongly refused a fact finding hearing, the reality is that there would not be sufficient court time for everyone who needs one. In another effort to reduce court time, review hearings have been all but abolished and judges are directed not to adjourn cases.

So in the good old days contact may have started at a contact centre and, after a couple of months, there would have been another court hearing to see how that had gone and to increase the contact if all had gone well. Then after a period of unsupervised contact you would have gone back to court to see whether it was appropriate to progress to overnight contact. But now the courts just assume that it will all go well so the judge makes one final order setting out the different increases in contact time over several weeks. This means that parents have to find the resources (time, money and energy) to take their case back to court if there are problems, instead of the court ensuring that the orders it makes are safe and workable.

And then there's Cafcass and social workers. There aren't enough of them either, which means they can't spend enough time with families to really get to know them and understand what's happening. That said, many respondents highlighted that Cafcass and social services assessments need to start with an open mind, which costs nothing and would bring a big improvement to many cases.

What does this report mean for the future of the family court?

Parents are not allowed to talk about their dreadful experiences in the secret family court. Journalists are allowed in, but they're not allowed to report anything that could identify a child, which means they can report so little they usually don't bother going. So this report has done what no individual could, and collated hundreds of experiences that have a few common themes. Now there's no hiding what children and survivors are enduring in the family court and we need to keep pressing for the recommended changes to be made.

How to use the report

If you're in children proceedings you can pick out parts of the report that fit your case and refer to it in court and/or your position statement. There is also a literature review (see the Resources section at the end of this book) where you should be able to find some useful research and statistics to use in your case. The judge may tell you it's not the law, which is correct, but you can say it's been prepared by the Ministry of Justice who are taking it very seriously so you hope much of it will be the law soon, and in the meantime you're asking them to protect your children in line with it.

If you're represented, don't assume your barrister will use this report. Give them the relevant part(s) and ask them where and how they will use them for you.

The report is long (216 pages) but don't let that put you off. As you can see from the few quotes I've given from the report, it's not full of technical or legal gobbledegook. It's easy to read, and read it you should.

The Domestic Abuse Act 2021

Another major step forwards towards changes in the family court, this statute received Royal Assent on 29 April 2021 and is due to come into force (hopefully) before the end of 2021. The new provisions include:

- For the first time, children who see, hear or experience the effects of the abuse will be recognised as victims of domestic abuse in their own right, instead of just being witnesses.
- The offence of controlling and coercive behaviour is extended to include separated or estranged partners.
- There is now a clear legal definition of domestic abuse, which includes psychological, emotional and economic abuse as well as threatening behaviour and coercive control, and of course, physical violence.
- Survivors now have access to 'special measures' enshrined in law, such as being able to give evidence by a video link or behind a screen.
- Perpetrators of abuse can no longer cross-examine their ex in court.
- Revenge porn, which has been a criminal offence since 2015, now includes threats to share private, intimate images.
- Non-fatal strangulation is now a crime, punishable with up to five years' imprisonment.
- The police have new powers including Domestic Abuse Protection Notices, which give victims immediate protection from abusers.
- Courts can make Domestic Abuse Protection Orders forcing perpetrators to take steps to change their behaviour, including seeking mental health support or drug and alcohol rehabilitation.
- Local authorities are now legally obliged to provide refuge accommodation and to prioritise homeless victims.

Academic research

Cafcass sometimes quote a sentence or two from some research to support a recommendation they're making. And sometimes the research quoted is out of context, or doesn't actually support what they say it does! So don't take what they say as gospel. In your role as a detective who leaves no stone unturned, research the research for yourself. Cafcass will usually name the author and the year of the research, so you can easily google it.

You can also do your own research to support your statements and evidence in court. Experts to research here include Dr Claire Sturge and Dr Danya Glaser (in particular their 'Contact and domestic violence – The experts' court report'), plus Professor Joan Meier, Dr Adrienne Barnett, Dr Peter Jaffe and Dr Nina Maxwell.

Dr Emma Katz is a leading research specialist in the harm caused by perpetrators to children and mothers in the context of domestic abuse, and her research published in May 2020 could be helpful for protective parents to use in court proceedings where they are alleging coercive control (see Resources). Like Sarah's story (Chapter 6), the accounts of children and young people in this research show how children can continue to be harmed by their father's use of coercive control after their mother's separation from him. It explores how, in the post-separation phase, fathers can use the same tactics of coercive control against their children that they use against their ex-partners, causing children the same kinds of psychological and emotional harm and constraining their lives.

The Transparency Project's website has an article about various pieces of research and the Women's Aid website has a Research and Publications page which includes a link to 'What about my right not to be abused?' See Resources section for links.

Re H-N and others (children) (Domestic abuse: finding of fact hearings) 2021

This was four cases heard together as one conjoined appeal in the Court of Appeal (see Resources section for the full reference).

It was a big event with all those heavyweight barristers and we had high hopes of changes for the way domestic abuse is dealt with in the family court. The result was mostly disappointing, although we'll need to wait and see how it plays out in practice. The Court of Appeal stressed that they were not making any new law and that they were leaving it to the Domestic Abuse Bill going through Parliament and the Ministry of Justice implementing the Harm Report, so they were only going to give 'guidance'. It's most unfortunate after all the hard work of so many people to get this appeal heard so quickly that the Court declined to make the progress so desperately needed, particularly ending the culture of 'contact at all costs'.

Three of the four appeals were allowed and sent back to their original courts (Central Family Court, Guildford and Canterbury) for a different judge to decide whether or not there should be a new fact finding hearing. Sadly the fourth appeal was never going to succeed; the whole point of an appeal is to get a different decision from the one made by the original judge but by the time this appeal was actually heard contact was working well between the father and the child and the mother wasn't asking for a different order to be made. She just wanted different findings to be made, but unfortunately it doesn't work like that – findings of abuse are only made in order to determine whether or not contact is safe for a child and the mother was saying by her actions that it was.

The Court of Appeal confirmed that Practice Direction 12J does not need to be changed. It contains a good definition of coercive control and it works well if it's used properly. Unfortunately it isn't always. But the judgement sets out how it should be properly followed.

Helpfully, the Court of Appeal also clearly spelled out that:

'A pattern of coercive and/or controlling behaviour can be as abusive as or more abusive than any particular factual incident that might be written down and included in a Scott schedule. It follows that the harm to a child in an abusive household is not limited to cases of actual violence to the child or to the parent. A pattern of abusive behaviour is as relevant to the child as to the adult victim. The child can be harmed in any one or a combination of ways, for example where the abusive behaviour:

1. Is directed against, or witnessed by, the child;

2. Causes the victim of the abuse to be so frightened of provoking an outburst or reaction from the perpetrator that she/he is unable to give priority to the needs of her/his child;

3. Creates an atmosphere of fear and anxiety in the home which is inimical to the welfare of the child;

4. Risks inculcating, particularly in boys, a set of values which involve treating women as being inferior to men.'

If you're in children proceedings, do use this crucial part of the judgement. We currently don't have much else to use to persuade courts that children are also victims of coercive control and are harmed by it.

Another helpful statement was that we need to move away from using Scott schedules as coercive control is a pattern of behaviour that can't be reduced to five or six allegations in a schedule. Unfortunately, the Court of Appeal didn't give any indication as to what we should use instead, passing the buck to the Private Law Working Group and the Harm Panel's implementation group. In part they were ducking the issue because the family courts are 'currently overborne with work' and they didn't want to impose anything that could make fact finding hearings take up even more court time.

On the plus side, they did say that 'It is, however, our expectation that, in cases where an alleged pattern of coercive and/or controlling behaviour falls for determination, and the court has made that issue its primary focus, the need to determine a range of subsidiary date-specific factual allegations will cease to be "necessary" (unless any particular factual allegation is so serious that it justifies determination irrespective of any alleged pattern of coercive and/or controlling behaviour).' This essentially means that, when the court is being asked to decide whether coercive/controlling behaviour has occurred, providing a Scott schedule shouldn't be necessary. That's helpful guidance but the difficulty is always in getting the court to make coercive control its primary focus in the first place.

It's common for judges to dismiss allegations of domestic abuse as 'historic' but you can now use this judgement to show that the court should still take abuse into account even if it was a long time ago. The case of Re T (one of the four cases) especially could be cited against a judge who is trying to minimise the abuse, as Judge Evans-Gordon did in this case. The judge said putting a plastic bag over the mother's head, which made her feel as though she wanted to die, was probably just a prank on the father's part. She kept talking about the 'relationship conflict', as judges and others so often do when they're unwilling or unable to recognise the abuse.

It seems that the Court of Appeal viewed the abysmal behaviour of these judges being appealed as 'one-offs' but they are most certainly not. These judges have all behaved badly towards mothers in other cases and there are many other judges who are similarly bullying, dismissive and disrespectful.

The Court of Appeal judges said they were confident that most of the judges and magistrates sitting in the family court now understand that domestic abuse is not just violence but includes coercive and controlling behaviour, which may be continuing and impacting on the children. Unfortunately the evidence does not support that view. Some of the training all the judges supposedly have is outlined in the judgement, but either they don't all attend (even though it's said to be mandatory), or the training is woefully inadequate, or judges sleep through it, or they can't see how it applies to their cases. However, thanks to these appeals, judges have now been warned that if they don't deal properly with coercive control, which could be harmful to a child, they're likely to be in trouble if they're appealed. Unfortunately though, as the Court of Appeal acknowledged, far too few people appeal. Which is another reason why I'd urge you to appeal where relevant (see Chapter 15).

FINAL SUMMARY:
WHERE DO YOU GO FROM HERE?

It's important for your healing, and for any future dealings you have to have with the narcissist, that you have some understanding of his personality disorder and how it affects you. Hopefully there's enough information in this book to give you the knowledge you need.

If not, there are books and websites listed in the Resources section, and there is no end of information about narcissists online. You could spend the rest of your life reading and listening to it all! Not that you should. After all, this is someone you're trying to leave and to get out of your life as far as you can. By spending huge amounts of time reading about narcissism, you're continuing to do just what he wants – to always have him at the forefront of your mind. So limit the time you spend on him, and focus on yourself for much more of your time.

If you're in court proceedings you've more important things to research than him, such as how the court works, what the procedure is and what to do next. If you're in financial proceedings you'll want to research how much of the assets and income you'll need going forward, including mortgages and maybe even a cash flow forecast (an independent financial adviser can help with this). If you're in children proceedings you'll want to spend quite some time reading the reports and research in the previous chapter. In other words, you've no more time to dedicate to him!

Probably the most important piece of advice in this book is 'shutty shutty, write it down'. Instead of being at his beck and call – someone he can always rely on for his narcissistic supply – you're now a third-party observer. You coolly observe his antics and behaviour, but it doesn't affect you. You're simply a detective who doesn't miss a trick. You add it to your list of evidence, and move on.

Other key points to remember are:

- Use reverse psychology to get what you want.

- Repeat your mantras at least a hundred times a day.

- Take it one step at a time. It's a long process, but it will eventually come to an end. If you ever feel overwhelmed, refer back to the advice on dealing with overwhelm in Chapter 4.

Finally, I hope you will experience good judges and professionals in your journey through the family court. But if you don't, be sure to fight for what you and your children need. Mothers in one of the Harm Panel's focus groups said they'd been told by their lawyers that their abusers would be granted contact and there was nothing they could do about it. This of course is why many parents are so irate at the huge amount of money paid to their lawyers who then refuse to do the job they've paid them for – i.e. to fight for their client. My advice is always to fight as long and hard as you possibly can for your children. Appeal every wrong decision. Complain to your MP and anyone else who will listen (always bearing in mind what you can and can't divulge about family court proceedings). And make complaints against Cafcass and social services where appropriate.

Because if you don't stand up for yourself and your children, who will?

RESOURCES

Reference books

Court proceedings

- *The Family Court Without a Lawyer* by Lucy Reed.
- *Eyes Wide Open: How to present your own case in family courts against lawyers* by Graham Fletcher.
- *How to Annihilate a Narcissist in the Family Court* by Rachel Watson. (Deals with children proceedings in the Scottish courts, where they don't have Cafcass or the same procedure, but is still very useful in England.)
- *High Conflict People in Legal Disputes* by Bill Eddy. (American but very useful still.)
- *Divorcing a Narcissist: Advice from the Battlefield* by Tina Swithin. (Again, American but easy to read and very helpful.)

Abuse and coercive control

- *Recognition to Recovery: How to leave your abusive ex behind for good* by Caron Kipping.
- *Living with the Dominator* by Pat Craven. (Still useful even if you've left.)
- *The Devil at Home* by Rachel Williams.
- *How He Gets Into Her Head: The Mind of the Male Intimate Abuser* by Don Hennessy.
- *Why Does He Do That?: Inside the Minds of Angry and Controlling Men* by Lundy Bancroft.
- *One Mom's Battle* by Tina Swithin.
- *Look What You Made Me Do* by Helen Walmsley-Johnson. (Her own compelling story of coercive control, how people can be controlled from a distance, and why it was so difficult to leave.)
- *Brutally Honest* by Mel B. (Narcissists aren't specifically mentioned but they aren't hard to spot in this book. Shows all too clearly the effect of toxic, abusive relationships on the children, as well as how the 'double

whammy' plays out and how victims turn to alcohol and drugs. A brave and honest story.)

- *Remembered Forever* by Luke and Ryan Hart. (The story of two brothers whose father murdered their mother and sister, and the coercive control and bullying that preceded it. In addition, Luke and Ryan now campaign against domestic abuse, see www.cocoawareness.co.uk.)

- *Codependent No More* by Melody Beattie.

Narcissists

- *Divorcing a Narcissist: The lure, the loss and the law* by Dr Supriya McKenna and Karin Walker.

- *Narcissism and Family Law: A Practitioner's Guide* by Dr Supriya McKenna and Karin Walker. (An excellent education for your solicitor or barrister. If they won't read it – without charging you for their training! – should they be acting for you?)

- *The Narc Decoder* by Tina Swithin. (A wonderful little book explaining what the narcissist's emails really mean, together with suggested replies.)

- *Will I Ever Be Free of You?: How to Navigate a High-Conflict Divorce From a Narcissist and Heal Your Family* by Karyl McBride.

- *Outsmarting the Sociopath Next Door: How to Protect Yourself Against a Ruthless Manipulator* by Martha Stout.

- *5 Types of People Who Can Ruin Your Life* by Bill Eddy.

- *Psychopath Free* by Jackson Mackenzie. (About recovering from emotionally abusive relationships with narcissists, sociopaths and other toxic people.)

Parenting

- *Divorce Poison: How to Protect Your Family from Bad-mouthing and Brainwashing* by Dr Richard A Warshak. (A must-read for any parent who is being alienated from their child.)

- *BIFF for CoParent Communication* by Bill Eddy. (An invaluable little book which teaches you how to write brief, informative, friendly and firm emails, etc.)

- *How to Talk so Kids Will Listen and Listen so Kids Will Talk* by Adele Faber and Elaine Mazlish.
- *How to Talk So Little Kids Will Listen: A Survival Guide to Life with Children Ages 2–7* by Joanna Faber and Julie King.
- *Safeguarding Children Exposed to Narcissistic Parenting, Coercive Control and Parental Alienation* by Alison Smith. (This is a guide for practitioners – ask your social worker to read it.)

Books for children

- *Stuck Between Two Worlds* by Lisa Parkes.
- *Divorce Is Not the End of the World* by Zoe and Evan Stern.
- *The Divorce Journal for Kids aged 7–11* by Sue Atkins.

Websites and apps

Narcissists and court

- **Rebecca Zung,** a US attorney with lots of advice about negotiating with a narcissist: *www.rebeccazung.com*
- Expose a narcissist in court (also by Rebecca Zung): *www.youtube.com/watch?v=Kt0LSyLcW1w*
- **Christine Louis de Canonville**: www.narcissisticbehavior.net/divorcing-a-narcissist/

Children and parenting

- **Our Family Wizard (fees payable)** and **AppClose (free)**. These apps are better than using email and texts, etc. as all your events and correspondence can all be kept in one place and the date is clearly shown. Helpful as evidence in court, as well as keeping your ex out of your inbox.
- **Patrick Teahan**, for videos of role plays with a narcissistic parent: www.youtube.com/watch?v=SyLzds6ylOI
- **Coping skills for kids,** for US resources, activities and books: https://copingskillsforkids.com/

Empathy Test

- Baron-Cohen's empathy test. Most women score about 47 and most men about 42. www.psychology-tools.com/test/empathy-quotient

Courses, support groups and charities

- **NCDV The National Centre for Domestic Violence** Help with injunctions https://www.ncdv.org.uk/
- **The Freedom Programme**: https://www.freedomprogramme.co.uk/
- **Get Court Ready Programme**: https://thenurturingcoach.co.uk/get-court-ready-programme/
- **Court confidence course**: https://www.courtconfidence.com/courses/court-confidence
- **Witness familiarisation training**. Bond Solon are the main providers (Google will give you others which may be cheaper). They don't cover family law specifically but the training will give you a big confidence boost: https://www.bondsolon.com/witness-familiarisation/
- **Parenting after Separation**. Una Archer works with parents who are separating, including those leaving a narcissist, to get the best outcomes for their children: https://www.parentingafterseparation.co.uk/
- **Bill Eddy Coaching**. A supportive community to learn skills for high-conflict co-parenting: https://www.conflictplaybook.com/
- **Mothers Unite**. A lot of help and support from other mothers going through family court, although some of the stories are distressing. Best to set up a false profile on Facebook first as abusive exes do manage to infiltrate the group occasionally: https://www.facebook.com/groups/1672156316419986/
- **Mothers ReVolution** (website and Facebook group). A non-profit charitable organisation that assists protective mothers with legal matters, media strategies, trauma counselling, support groups, retreats, training, and networking: https://protectivemothersrevolution.org/
- **MATCH Mothers**. A charity supporting mothers living apart from their children, including those who have lost residence in the family court: https://www.matchmothers.org/
- **Kids Come First**. Separated parent support workshops: https://kidscomefirstuk.co.uk/

- **Young Minds**. Help for parents worried about a child's mental health: https://youngminds.org.uk/find-help/for-parents/
- **Mosac**. Support for parents whose children have been sexually abused https://mosac.org.uk/
- **Making Lemonade – The Single Parent Network**: https://makinglemonade.com/

Counsellors and coaches

UK

- **The Nurturing Coach** has counsellors specialising in narcissistic abuse and parental alienation and also runs webinars and courses https://thenurturingcoach.co.uk/
- **David Kilmurry** is a hypnotherapist recommended by survivors of domestic abuse: https://www.kilmurrylifecentre.com/
- **Eleanor Pool** is a therapist who works (online and in person) with clients leaving narcissistic relationships: https://eleanorpoolcounselling.com/
- **Caron Kipping** is a coach specialising in helping people leaving abusive relationships: https://caronkippingcoaching.com/

For children

- **Smiley** (children's life coach and mentor). Lisa Parkes provides online support for children, including those who have a narcissistic parent, or parents going through a toxic divorce: https://smileyforlife.com/

US and Australia:

- **Lisa A Romano** is the 'shutty shutty' originator and life coach for co-dependency and narcissist abuse recovery: https://www.lisaaromano.com/
- **Melanie Tonia Evans** provides information, advice and recovery programmes to help you understand narcissistic abuse and empower you to take control of your life again: https://www.melanietoniaevans.com/
- **Dana Morningstar** provides red flags of a narcissist and other resources for education: https://www.thriveafterabuse.com/
- **Patricia Evans** is a specialist in verbal abuse: https://verbalabuse.com

Legal help

- **Dealing With Divorce** (my own website, where I provide legal help for litigants in person or anyone who is dealing with a narcissist in court): https://dealingwithdivorce.co.uk/

- **Rights of Women** (charity helping women through the law): https://rightsofwomen.org.uk/

- **Help to appeal family court decisions** (by Rights of Women): https://rightsofwomen.org.uk/get-information/family-law/how-to-appeal-family-court-decisions/

- **Family Rights Group** (including good information on making complaints): https://frg.org.uk/get-help-and-advice/what/complaints/

- **Support Through Court** (charity providing volunteers who act as McKenzie Friends): https://www.supportthroughcourt.org/

- **Law Works** (charity providing legal advice clinics): https://www.lawworks.org.uk/

- **Advocate** (barristers who give free legal help): https://weareadvocate.org.uk/

- **Advice Now** (lots of really helpful legal information): https://www.advicenow.org.uk/divorce-and-separation

- **No Family Lawyer** (website that accompanies the book *The Family Court Without a Lawyer*): http://www.nofamilylawyer.co.uk and for useful documents for court see http://www.nofamilylawyer.co.uk/useful-documents.html

- **The Voice of the Child** (putting children first in family law): https://voiceofthechild.org.uk/

- **Guidance for McKenzie Friends**: https://www.judiciary.uk/wp-content/uploads/JCO/Documents/Guidance/mckenzie-friends-practice-guidance-july-2010.pdf

- **Letter from parent consenting to child going abroad**: https://assets.publishing.service.gov.uk/government/uploads/system/uploads/attachment_data/file/348110/Letter_of_Consent_for_Minors_travelling_to_UK_Apr08.pdf

- **Information Commissioner's Office**: https://ico.org.uk/your-data-matters/your-right-to-get-copies-of-your-data/preparing-and-submitting-your-subject-access-request

Help for men who are abused

- **Help Guide**: https://www.helpguide.org/articles/abuse/help-for-men-who-are-being-abused.htm
- **Paul Lavelle Foundation**: https://paullavellefoundation.co.uk/
- **The Nurturing Coach** https://thenurturingcoach.co.uk/

Relevant cases and reports

- **The Harm Report**:
  https://assets.publishing.service.gov.uk/government/uploads/system/uploads/attachment_data/file/895173/assessing-risk-harm-children-parents-pl-childrens-cases-report_.pdf
- **The literature review** (gives valuable research you can use):
  https://assets.publishing.service.gov.uk/government/uploads/system/uploads/attachment_data/file/895175/domestic-abuse-private-law-children-cases-literature-review.pdf
- **R v P** (Children: Similar Fact Evidence):
  https://www.bailii.org/ew/cases/EWCA/Civ/2020/1088.html
- **Re F** (Children; contact, name, parental responsibility; HHJ Duggan):
  https://www.bailii.org/ew/cases/EWFC/HCJ/2014/42.html
- **Re P** (A child) 2015: (NPD, no order for contact):
  https://www.bailii.org/ew/cases/EWCA/Civ/2015/170.html
- **Court of Appeal judgement: Re H-N and others (children) (Domestic abuse: finding of fact hearings) 2021**:
  https://www.judiciary.uk/judgments/re-h-n-and-others-children-domestic-abuse-finding-of-fact-hearings/?fbclid=IwAR2FZMO2svs51wNEb5As5rUxUUL6g53G7C4QSJ5YZzKezp3ZYU6T8tdPW-0
- **PD12J**: https://www.justice.gov.uk/downloads/fjr/pd12J.pdf
- **Cafcass 'tool' for distinguishing domestic abuse and harmful conflict**:
  https://www.cafcass.gov.uk/grown-ups/professionals/ciaf/resources-for-assessing-harmful-conflict/

Academic research on how abuse affects children

- *Child Custody and Domestic Violence: A Call for Safety and Accountability* by Peter Jaffe, Dr Nancy Lemon and Samantha Poisson. This book shows the likelihood of abuse with a new partner, or abuse of the child in the absence of a partner and that the abuse should not be dismissed by the court as 'historical': https://sk.sagepub.com/books/child-custody-and-domestic-violence

- *When Coercive Control Continues to Harm Children: Post-Separation Fathering, Stalking and Domestic Violence* by Emma Katz https://onlinelibrary.wiley.com/doi/full/10.1002/car.2611

- The Transparency Project's website provides information on useful research: https://www.transparencyproject.org.uk/independent-research-on-domestic-abuse-and-family-courts/

- The Women's Aid website also has a Research and Publications page: https://www.womensaid.org.uk/evidence-hub/research-and-publications/

- You may also want to check out research by the following experts: Dr Claire Sturge and Dr Danya Glaser (in particular their 'Contact and domestic violence – The experts' court report'), plus Professor Joan Meier, Dr Adrienne Barnett, Dr Peter Jaffe and Dr Nina Maxwell.

Novels

- *Picture Perfect* by Jodi Picoult. The world thinks your marriage is perfect. You know it's a lie. What would you do?

- *Keeping Faith* by Jodi Picoult. What happens to Faith may be extreme, but the custody battle isn't although it is American and we don't have 'objections' in the UK!

- *The Storm* by Amanda Jennings. A good description of a controlling, narcissistic husband and father, with an extra twist. Unfortunately the author failed to take advice from a family lawyer and perpetuates the myth that assets are divided equally on divorce.

- *Big Little Lies* by Liane Moriarty. The book that was later turned into a popular HBO series.

ABOUT THE AUTHOR

Diana Jordan is a former solicitor with over 30 years' experience in family law. She now works with people who can't afford a solicitor, and particularly those who need help dealing with a narcissist in court proceedings (something that most lawyers unfortunately don't understand).

As a divorce consultant, Diana provides the support people need to represent themselves effectively – helping them to correspond with their ex (or their ex's solicitor), prepare court documents, navigate the family court system, and get the best from court hearings.

Diana is also the author of *A Better Way of Dealing with Divorce: A guide for parents who want to keep out of court, and save their money and sanity* – written for those who aren't divorcing a narcissist!

Find out more about Diana and her services at

www.dealingwithdivorce.co.uk

Printed in Great Britain
by Amazon